The Manipulative Child

The Manipulative Child

HOW TO GAIN CONTROL AND RAISE RESILIENT,
RESOURCEFUL, AND INDEPENDENT KIDS

Ernest W. Swihart Jr., M.D.
Patrick D. Cotter, Ph.D.

Macmillan • USA

Many case examples appear throughout this book. In all cases, significant identifying details have been altered to protect the identity of the persons described. Any resemblance to real people is coincidental.

MACMILLAN

A Simon & Schuster Macmillan Company
1633 Broadway
New York, NY 10019

Library of Congress Cataloging-in-Publication Data
Swihart, Ernest W. (Ernest Walter)
    The manipulative child : how to regain control and raise
resilient, resourceful, and independent kids / by Ernest W. Swihart,
Patrick Cotter.
        p.   cm.
    Includes bibliographical references and index.
    ISBN 0-02-861254-X
    1. Problem children—behavior modification.   2. Manipulative
behavior.   3. Self-esteem in children.   4. Child rearing.
5. Parenting.   I. Cotter, Patrick.   II. Title.
HQ773.S95   1996
649'.64—dc20   96-15974
                                                    CIP

10 9 8 7 6 5 4 3 2 1

Printed in the U.S.A.

We dedicate this work to our parents, Ernest and Ida Swihart and Vince and Dorothy Cotter. They guided us using the values they held dear, gave us steadfast support, believed in our abilities, and offered us the freedom to discover ourselves, make our own mistakes and accept responsibility for our own lives. They could not have done a better job.

We also dedicate this work to our families: Karen, Kay, David, Daniel, Gretchen, and Jason. Our families, especially our wives, wholeheartedly supported our efforts over the years, offered help and advice when asked, patiently endured our musings, ramblings, and diatribes, and believed in us even when we weren't so sure.

Contents

Acknowledgments

I (PDC) wish to thank my co-author and friend, Ernie, for his helpful editing of my writing. Ernie skillfully modified text that rambled on with too much detail (read boring), into manuscript that was readable and interesting.

I (EWS) want to thank Pat for his careful scientific thought and critique. His is truly an independent mind. He can always be trusted to keep his own counsel and maintain healthy skepticism when I'm having a "great idea." This effort was truly a partnership.

We would like to acknowledge the help we received from Karen and Kay who typed when asked, edited our sometimes shaky grammar, offered honest critique of our ideas and expression, and provided succor when we were discouraged.

We would like to extend our heartfelt thanks to all the children and their families who provided, through openness, candor, and courage when trying to change, the clinical information that became the hypotheses that form the foundation for this book. Without them, the ideas and insights expressed here would never have happened. They openly encouraged us, but their success in their lives provided us with the knowledge we were on the right track.

To all those who offered help in crafting the manuscript, we couldn't have done it without you. Jason Swihart provided invaluable editorial critique on everything we wrote. His ability to help us clearly express our ideas, to ferret out the ambiguities in what we had written, repeatedly amazed us. How could a mere college punk be so good at this? Jean Tasa and Sue Kimmel typed and Tom Langenfield edited early in the process until we finally learned to do it ourselves.

Many people along the way have offered encouragement and support for our persistence on this project. Al Heimel and Linda Kellog must have asked about our progress every time we saw them for the last six years. Orv Huseby expressed his belief and support to Ernie most every Tuesday at noon during racquetball. Bill Hebert and Jack Rosberg were always ready to listen and comment. This list could go on indefinitely.

Jonathan and Wendy Lazear, who guided us through the process and didn't give up when the idea of the book wasn't easy to sell. They believed we had something useful to say.

Finally, Emily Heckman, Pam Hoenig, and Nick Bakalar, our editors at Macmillan, provided the insight to help us focus our work and refine our presentation, while acting as boosters and cheering squad along the way. Without their help this book would have foundered.

Introduction

The idea to write this book occurred over lunch several years ago. We had just given a workshop entitled "Manipulation and Self-Esteem." The enthusiasm of the audience told us that parents and others who work with children shared our fascination with a clinical observation we had made: Highly manipulative children and teenagers seem inevitably to develop poor self-esteem. Our audience wanted to know more; they wanted to know what they could do to prevent this poisonous interaction from developing in their children. We've written this book to describe the relationship between the two, the process of acquisition and destruction of self-esteem and, most importantly, to explore what each of us can do to ensure that children learn the skills necessary to generate and maintain their own self-esteem.

We're deeply troubled by what we see going on with children in this country. We believe that there is an epidemic of difficulties among our youth that has gone on now for more than twenty-five years. This epidemic grows every year; no end is in sight. Worse, it appears that much of what parents have been told to do and what schools have been mandated to do in response to this epidemic has resulted in the escalation of the problems that youth experience. Simplistic explanations and answers abound—the problems of youth are fair game for politicians, pundits, and authorities—yet few seem to have a good idea of what's wrong, let alone what needs to be done.

Pat is a child psychologist with twenty years experience treating children (and their families) with just about the whole gamut of psychological ailments. He has spent time both on the staff of a major children's hospital and in private practice. I am a pediatrician who spent several additional years after my pediatric residency learning about and then teaching behavioral pediatrics at the University of Wisconsin. (Behavioral pediatrics is a broad subspecialty that attempts to address the psycho-social-behavioral problems of children—from parenting difficulty and training to specific problems such as bedwetting, ADHD, eating disorders, or adolescent depression.) Since then, I have practiced a combination of general and behavioral pediatrics for twenty-plus years. The two of us find an amazing synthesis when we share our unique experiences, observations, and vantage points. I've had the experience, as only a pediatrician can, of watching hundreds of children grow up from cradle to college. My observations both of healthy kids developing into resilient and effective adults and children who've gone on to have difficulty, combined with Pat's considerable clinical experience and theoretical expertise, have allowed us to analyze not just what is wrong with problem kids but what is right in well-adapted kids. (Most psychologists and psychiatrists don't have this vantage point because they see only kids with problems and then, often, for only a short segment of the child's life.)

When we recognized the reliable presence of manipulative behavior among teenagers with problems and low self-esteem, we began to understand that all these seemingly disparate problems—from eating disorders to drug abuse—might be somehow fundamentally related to one another. If we could understand this commonality, we might understand something more useful than if we remained focused on individual problems.

We noted that the epidemic seemed to afflict a unique population of children. While kids raised in poverty have always had a lot of difficulties, this epidemic was laying waste children of the middle class—indeed, the most enfranchised, most affluent, and best-educated middle class the world has ever known. The parents of these kids were highly motivated, well-read, successful people—just the group that most would predict to be unlikely to produce children with problems.

As we accepted the universality of manipulation among troubled youth, we were afforded our first glimpse of the larger picture. These children were using manipulation to adapt to life's circumstances. Since manipulation requires the involvement of other people, it is dependent behavior. When we compared children who were doing well, the contrast was striking—this group eschewed manipulative behavior; they operated independently.

Putting this all together, we arrived at an inevitable series of conclusions: There is a central cause for the epidemic; manipulation (dependency), the principal adaptive strategy of troubled children, is not a result of the difficulties these children suffer, but is intimately related to the cause of their problems; well-meaning, successful, well-read, motivated people are raising children who've learned to adapt to life in this dependent fashion.

We've been led to ask many more questions. What is manipulation? How is it related to the cause of the epidemic? How does manipulation manifest? Are there types of manipulation? What role do the people who are manipulated play? Are there personalities that are predisposed to manipulation? What are the antecedents to this sort of dependency? What is it we do as parents, as a society, to foster the development of dependent children? What is independence, anyway? And, finally, what can parents, teachers, and others who work with children do to promote independent, nonmanipulative adaptation in children? This book answers these questions.

It is our goal that this book guide you in teaching your children to become strong, resilient, independent adults, capable of generating their own self-esteem and adapting to life as they find it rather than asking life to adapt to them. Surprisingly, the changes we propose are simple and easy to understand, though often difficult to do. They involve empowering parents to be parents. They involve subtleties of technique and approach that are mastered only with patience and practice. They involve viewing your children as capable but inexperienced, and needing your clear guidance and loving discipline as they grow up. And, most of all, they involve avoiding defeat in one of life's most demanding and important occupations: raising children.

EWS
Minnetonka, Minnesota

CHAPTER 1

Manipulation:
A Clue to the Mystery of Failure

Amerian children are in a great deal of trouble. Statistics reflecting the overall social health of our children scream out the same message: We've got problems. In Minnesota, where we live and practice, suicide rates among teenagers tripled in the four years prior to 1991; one of three teenage boys and one of six teenage girls had thought of suicide; teenage pregnancy had tripled during the previous fifteen years, despite widespread contraceptive availability; and 11.8 percent of youth carried a major psychological diagnosis. Across the country, teenage gangs run rampant in many cities, drug use continues to increase, and eating disorders, once a medical rarity, are commonplace. It appears that we are witnessing not just the age-old phenomenon of adolescent rebellion but something else that cannot be dismissed as hijinks, hormones, or coming of age—these are kids with no goals, structure, or sense of self.

How can it be that our affluent society, awash with possibility, can produce several generations of children who can't manage to get their homework done, who score badly in any international measure of academic achievement, who show little self-control at home or in public, and who, as they become adolescent, are increasingly afflicted with depression, suicide, unwanted teenage pregnancy, eating disorders, chemical dependency, and violent behavior? One editorial in the journal *Pediatrics* called this national malaise "Failure to Strive." Explanations for the problems of American youth abound, but somehow none provide a coherent, thorough understanding of the genesis of our problems, let alone a useful prescription for action.

We've been on the scene long enough to watch an entire generation grow up. As the kids we've known and observed have matured, many have developed problems, and we've been there to see, wanting to understand what was going on. We've looked for clues to the mysterious cause of all this difficulty. We've asked ourselves, "What's so different today as compared to forty or fifty years ago?" We've examined society's responses to these problems and asked, "Why have our attempts to cure or prevent the problems of youth been so uniformly ineffectual?" The New York Public Library has more than four hundred parenting books in vigorous circulation, yet with all this information, the situation seems to worsen. Why, despite enormous efforts by parents, schools, and the judicial system, are we going backwards? Does anyone have a clue? We must be doing something wrong, and whatever it is, it is fundamental, critical to the development of healthy, well-adapted people.

Parents today approach childrearing with fear and trepidation rather than with the joy and high hopes of yesteryear. Many parents seem to regard their children as time bombs, sure that some unwitting parental transgression will start the clock ticking—with good reason; the facts aren't very heartening.

Recently, a devoted mother, who has so far raised her three children successfully, asked us, "Why is it that when I say 'no' to my kids, I feel guilty?" Indeed, why? Since we know her well, we know that when she says "no" to her children, she has made a responsible adult decision about what she will allow them to do. We know she has done the right thing, but she feels guilty about denying her children's wants. That sort of a bind doesn't lead to long-term consistency, and, if it interferes with parenting, it won't bode well for her children. She went on to say, "We're all afraid of our children, afraid to upset them, afraid we may make a mistake, and we're unwilling to take a chance, to be in charge." We agreed with her and told her so. It's time we accepted that our timid approach to raising children isn't working.

This mother's dilemma is a bellwether we should heed. If anything characterizes parents today, it is the fear and guilt they feel while trying to do the best job they can of raising children. Their uncertainty has made child-rearing advice big business. We see parents all the time who read everything they can find and end up more confused than they were before they started, further from the real source of guidance they want and need.

This book is not meant to be an exhaustive review of the literature and research about childrearing. We don't pretend to have all the answers, and we know that no one else does either. We intend to explore one aspect of the problem—manipulation—that gives us considerable insight into the difficulties of our children. When we understand the significance of manipulative behavior—how it works and what it does to children—we can draw some conclusions that parents and teachers can put to good use in raising well-adapted, responsible children.

We are not apologists for the current crop of parents: We don't want our analysis to be used as an excuse for the failure of efforts to raise children who have the wherewithal to survive and thrive. Instead, we decided to write this book because our clients and patients have found our ideas useful in helping their children achieve self-sufficiency and independence. If you are looking for a simple explanation for your childrearing difficulties, or if you're looking for an easy, no-stress answer to childrearing, read no further. This book is intended to cause you to examine your basic assumptions about children and childrearing, and challenge you to make some fundamental changes in how you operate with your children. Much of what we will ask of you takes time and can be, at times, emotionally difficult, but the reward—the strong, resilient, independent, self-directed, self-confident people your children can become—is well worth the effort.

Our childrearing difficulties have historical roots that go back well over a century. Trends established years ago are bearing their bitter fruit today. Parents today are caught up in the confluence of these trends, which render them immobile and ineffectual, impotent to do the hard work of raising children. Some of the historical antecedents to today's malaise are well chronicled in Charles Sykes important book, *A Nation of Victims*. Two are worth mentioning here.

The foundation for how we see children and childrearing was laid shortly after the turn of the century by Sigmund Freud. He theorized that adult mental ills were the result of damage done to the developing "psyche" by parents who traumatized their children during critical stages of their early development. This idea was popularized and began to alter childrearing practice significantly after the Second World War, through the efforts of Benjamin Spock and other writers. Parents, who previously would have been more concerned with teaching their children the difference between right and wrong, or with raising children with good character and the will to do hard work, suddenly became wary of the possibility of doing damage to their children. The theory behind this was complex and confusing, the pitfalls along the way hidden from the uninitiated. As a result, childrearing practice became the venue of experts; no mere mortal parent could hope to avoid disaster without the advice of professionals. Traditional reliance on family and community for support and advice was now eschewed; never before in human history had anything like this happened. Suddenly, and pervasively, we came to regard children as if they were fragile eggs requiring very careful handling, under the guidance of someone with a Ph.D.

A second trend came from a book published in 1950 called *The Authoritarian Personality*. The authors, Theodor Adorno and colleagues, attempted to define, for all time, the characteristics of authoritarianism. In this postwar period, they equated firmly held beliefs and strong moral footings (and, therefore, the willingness to impose these upon children) with fascism. This notion—that anything other than willingness to accept all things without moral judgment, was fascist—took hold in the fertile ground of a population that had experienced, firsthand, a war waged against fascism. As anti-authoritarianism took root, parents began to doubt themselves, to question the worth of their beliefs. They felt guilty imposing their idea of right and wrong upon their children. Spock's emphasis on permissive parenting dovetailed nicely with this national mindset, and a whole new way of childrearing began. We have seen the emergence of the generations reared according to that approach, starting in the 1960s and continuing right on up to the present, and they're not doing very well at all.

The mother at our office demonstrates all of this: She feels guilty while doing what she knows is right because she feels she is being authoritarian. She is worried she might do some sort of damage to her children if she makes decisions they don't like and, caught in this bind, is finding it hard to be an effectual, confident parent. Most parents experience the same bind at least some of the time.

But the Trouble Isn't Just at Home

Sykes, in his penetrating investigation of our nation's malaise, quotes Jaime Escalante, the highly successful Los Angeles schoolteacher portrayed in the movie *Stand and Deliver*:

> Our schools today . . . tend to look upon disadvantaged minority students as though they were on the verge of a mental breakdown, to be protected from any undue stress . . . Ideas like this are not just false, they are the kiss of death for minority youth and, if allowed to proliferate, will significantly stall the advancement of minorities.

Well, we agree with Mr. Escalante, but the problem he sees isn't confined to underprivileged, inner-city youth. The exact same thing is happening in the privileged middle class. Not only are parents unable to assume leadership roles in families, but uncertainty afflicts schools even more. A few days before this was written, we saw a thirteen-year-old boy, Randy, with whom we've worked since he was a preschooler. His parents are basically strong, effective people, but he's been a handful from the get-go. Their effectiveness in parenting Randy has also been compromised by a younger child with a very serious and time-consuming chronic illness. While they've done reasonably well with Randy at home, his school progress has been a series of ups and downs, with the downs often winning. His sixth-grade year in a "progressive" public school had been a total disaster despite special help, attendance in friendship and family stress groups, regular sessions with his counselor, and frequent meetings between his parents and the "team" of teachers and social workers.

At the end of the school year, the family moved to another community, and this presented the opportunity to send Randy to a nearby parochial school. After lengthy consideration and a bit of consultation with us, Randy's parents decided to have him repeat sixth grade in the parochial school, believing that neither his academics nor his sense of personal responsibility were ready for the challenge of middle school.

In mid-March we did a routine follow-up on his progress. When he walked into our consultation room, it was immediately apparent that something had changed dramatically. He made direct eye contact, he smiled the biggest smile we had ever seen from him, and he held himself erect. "So, Randy, how's it going?" we asked. "Great," he replied, "I'm at the top of my class in math and English!" He beamed, and his self-confidence filled the room. We were stunned and happy for him.

Later, we asked his father what had happened to make such a difference. He told us that the change had everything to do with Randy's teacher. "The first two months were real tough. It was sorta like boot camp for Randy. His teacher wouldn't let up, wouldn't back off. She dominated him, not angrily or spitefully, but in a way that said she cared for and believed in him and wasn't going to let him avoid his work and fail. He just hated it. He hated her, but she just kept smiling and demanding performance. He was really angry with us for sending him to that 'awful' school. He wanted to continue to be the victim he had always been before. After the first two months, he caved in and began to perform. He found out he could do school after all!"

We wish we could run this teacher through a giant copy machine. She is rare. She knows what she wants from her pupils, she knows she must establish her unquestioned leadership at the beginning of the school year, and she knows her pupils aren't going to like it one bit. She also knows that once she's done this, she'll be respected, even loved, by them. More importantly, she knows that once they start performing, her students will begin to like themselves and even school. But teachers like Randy's and Mr. Escalante are unusual. It is an uncommon teacher who isn't worried about doing damage by stressing or frustrating a child. Not many teachers recognize the absolute need to establish leadership, without worrying whether their students don't like school or them for awhile. And it is a rare teacher who isn't concerned about parental disapproval and the potential for legal entanglements when children are unhappy with their teachers.

Worse, yet, is the lack of administrative support for the teacher who is actually willing to take these risks. There are many potentially excellent teachers in our schools, but they know they'll be completely on their own if they really demand performance and end up in conflict. Incredibly, the ingredients that make an outstanding teacher are simple, yet we've somehow so complicated the classroom with worries and fears that many good teachers have been rendered ineffectual. It takes real courage to do the right thing for kids, to stand up to their anger and indignation at being asked to perform. We've sapped the courage of teachers with a smokescreen of supposed disabilities, with concern for giving children self-esteem rather than teaching them the skills to acquire their own self-esteem (such as demanding academic performance), and with educational programs and policies that diffuse and muddy responsibility for both students and teachers.

"Failure to strive" is evident in all socioeconomic groups—the great American middle class is no exception. And, it seems to us, the more that's done to try to cure the problem, the worse the problem becomes. We have watched, over the time of our clinical careers, as more and more children are referred for help, as schools and families experience more misbehavior and lack of achievement, as kids are less able to deal with stress. We've watched entire schools become "therapeutic" in an attempt to help children cope with academic and behavioral demands that a few generations ago would have seemed meager. We have watched as schools blame parents for the difficulties of children and as parents blame schools for the same difficulties. We have watched as teachers lower expectations to try to help children achieve success in an attempt to give them a boost in self-esteem, only to find that children underperform just as much when expectations have been lowered, their self-confidence further eroded by this patronage. We have heard the cry for more school days in the year, as if additional mediocrity will cure underperformance. We hear the real problem is money, that we can buy better performance. We doubt it.

Marva Collins, the legendary teacher who runs a private school in the ghettos of Chicago, pointed out just how low our expectations for children's school performance have sunk by simply reciting the contents of the *Rhetorical Reader*. Published in 1862, it was a textbook intended for elementary children and included writings from John Ruskin, Oliver Goldsmith, John Milton, and Leo Tolstoy. Apparently children were smarter in 1862 than today. We doubt it.

What's going on here? Are we to believe that our children are somehow less able to perform than children in Taiwan, South Korea, or the former Soviet Union (international test scores suggest this is the case)? Are we to believe that the decline in SAT scores (verbal 477 to 428, math 498 to 476) from 1960 to the present, despite a real dollar expenditure increase of almost 300 percent per pupil, represents a mysterious population shift toward less able children? Are we to believe that additional funds will help when we note that we are second only to Switzerland in total expenditure per pupil and that we spend double what is spent in Japan? Are we to believe that the real answer is smaller class size when we realize the average elementary class size in Japan is forty-five? Are we to believe that the legendary success of Asian immigrant children in school is because they are, on average, smarter? We don't think so. It is clear to us that something has happened to the way we rear children, to the way we prepare them for the world. Whatever has happened is a relatively recent phenomenon, though its roots may be buried deeply in our past. This phenomenon is pervasive—it affects not just families but schools as well.

Society's response to the problem has been worse than useless. We asked a young patient, referred because of poor school performance, how he thought he was doing in school. "Fine," was his reply. "How do you know?" we asked. "Because my teacher gives me lots of happy face stickers on my papers!" Chester Finn, who surveyed teachers' reports on student progress, calls this the "unholy marriage of low expectations and high marks . . . a poisonous brew of humanitarianism and condescension." Virtually all of our responses, as professionals and as a society, have been aimed at the preservation of children's self-esteem, at protection from reality and stress, rather than at the goal of development of character and learning. It seems that as we have put more and more effort into giving children self-esteem we see less and less success from our efforts. One school we're acquainted with has therapy groups for a multitude of problems. The entire school orients itself around the self-esteem of its young charges. Viewing this school from the outside, we have watched as children there underperform more and more, become sadder and less responsible than their counterparts in other schools. The response of the school to the increasing evidence of lowered self-esteem has been to increase the number and variety of therapy groups for students! If a little therapy doesn't do it, perhaps a lot will.

As schools became more therapeutic in the 1970s, a pernicious trend began. States passed laws that allowed schools to identify children having difficulty as learning disabled. Criteria for this labeling were established, and once a child "qualified," money from state funds became available to the child's school district to provide services for the child. The testing process that schools employed was designed to satisfy the particular state's requirements, and the label "learning disabled" was just a legal appurtenance, not an exhaustive clinical or scientific diagnosis. But schools, teachers, and parents either never understood that significant fact or forgot it. The whole field of learning disabilities is a confused mess of opinion, a few scientific facts, and legal mandates. Fancy language obfuscates the little we really know. Kids have auditory processing disabilities (that means they weren't listening when asked to perform), decoding-encoding disability (that means they don't use the phonics they learned or never learned and instead guess at or skip words they haven't seen before), problems in visual-motor integration (your devoted authors have sloppy handwriting, too!).

We have little doubt that there are a few children and adults out there who have true neurological deficits that interfere with learning, just as there are tone-deaf people or persons with fine-motor handicaps such as chorea that make handwriting difficult. But the sheer size of the population now identified as learning disabled calls into serious question the current definition. Instead, it would appear that what we have here is just a convenient way to explain failure, not of students, but of the teaching methodology being employed. The emotionally trying, hard work needed to ensure the learning performance of children in school has been sidestepped. This has also guaranteed the continued employment of special education personnel. But this is not without cost, paid by all the children who will carry their labels throughout their school careers, convinced that they cannot really perform like other kids.

Patti is a seventeen-year-old we recently saw for evaluation because of mediocre school performance. She's bubbly and vivacious, very articulate, and obviously quite bright. Her mother is a schoolteacher, her father a gastroenterologist. Patti had difficulty learning to read in first and second grade, and was evaluated for a learning disability when she was eight. The evaluation resulted in a label of learning disabled for Patti, and she has received help in school since. When we first saw her, she still had difficulty reading. As a matter of fact, she hated reading. Further investigation showed that Patti can't or won't sound out new words. When pressed on a word she didn't recognize, she guessed from context and her guesses were only fairly accurate. Most of the time, she just skipped the words she didn't recognize. Her reading comprehension was, understandably, poor. We arranged for phonics remediation, which Patti initially resisted vigorously. She couldn't comfortably give up the learning-disabled label; she argued vehemently that our approach would never work. As it turned out, Patti knew more phonics than she realized and her progress was swift. Her real problem was learning to apply what she knew. Her guess-or-skip style was so ingrained that considerable practice was required for her to unlearn it and learn a new approach. But soon her work with a determined phonics tutor paid off, and her reading rapidly improved, as did her school performance. She now sees herself as a normal, capable student, not a disabled victim.

So why didn't Patti learn to read in the first place? Did her learning disability magically disappear under our care? Patti, like many children, walked into first grade a non-reader. She noticed, though, that a few kids could already read and she wondered why she couldn't. She became frightened and unsure. Her parents and teachers gave her lots of attention and help. Whenever she came to a word she didn't know, she became frustrated and asked for help. She said "I can't" a lot, and everyone believed her. Her parents and teachers feared she would give up. They couldn't tolerate watching her frustration, so they helped her by giving her the words she didn't know rather than insisting she sound them out. Patti learned that she could sound out the first phoneme of a word, and then she guessed until she got the right word. Then her parents and teacher praised her correctness. She became a sight reader: She memorized all the words she needed to know to read at a second-grade level. But in third grade, this didn't work so well. Phonics is generally taught only in first and second grade, and by third, reading becomes more independent. She couldn't decipher all the new words that third grade presented without someone's help, and she quickly became convinced she wasn't capable of reading. No one ever thought to go back to the basics, which she had never learned; so for Patti, reading was difficult and meaningless. She became apprehensive just trying to read, so she learned to avoid it. And her learning-disabled label and all the special help she received further convinced her of her inability to perform academically without help.

The reader might think Patti's story unusual, but it's not. Quite the contrary. It illustrates a central problem with our approach to parenting and teaching, a problem we must address if we're going to raise self-confident, competent children. We cannot continue to regard children, in Mr. Escalante's terms, as "on the verge of a mental breakdown, to be protected from any undue stress" if we expect to be able to see them through the hard and sometimes frustrating work of learning.

A universal feature of junior and senior high schools today are study halls. Years ago, study halls didn't exist. They were created in response to a decrease in the completion of homework, and the belief that children needed a supervised environment in which to study. Some schools have study halls for specific subject areas, with a teacher available for questions. This may seem like a good approach to improving performance, but the amount of studying that takes place in most study halls is questionable—many would be better labeled social halls. Worse, many study halls are great places for students to hone their manipulative skills: Friends or teachers in charge are often too glad to help out. The attitude we hear from many of our underachieving clients is "If you can't get it done at school, it isn't worth doing."

Recently, the parents of an underachieving client of ours attended a meeting to go over his Individual Educational Plan (IEP). The parents told us that the plan specified that their son was to get 80 percent of his work done and turned in and that his work was to be 80 percent accurate. "Let's see," they said, "that means that they would like him to do roughly 64 percent of his work well. Does that make sense?" Rather than insisting that this child perform, the school had proposed a formula that would hardly earn a "D" in most courses. They ensured, by the very statement of goals, that he would continue to underachieve!

We're troubled by these trends. As society becomes more protective of children, as we attempt to "support" them more, as we try to "give" them self-esteem, as we try to be more "positive" with them, it appears they do worse. As we involve ourselves more in their relationships with one another, they fight and tease more. As we offer them more individualized help with their studies or diagnose them as learning disabled, they underachieve more. As we give them more to be happy about, they become more depressed. As we broaden the agenda of items for which schools are responsible, the focus on the primary job of education becomes lost. We watched these approaches for all the years we've been in practice and cannot escape this conclusion: Helping children by making life easier for them has created more problems than solutions.

A Clue to the Mystery

Let us tell you the stories of two young women we know well:

Kathy, the youngest of three children, is a sixteen-year-old junior in high school. We saw her for long-standing problems with insomnia. Kathy has two brothers, one a sophomore in college and the other a senior in high school. She gets along well with both. Kathy's parents have a stable, 20-plus-year marriage. She carries a B+ average in school, completes her work on time and, in most instances, does quality work. She is achieving at a level consistent with her abilities and usually works hard on her homework, though on rare occasions she might rush through an assignment just to get it done.

Kathy is well known in school and has quite a few friends, some very close. Kathy tells us that her friends feel they can always count on her, that she's loyal and honest, "fun to be with," "not a prude"—high praise in the adolescent caste system.

Kathy is an athlete. She enjoys basketball and softball, but soccer is her true love. As a freshman, Kathy tried out for the soccer team but didn't make the team. The coach liked Kathy's drive and determination, but simply felt she wasn't seasoned enough. The coach encouraged her to get more experience with the Park and Recreation League before trying out for the school team the next year. Kathy, telling us this story, said, "Bumm-aire! I thought I could do it. I tried my hardest, but I just wasn't good enough. So I did what Coach told me to do."

Over the next year, Kathy played both indoor and outdoor soccer at Park and Rec. The following spring, as soon as the ground was free from snow, she could be found outside practicing dribbling, kicking goals, or running to get in shape.

When Kathy made the school team the following fall, she was thrilled. "I was pretty sure I could do it," she told her parents excitedly. "I wasn't always sure during some of the tryout games, but I did it. I'm sure glad I didn't give up." Although she was far from being the marquee player during her first full season, Kathy's game was defined by stability and consistency. At the end of the year, her coach commended her tenacity: She told us that he said, "I can always count on you to do your best."

Kathy is engaged and elated with the world. She's a delight to talk to, and has something to say on topics that range from soccer to state politics to school gossip. She has a particular interest beyond her years in pragmatic living skills and often talks with her corporate-executive father about the management of personal and business finances.

Kathy's parents have always insisted that their children have household responsibilities, so Kathy shares household chores with her brother, and she is required to keep her own bedroom neat and orderly. Less than thrilled with these duties, she nevertheless does them—albeit with minor complaints. "I do them," she said resignedly, "but they aren't exactly the high point of my week."

Kathy will test rules and stretch limits like any teenager. One parental mandate is no food in the carpeted family room. Kathy has broken this rule on occasion, and always seems to get caught—errant Doritos and Coke cans give her away. When confronted by her mother, Kathy reluctantly admits her transgression and goes off to clean up after herself.

A year ago, before she was allowed to date formally, Kathy and her brother John worked out an under-the-table deal: He would ferry her to McDonald's so that she could see a boy who had caught her eye. She would meet the lad, spend a few hours with him, and later join up with John so that they could go home together.

Ultimately, Kathy's parents became suspicious. They asked whether she was dating. She reluctantly confessed the arrangement, complaining that all of her friends were able to date before they were sixteen, that it wasn't "fair." Her parents' response? "We're sorry that you don't think the rules are fair, Kathy, but you still have to follow them." Kathy reluctantly agreed and, until she was sixteen years old, didn't date. Nonetheless, she continued to believe the rule was archaic and unfair, but, to her credit, she honored it until she was sixteen. She wasn't happy about it, but she went on with her life.

Another young woman, Margie, is a sixteen-year-old we've seen at the clinic for several years. Margie comes from a seemingly "nice" family. Her father works in a skilled trade, and although he is on the road a lot with his business, he is attentive to Margie and her siblings and seems to be a loving father. Margie's mother, a devout woman who attends church regularly, has insisted on a religious upbringing for her children. One of Margie's sisters is in college and doing well. Her other sister, the younger one, is confined to a wheelchair with cerebral palsy. Margie is an appealing, very attractive girl who excels in high school both in academic subjects and several sports. She is always neatly dressed, never a hair askew. Boys are attracted to her, but she has had no serious relationships. She comes across as demure and charming in a shy and quiet kind of way.

But Margie has a problem: She weighs only eighty-seven pounds. As we got to know her better, we discovered some frightening behavior patterns. Margie gets satisfaction from only one area of her life—controlling her weight. In all other aspects of life, this young woman finds little pleasure. She cannot tell herself she is okay in any other activity. She neither praises herself nor is she proud of her accomplishments in sports and academics— she is never "good enough." She is unable to see herself as a worthy person; instead she sees herself as someone with deep and terrible secrets. She is sure that if anybody ever really got to know her, they would find her lacking. Believe it or not, her big secret is something most people accept about themselves: She's not perfect! But she cannot see herself as worthwhile unless she's perfect, and she loathes the very human part of herself that's not. Her goal is absolutely unreachable, even when she narrows her aspiration for perfection down to just her weight. She does not, cannot, see herself as attractive to boys, but regards herself as dowdy and undesirable. She has had no lasting, deep friendships and is scared stiff by intimacy. Her closest relationships are with therapists, but she tells them only what she wants them to know—and that's darn little. She feels isolated and inefficacious, and has thought about suicide on a number of occasions.

Margie's family seems stable. Her parents have never considered divorce and, indeed, don't appear to have any difficulty. But Margie's mother is terribly concerned about her teenager. Her sister goads Margie constantly to eat more, and at mealtime time the entire family focuses on Margie's food intake, which is minimal, or on her exercise regime, which is fanatical.

Margie's mother describes her as the nicest girl in the world. When little, she was always good, always did nice, pleasing things for mom, particularly when she had to deal with Margie's sister who was chronically ill and developmentally disabled. Margie never said a cross word. Margie always did what she was told. Margie, indeed, seemed to live for her mother's needs.

Margie's biggest concern is whether other people will like her. She worries that she might do something to upset or disappoint others, in particular her parents. Margie frets continually about others' feelings, never her own. She always tries to be proper and perfect. Yet she lies, both to others and to herself, about her food intake, exercise, and weight. Margie has been through one doctor after another and program after program. Despite all the help she's received, she has no interests other than exercising, weighing herself, and agonizing over what goes into her mouth. She has no idea how to make herself happy, only how to make others happy. Margie is chronically depressed—and doesn't seem to have the resources to improve her situation.

From the therapist's clinical point of view, the people in Margie's family are very enmeshed with one another. That is, they're overly involved in one another's business and don't tend to their own. They lack independence; they cannot support each other's efforts at finding solutions for problems without meddling in the solution. Rather than caring for one another, they caretake one another. Each family member has difficulty recognizing the personal boundaries of others, invading privacy without a second thought. The family message is "we are all responsible for one another" rather than "each of us is responsible, first and foremost, for ourselves." Margie feels responsible for everyone's problems but her own.

Margie does not particularly enjoy her athletic activities, but she has found that swimming and running help greatly in controlling her weight. She also believes a perfect body must be in perfect physical condition, and she feels a little more normal as a result of her participation. Her "jock" status, her nearly perfect grades, and—most of all—her skeletal frame are the only things Margie calls her own. Despite the concern of others, Margie's sense of personal competence comes only from being able to run vast distances and remain emaciated.

Margie and Kathy are both attractive and intelligent girls, and excellent athletes. Both come from homes with stable marriages with parents who want the best for their children. Yet one of the girls is marinating in self-induced misery while the other is a vivacious, thriving young woman. Why is there such a difference in the lives of these two young women? We believe that Kathy's family fostered, even insisted upon, independence and self-sufficiency, whereas Margie's family stifled and discouraged independence. Margie's family actively, though unknowingly, encouraged, nourished, and required dependence.

In Kathy's family, feelings were private experiences and were owned by the individual experiencing them. Feelings were respected for what they were. Discussions of feelings were encouraged. In Kathy's home, you were responsible for managing your own feelings. Empathy towards another was encouraged, but it was not okay to meddle, to attempt to make another feel better by taking action beyond a compassionate and supportive response. In Margie's family, everyone's feelings were the purview of others; Margie never learned to take care of her own feelings. If you felt sad, it was the job of others in the family to do something to make you feel better, to solve your problem for you. If this didn't happen, your bad feelings were their fault. Margie grew up expecting her family to make bad feelings go away. Margie learned to have others take care of her, while Kathy learned she could, and must, take care of herself.

Despite their religious faith, Margie's family values were always changing to accommodate each member's immediate desires (to feel good). Not so in Kathy's family. Family values superseded an individual's feelings. Rules and values were never altered or modified to make a family member happy.

Margie's world is threatening and fearful. She is constantly on guard to protect her secret—that she is human and not perfect. Image management is her sole goal. She believes she must be the perfect child, student, and friend, disappointing to no one, approved of by all.

In contrast, Kathy has learned that failure isn't the end of the world—that it's an unpleasant experience but not a catastrophe. She has learned that failure can be attributed to two things—insufficient effort or an unreasonable goal, and she has learned to distinguish between the two. She has also learned that persistence and patience are the keys to success.

Margie never learned to follow her parent's rules because they could always be changed. If she can't change a rule, she finds a way around it, offering either reasonable explanations or excuses that evoke sympathy for her transgressions. Margie is dishonest, both with herself and others. Much of her dishonesty is focused on rigid weight control in her pursuit of perfection and her half-hearted attempts to correct her problem. She blames others for her failures. When asked how she is doing, she replies in a defeated, mournful tone, "I'm trying . . . I'm doing the best I can." At other times, she resorts to blame: "I know I could be doing much better, . . . things have been so stressful lately. I just don't get enough support from my family. After this next week when life is less stressful, I'll get back on track." Or "this isn't my fault. I just can't deal with all the craziness in my family." Each time we see her, she offers up excuses, someone or something else to blame for her failure to make progress.

Kathy, in contrast, has learned to accept responsibility for her behavior. She doesn't often make excuses or attempt to justify her behavior. She could have conveniently lied about her dating, blamed her failure to make the soccer team on her coach, or denied leaving the pop cans in the family room. Instead, Kathy accepts responsibility for what she does. She might not agree with the rules about dating, but she follows them nonetheless. It would have been much less immediately stressful for Kathy to have lied about dating, evading her parents' wrath. She could have made excuses or denied the pact she had with her brother. But what she did was recognize her failings and go about the hard business of correcting the problem. Kathy expressed her feeling that her parents' rules about dating were unreasonable and unfair, yet she knew, in the end, that she would have to observe those limits. From her life experience, Kathy has learned it is not always easy to adapt to the world, things are not always fair or reasonable, and the world won't bend to her interpretation of life. Instead she has to learn to deal with things the way they are.

We spent a lot of time treating kids who exhibit behavior similar to Margie's, and we puzzled over the lack of success—in our practice as well as in those of other doctors—for a long time. We noticed that although their problems are many and varied, most of the children we treated found it difficult, if not impossible, to play by the rules in their lives. They were typically frightened, fearful, angry, and sullen. Rather than recognize their own failures, they blamed their failures on circumstance—or on others—instead of learning to accept responsibility for their lives. Their universal refrains were "I can't; I won't; I don't, it's not fair; it's not right; it's not my fault." For these sad, maladjusted children, failure is devastating. They often don't get along with their parents, siblings, schoolmates, and teachers. When things get hard, they can usually be found asking others to correct the world for them.

The upward trend in the statistics reflecting problems among our nation's youth had us just as perplexed as anyone else until one day, six years ago, we made an observation that changed our understanding of these problems and our approach to them. It has taken the intervening years to grasp the meaning of this new view, but the resulting understanding has been worth the work.

We were having a working lunch one day at a local Italian restaurant. We get together at least once a week to swap stories, consult about patients, and discuss the plight of American children. I (EWS) was relating the stories of three teenagers who, while having very different problems, all had managed to defeat the best efforts of many helping professionals in school and the community to improve their lot. All three were highly manipulative. I wasn't making any more progress than any of the other professionals who had treated them, and I was frustrated with my ineffective efforts. Finally, I blurted out, "Pat, is everything manipulation?" Pat frowned and thought for a moment. Finally, he said, "Well, maybe so. That's an interesting idea." The idea took root in our minds and we talked about manipulation over many lunches after that, exploring the possibility that manipulation was a real clue to the mystery of all these failing children.

We were already well aware that manipulative behavior was commonly present in children who were having problems. But, like most professionals in the field, we saw it as a manifestation of their difficulties, a secondary effect. Suddenly, we were looking at manipulation differently, as a more fundamental behavior somehow directly related to the cause of their difficulties. As we paid more attention to manipulative behavior, we realized that virtually every child with problems we studied was using manipulation as their primary problem-solving mechanism. When things were easy and smooth, many of these children operated just like any other child. But when the going got rough, they immediately shifted to using manipulation to eliminate or circumvent the problems they faced. Some children used manipulation all the time, spending virtually every waking hour trying to influence and manage the behavior of others.

Then we looked at children who were doing well. Eureka! These kids manipulated very little. When they tried, their parents, siblings, and friends rebuffed them. The difference was so striking we began to suspect that the very criteria we used to define a healthy child—being responsible for self, being honest, having goals in life, taking both failure and success in stride, being emotional without being emotionally labile—were inherently nonmanipulative characteristics. Healthy children were healthy precisely because they did not attempt to solve life's problems through manipulation.

We realized that the common denominator among children with widely disparate problems was the use of manipulation as a method of adaptation. That is, kids experiencing difficulty, no matter the type of difficulty (excluding children who were frankly psychotic or who had neurologic conditions that accounted for their problems), were joined together in one large group by this single variable. The manner of their manipulation, who they manipulated, and the conditions under which they manipulated, differed greatly, but the manipulation factor remained a constant.

Self-Esteem versus Manipulation

Self-esteem is a dynamic, ever-changing set of beliefs about oneself. It is manifest in a sense of personal competence, self-confidence, and worthiness. It varies from time to time and situation to situation. It is self-generated and requires effort to maintain or expand. It is not a possession that, once acquired, is permanent; rather, it is a set of feelings about oneself that require constant renewal. Self-esteem cannot be given to someone, but the skills to build it can be taught. It is not egotistical; it does not thrive on the defeats and failures of others or even comparison with others. Self-esteem is most apparent in individuals who have excellent knowledge of their own personal goals and values and live their lives in strict accordance with them.

Self-esteem is not feeling good or happy. As the proverb goes, "Gold and silver are forged in the fire of the furnace; character in the fire of adversity." People learn self-esteem by overcoming difficulty. The biggest lessons we learn about our own self-worth come from the hardest, most fear-ridden things we do. Engineered success, easy accomplishments, or avoidance of situations that frighten us do not bolster our self-worth. Self-esteem is built on the bedrock of many experiences that, taken together, prove our overall competence to accomplish what we set out to do. When we find the easy way out or accomplish our ends through someone else, we may feel relief or happiness for the moment, but our self-esteem suffers in the long run.

As we continued to compare children who believe in themselves, who feel competent in the world, and who know they are worthy and worthwhile, with their less fortunate counterparts, we realized that they use manipulation very little. Children who have an overblown idea of their own importance are egotistical and self-centered, or children who believe that they are worth little and therefore dislike themselves, manipulate their way through life. We realized that there exists an inverse relationship between manipulative behavior and self-esteem. Virtually without exception, it became clear to us that the more children manipulate, the less able they are to develop enduring self-esteem.

From this realization many questions arose. What is manipulation? Can we define it scientifically? What are the different styles of manipulation? Where does it come from? How is it learned? Can we prevent its devastating effects on self-esteem? How do we treat patients who are manipulative? What advice can we give parents that will steer them on a course of childrearing that will reduce the likelihood of their child becoming manipulative? The rest of this book will attempt to answer and address these questions.

To Do List:

1. Make an assessment of your own self-esteem. What were the events in your life that contributed most to your sense of competence, of worth in the world? Are there areas you actively avoid because you don't feel you can deal with them? Characterize recent activities and pursuits that have resulted in a feeling of self-worth. What conclusions can you draw from these experiences?

2. What role did your parents play in the development of your self-esteem? If they had a beneficial effect, try to characterize what it was they did. If you feel they had a negative effect on you, what was it they did? Remember, we're talking self-esteem, not feeling good or happy. How did your parents transmit their belief in you?

3. Do you try to parent in a way that avoids the mistakes of your parents? What were these mistakes? Were they really mistakes in the long run, or just unpleasant at the time? Did you learn anything useful in the process? Basing your parenting on avoidance of the mistakes your parents made will decidely not help you to raise nonmanipulative children. You should have a clear goal as to what you want to achieve as a parent, rather than reacting to the past experiences you had as a child.

4. What is your primary job as a parent? Write it down, and then ask yourself whether you are successful. Will your child learn to be independent and self-sufficient as a result? Are the things you wrote down really your job, or perhaps the job of the children in question? What do you want to accomplish with your children?

CHAPTER 2

What Is Manipulation?

When we first realized the importance of manipulation in the lives of the children we treated, we didn't have a useful, accurate definition. Everyone seems to have their own understanding of what manipulation is and what it does, but we needed a precise, inclusive, scientifically correct definition. We needed to understand the ways in which manipulation actually works, the styles of manipulation, the kinds of people who manipulate, and the reasons they manipulate.

We noticed that most descriptions of manipulation assumed or implied that these behaviors were guided by conscious thought. From novelist to scientist, all assumed manipulation to be consciously planned behavior. When we looked at our patients who were manipulating their way through life, however, we discovered just the opposite: They did not seem particularly aware of how they were operating or why they were doing what they did. Manipulation turned out to be just a way of carrying on life's business, a mode of adapting to the world. Learned from doing, it becomes habitual and quite unconscious behavior. Remarkably, we found that patients used manipulation even when other more honest and straightforward methods would have served as well or better.

We found little to help us understand how or why manipulation works. While manipulation is the stock-in-trade of many excellent fiction writers, we discovered little about the actual process of manipulative interactions. Likewise, there were no clues to help us comprehend how and why manipulation had been learned in the first place, or why it eventually and inevitably led to failure. Descriptions and definitions didn't describe the personal characteristics of the manipulators or their subjects or the problems they inherited along the way, or much about the goals of the interaction. Novelists have addressed these questions often, but their descriptions, which imply that manipulations are usually consciously planned, mislead us. Clearly we had work to do, so we set out to describe what we saw in our patients, to try to make sense of what was often very confusing behavior.

We needed investigative tools that would allow us to tease out the important facts. For the most part, we used a method called Applied Behavioral Analysis. Using observable behavior as data, this approach analyzes the temporal relationship of specific human responses to one another: When a target behavior occurs, the conditions that were present just before and immediately following are recorded and analyzed. By using this method, one can understand why a specific behavior is occurring and, if one chooses, design a treatment program to reduce, increase, or change the behavior. Tedious but reliable, this method allows dissection of situations that would otherwise be thoroughly confusing.

When we started our analysis, we guessed that we would discover that manipulators were positively reinforced for their manipulations—that their manipulative behavior produced a desired, immediate, and added response from those being manipulated. But we soon found we couldn't make this hypothesis work—it just didn't fit the observed data. Yes, manipulations often were rewarded and the manipulator got his way, but often, manipulations seemed to go nowhere, to end in an inextricable stalemate. We knew that positively reinforced behaviors tend to disappear when the desired immediate result doesn't happen; our clients tenaciously continued to try to manipulate even when there was no desired added outcome.

We were puzzled. Finally, we concluded that there must be another mechanism working here—something that would explain the persistence of these behaviors despite their failure to achieve the obvious desired result. One day, Pat had one of his semimonthly brainstorms:

"Could all this be negatively reinforced? Is all this avoidance behavior?"

Bingo. It fit. We had observed, over and over, that the manipulator and his subject were often (perhaps we should even say, always) avoiding something. This explained our observations; we could now make sense of our experience.

So, you ask, what's the big difference here? To clarify, we'll need to acquaint the reader with a few concepts from behavioral science:

Reinforcement is any immediate response to a behavior which makes it likely that the behavior will occur again in the future.

Positive reinforcement is something that happens immediately following a behavior that is added. The word positive, in positive reinforcement, does not mean good, warm, nice, or even desirable. It means that something happened immediately following a behavior that was *added,* rather than subtracted. For instance, if we say something to someone and they reply immediately and appropriately, their reply acts to reinforce us, and we are likely to continue the interaction. If there is no response, we are less likely to try to continue the interaction. Most of what we learn to do is shaped (modified) by the ongoing feedback we perceive—whether it's interacting socially, playing tennis, or driving a car. Very little of this requires cognitive analysis unless the feedback is significantly delayed. Behavior learned and shaped by positive reinforcement is not very enduring; instead, it is very flexible and adaptable to situational change because the feedback changes.

The negative in negative reinforcement means that something is subtracted from the system as an immediate result of a behavior. When you get in your car and switch on the key and the radio erupts with 110 decibels of screeching electric guitars accompanying some pitiful attempt at singing (because your teenage son was the last to drive the car), you immediately reach for the knob and turn the volume down. You are negatively reinforced: The full-blast heavy metal is removed from the system, and you feel relief. Contrary to popular understanding, negative reinforcement is not punishment, and the difference is very significant. Punishment occurs when something unpleasant immediately follows a behavior—it is added to the system. Like positive reinforcement, its effects don't last if the conditions for punishment are removed (for instance, mom and dad aren't watching right now). In contrast, behavior learned through negative reinforcement is very enduring, even when situations change.

There are two special kinds of behaviors learned through negative reinforcement that are essential to understanding manipulation: escape and avoidance. Quickly learned and amazingly persistent, they are the basis for manipulative behavior. Here is an example of how they work: If a person experiences an unpleasant or painful event, like an electric shock, s/he will learn to avoid situations in which an electric shock will occur again, or to escape the potential for a shock. The precautions people will take to avoid or escape future shocks may be elaborate and inventive. A research psychologist named R. L. Solomon did some of the original animal experiments in this area. In his experiments, dogs learned to jump out of a box when a light was turned on, because otherwise they would receive a light electrical shock through the floor of the box. They learned the behavior after only a few experiences. Unlearning this response, however, was another matter. The behaviors persisted for years even when the conditions that taught the dogs to avoid the shocks were removed. Only after hundreds of tries, without the threat of shock, did the learned response begin to falter.

Think of a situation you avoid—like getting an electric shock or meeting someone you dislike intensely. Now think of all the ways you use to get around or away from this situation and how persistent your response to these situations is over time! A lot of basic behavior is based on this response, most of it perfectly healthy and adaptive (for example, would you wear only your underwear to the shopping mall, or would you eat with your hands and belch loudly at a formal dinner party?). Once we've learned an avoidance response, we carry around a memory that results in discomfort, apprehension, or anxiety whenever we even think about the situation—this maintains the response. Avoidance and escape responses are not rational, and are not likely to be unlearned through reason.

Behavior learned through negative reinforcement can produce all sorts of unpleasant bodily reactions. Some years ago a Stanford University psychologist whimsically described what he called the "Sauce Béarnaise" Phenomenon. This college professor's favorite meal was filet mignon with sauce béarnaise. One evening he went out to a restaurant and ate his favorite meal. Later that night he became ill with a stomach flu that was going around and experienced nausea and vomiting all night long. You can guess the rest of the story: From then on, the mere thought of sauce béarnaise made him queasy, and he never ate it again. Many people react viscerally to specific situations or thoughts; their responses have been learned in just this way, and their reactions may endure for years or life.

So how is it that manipulation is based on avoidance and escape? The manipulator has a keen awareness of what his target will avoid, and uses it as a ploy. Manipulation will not work if the person being manipulated will not avoid whatever the manipulator is trying to sidestep. Since the manipulator is also avoiding something, and will go to great lengths to succeed in his manipulation, the manipulative interaction is characterized by mutual avoidance.

Let's look at an example. Joey is a six-year-old who is somewhat anxious by nature. New experiences frighten him, and he would much rather hang around his mom or dad than try something he has not experienced before. His parents have learned this about him, and are afraid of upsetting him because they believe this may do harm to his developing personality (they assume he is fragile). They live in Minnesota, land of ten thousand lakes, where the ability to swim is an absolute requirement to enjoy life safely. Joey's mom, Katie, signed him up for summer swimming lessons at the local YMCA, and initially Joey agreed. But as the day of the first lesson approached, Joey began to express his reluctance to participate, and when the day finally arrived, he developed a mysterious stomach ailment and refused to get out of bed. Katie, who felt his stomachache was probably caused by his anxiety about the lessons, reassured him that everything would be okay and insisted he get himself up and ready to go. Joey cried louder about his tummy, and, when this didn't work, threw a fit, accusing his mother of not caring about him.

"You never listen to me. My tummy hurts," cried Joey.

"Your tummy will be just fine as soon as the lesson is over. You have to learn to swim, otherwise you won't be safe around water. Now please get up," Katie said.

"I hate swimming; I already know how to swim."

"You do not know how to swim, and how can you say you hate swimming? You love to be in the water."

Joey became all the more upset, crying so hard that he finally threw up. His mother relented, telling herself that Joey would be more willing to take swimming lessons next year. "Besides," she thought to herself, "I shouldn't push him—he'll do things in his own time."

Both Katie and Joey avoided situations they feared: Now Joey didn't have to face an unfamiliar situation and the loss of control that might mean, and Katie, who felt guilty about insisting Joey participate against his will, was relieved by acquiescing to Joey's refusal. Joey lost both the opportunity to gain self-confidence by learning a new and useful skill and by overcoming the fear of tackling a new situation. Katie lost the opportunity to see her child take a step toward independence, and, in the process traded a very real risk (drowning) for an imaginary risk (damage to Joey's psychological development). When Joey was seven, they played out the same scene, only more vehemently because by then both he and his mother were more determined to avoid things.

This simple scenario illustrates the essence of manipulation. Both participants had hidden agendas, and neither was truthful about their true feeling (fear). Both had knowledge, gained from past experience, of what the other would avoid. Neither's fears were rational, and the only immediate payoff (reinforcement) at the end was relief from anxiety and guilt. Both could justify their actions and positions, but an outsider could easily see through their explanations. The outcome did not serve any kind of long-term goal for either participant. Principles (swimming is essential to safety in the water) were confounded by emotions. Neither planned or consciously guided the scenario, but each reacted predictably out of fear or guilt.

Over several years, we've analyzed many clinical scenarios like Joey and Katie's, in which manipulation was present, and derived some characteristics common to all manipulative situations:

- All participants in a manipulation are avoiding something; what they are avoiding is usually hidden.

- Self-deception is commonly present in both the manipulator and the manipulated.

- Manipulative interactions tend to maintain the status quo rather than serve a long-term goal.

- Manipulative interactions are guided by expediencies of the moment, not principles: They are opportunistic.

- Independence is lost and dependence is strengthened in a manipulation.

- Manipulations can be justified, but the reasoning employed won't survive critical outside analysis.

- Manipulations are rarely planned or even conscious; they are just how one goes about life's business.

- When manipulations are not working, manipulators redouble their effort and often use cruder forms of manipulation to achieve their end.

Forms of Manipulation

When we began to identify and study manipulation in our clients, we immediately recognized that there were many kinds of manipulation. Some were blatant and crude, others very subtle and sophisticated. Some worked in only certain situations, others were more generally used. Crude and obvious manipulations were learned very early on; older children often employed much subtler forms. A particular child's manipulative style often seemed more determined by inborn temperament than by the temperament of the parents. We developed the following classification of manipulative styles from our experience:

Internal/External Untruth

These are lies one tells about oneself to avoid something. They may be subtle or obvious to an outsider, but if the target of the manipulation accepts them, the manipulation can proceed. Generally these self-lies are incapacitating. While they may start out as a deception to avoid something, they often turn into beliefs about self based on and verified by failures—failures that are exclusively the result of lack of effort or risk taking. If one believes that one can't do something, one won't try or will make only a half-hearted attempt, confirming one's belief about one's self. Confronting these lies will produce vigorous self-defense and dislike—often short-lived—of the confronter. If we continue to insist that the manipulator do something inconsistent with his erroneous self-concept, he will often resort to a cruder and more abusive style of manipulation.

Examples are "I can't . . . ," "I'm just too scared to . . . ," "I just don't understand . . . ," "I hate . . . ," "I'm bored with . . . ," "I'm dumb," "I'll do it later."

How often have we accepted a statement by a child like these, relieving the child of responsibility for his own life or happiness? When we feel sorry for a child with these complaints and act on our pity to "help," we erode independence. If we continuously do this to a child over years, we will create a very dependent person. There is a better way that is both compassionate and promotes independence and responsibility for self.

Mary started a career of underachievment in school in the first grade. She had difficulty learning to read, but she got along because of a winning smile and pleasant ways. She was diagnosed with Attention Deficit Disorder, and treatment was started. Her attentiveness in school improved some, but she never learned the most basic skills—she could neither read nor spell. By seventh grade, things were going very poorly. She did her homework only with constant parental prodding, and then poorly. She did her assignments late or did not turn them in at all, or she did them with the help of friends or study hall teachers. In the eighth grade, she wanted to do better, but failed because she could not find enough help to get her through. One day when she was fourteen, she decided that the pressure was too much and wanted to move out.

When Mary had trouble learning to read in the first grade, she experienced what many children who have the characteristics of ADD experience: Learning phonics is tedious and repetitive—just the sort of work these children find odious. She looked for help, for relief, and she found it. She successfully got around learning to sound out words, and learned enough words by sight to make it to the third grade. From there on, things became increasingly difficult. Reading new words became nearly impossible without the help of others, so she concluded that she was not capable. At that point, she gave up, and explained her failure and lack of effort to herself and the world by relying on the crippling belief: "I'm stupid."

Shifting Responsibility and Blame

In this more obvious form of manipulation, a skillful sleight of hand removes the responsibility from the self and places it elsewhere. If we allow this type of manipulative behavior, we enable the manipulator to escape dealing with his own life.

Let's revisit Margie's situation as an example. Margie is the young woman with Anorexia Nervosa mentioned in chapter 1. She was a master at this manipulative technique, which made her treatment very difficult. She could always be counted upon to have a litany of excuses for her failure to make progress: "Things are really stressful at home," "School is so hard this semester," "My sister is always on my case."

School underachievers, like Mary, often offer excuses like: "I loaned my books to a friend," or "I forgot my stuff at school." The excuses are many and diverse.

Every time we ask children the question "why?" when we know they've behaved inappropriately, we may be encouraging them to shift blame and deny responsibility rather than encouraging them to own their own lives and behavior. If we are lucky, they'll answer honestly with "I don't know." But more often than not, the question "why?" asks children to fabricate a little lie, to explain their misbehavior or misfortune. Worse, it suggests to them that if their answer is good enough, they may be off the hook. Unfortunately, this practice is widespread—watch what many teachers do when misbehavior occurs. Parents who wish to counteract the prevailing approach and teach their children to become responsible for themselves must steadfastly place responsibility for self back on their children's shoulders.

Asking the question "why?" is done with good intentions by people who believe that our behavior is under continuous, conscious cognitive control. A little introspection by these people would demonstrate that few human acts are decided upon before doing. Imagine how your day would go if everything you did had to be planned and decided upon before execution. How much thought do you give, once you've decided to get up, to your morning routine? While you shower, eat breakfast, get dressed, and drive to work, you think very little about what you're doing. During this time you may be planning your day, making a checklist of things you need to do, but you aren't likely to be consciously guiding your immediate actions. The only time we really guide our immediate behavior is when we're doing something new—and then we usually don't do a good job because we haven't practiced what we're doing until it has become automatic. Worse, if we begin to try to guide well-practiced behavior consciously, we mess it up. For instance, any athlete who becomes self-conscious, who tries to guide his performance consciously, will start to make mistakes. Even academic performance will suffer if focus on the topic shifts to focus on one's performance. Test anxiety has its roots here.

Instead of conscious direction of our behavior, we may make the decision to engage in a particular activity or project, and once we've made that decision, our learned "repertoire" of behavior takes over from there—thank goodness. Otherwise we would accomplish very little. Some human acts are purely impulsive. We think of something and act—there is no conscious decision to act. Misbehavior is typically impulsive, not planned or decided in advance, so asking a child why s/he did something only teaches the child to make up a plausible explanation. Worse, "why?" teaches a child to make up an explanation to gain absolution. Trying to find a reason for our behavior is rarely helpful. Learning to accept responsibility for our actions and their consequences may be momentarily uncomfortable, but it is the essential step we must take to become self-directed—and nonmanipulative—in our lives.

How many of us have worked with or known people who constantly explain away or shift blame for their misfortunes and misadventures? Are they effective people? Every time someone shifts blame and responsibility, they acquire the mantle of a victim and, thereby, give up power over their own life. When we allow children to do this, when we train them to shift responsibility by asking the question "why?" we eliminate the possibility of taking a step toward independent control of their existence.

Shifting blame and responsibility avoids the discomfort of dealing with the things that happen to us in our lives, and eliminates the possibility of learning from our mistakes and failures. We must not teach our children to engage in this mechanism; it will paralyze them in the long run. We'll discuss this more in a later chapter, when we discuss parenting styles.

Seduction and Coercion

Seduction and coercion are like two sides of a coin. Occasionally, manipulative children use one of these styles exclusively, but most employ both, depending on the circumstances. Commonly, when seductive tactics aren't working well to control a situation, the manipulator will switch to coercive tactics.

The seductive manipulator seems to offer something the manipulated desires in exchange for favors from the manipulated. But what seems offered is really just smoke and mirrors, an act to attain an end. Sexual seduction is common, but many other forms exist: the promise of attention, overniceness, the promise of money or material things, the promise of future favors, and so on. Seductions are difficult to confront because they are so pleasing to the manipulated, who also fears the loss of the favors. Often the behavior involved appears desirable and even appropriate until, on closer examination, we realize that the behavior occurs only to achieve the manipulator's end. If the seduction doesn't work, anger often results. The manipulator commonly puts down the unsuccessfully manipulated, classifying him in a simple, pejorative category (jerk, nerd, uncaring, self-centered, egotist, and so on). The anger may lead to reprisal spanning the spectrum from simply bad-mouthing the person, to lawsuits or violence.

Some manipulators coerce people around them to do their bidding by using unpleasant and frightening tactics like threats of violence or actual violence, angry outbursts, and temper-tantrums, but the average coercive manipulator uses much more subtle methods. For instance, the coercive manipulator may elicit guilty feelings in his target, who then assuages these bad feelings by cooperating with the manipulator's demands. A manipulator may know something we don't want revealed, and we allow ourselves to be emotionally blackmailed to avoid having the truth come out. Embarrassment or the threat of embarrassment is a great tool used by toddlers in public places, but it is perfected by teenagers. A manipulator may be a "nice" person whom we wouldn't want to challenge and risk losing their friendship and goodwill. We may try to teach a daughter to behave well through reasoning with her, but soon find we're being controlled by the same tactic. If we are emotionally coercible, we may not be honest and direct, thereby avoiding unpleasantness ourselves or avoiding causing unpleasant emotions in others.

Manipulators who are skilled in the subtleties of seduction and coercion will usually resort to more primitive and obvious forms when more sophisticated methods fail. Thus, the "nice" manipulator suddenly becomes a violent or spiteful person, the "logical" negotiator has a temper-tantrum, or the guilter pulls out all they've got on us. When we yield, these manipulators magically revert to their previous modes, becoming nice or reasonable or subtly guilting, until they need to resort yet again to the coercive or seductive tactics they need to get what they want.

Here are some examples of this type of manipulation:

Julie's parents, concerned about her grades, confront her: "Julie. You got a 'D' in English. What's going on?" Julie responds, "I was so upset by you and Dad fighting, I just couldn't concentrate." Rather than talking about her own feelings, Julie immediately put the blame on her parents by trying to make them feel guilty and responsible for her poor performance.

George, Julie's brother, who rarely lifts a finger to help around the house, is asked to take out the garbage: "Why do I always have to do it? I did it yesterday and Julie never does it." His mother replies, "Julie has other responsibilities." George, too, plays the guilt card: "Oh, sure, and I suppose she has to interrupt her homework to do her work." The volley continues when George's mother responds: "But you're not doing your homework. You're watching TV." All the while, the task at hand never gets done.

Then there are the perennial favorites: "All the other kids' parents let them . . . and don't make them . . ."

Jane was in eighth grade when a boy she was dating made sexual advances toward her while they were lounging around the family swimming pool. She was wearing a skimpy bikini, and he had managed to remove the top of it before being interrupted by a friend who dropped by to visit. The boy had used no force, but Jane had been unable to tell him to stop. When she told her mother about it, they concluded this was an attempted rape and was, therefore, entirely the fault of the boy. Jane became depressed after this incident, but continued to go out with boys. Again, at age sixteen, she was visited by a boy she considered a friend. They were alone, lying together on the floor, legs entwined, listening to music, when he began to fondle her. He began removing her shorts. Again, no force was used, but she was unable to say no. And again, she was saved by the bell—a neighbor dropped by, giving her an excuse to go upstairs and visit. When she told her mother about this, they concluded that this was another attempted rape, never addressing the issue of Jane's involvement. For some reason, Jane was unable to speak up for herself and tell these boys to stop. In both cases, Jane's body language and manner of dress were suggestive, but this fact was conveniently forgotten in her discussion with her mother. When we pointed out these omissions to Jane and mentioned that sexual advances are a part of life one must deal with, Jane began to cry. When asked how she felt, she replied, "stuck between a rock and a hard place." Her dependent understanding of how the world is or ought to be was being challenged, and she didn't like it one bit. Boys were supposed to play it her way, no matter the skimpiness of her bikini or the suggestiveness of her posture. And while we cannot condone the behavior of the boys involved, for Jane's benefit, her part in these two scenarios cannot be ignored.

Jane began to see herself as a victim after the first so-called attempted rape. Since then, on several occasions when she has been upset about something in her life, she has overdosed on common medications like Tylenol. She says she does this when she's sad and "just can't go on." She's never taken enough to do much harm, but her parents have been in a constant state of worry for several years. On one occasion, she demanded to be allowed to go to a friend's cabin for the weekend for a unsupervised party. When they said no, she simply told them, "Then I'll commit suicide if I can't go." They gave in, and she went.

Jane is a very dependent person. She wants things to be just her way. Despite her view of herself as a victim in all this, she says that all her best friends are boys and she really has no close girlfriends. Jane is a pretty girl with a striking figure. In our view, Jane has used these attributes for years to get her way with boys, but sometimes her seductiveness backfires, and when this happens, she can't accept responsibility. As she's grown up and found that fewer aspects of her life yield to these control tactics, she has grown increasingly depressed and despondent. When nothing she does makes things go her way, she resorts to her ultimate weapon of coercion, suicide.

A local billboard announces, THE LEADING CAUSE OF TEENAGE SUICIDE—UNTREATED DEPRESSION. Over the past few years, suicide among youth has become increasingly common and well publicized. There is little doubt that people who commit suicide are commonly depressed and that effective treatment is available. Unfortunately, however, many children have discovered that the mere mention of thoughts that smack of suicide produces an amazing response from adults. We seem unable to distinguish between depression and the pique of someone denied their way. Sykes refers to SWAT teams of school social workers descending on school situations to make things all right for the child, to rearrange the child's environment so that the child is happier. Rarely is the child asked to change, to cope, to adapt to the real world, to give up victim status. Risky as it may seem, we would prefer an approach that addresses the child's dependency, which demands adaptation to the real world, rather than one that ameliorates the child's emotional state. It is usually much easier, for the moment, to help a child feel better, to relieve a child of demands for self-direction and self-responsibility; it is easy to convince oneself that something useful has been done for the child, all the while feeding the child's dependency. Perhaps, rather than seeing all

WHAT IS MANIPULATION? **33**

the unhappy children out there as depressed, we should take a hard look at the dependency we've created that is the root of their unhappiness.

Let's be clear here: We treat lots of depressed children and adolescents. There is little doubt that depression is a chemical state of the brain just as happiness or anger or irritability are and that there are often inherited predispositions to this altered chemical state. There is also excellent evidence that much depression is in part environmental. There clearly are life events that precipitate depression. We are here concerned with the powerful tool of control children have been given to coerce adults to do their bidding by mentioning the "s" word.

Coercive tactics often involve asking the parent the question "why?" This opening gambit leads to a game of explanation, denial, guilting and shaming, threat of withdrawal of love, attention or privilege, anger or violence. "Why?" on the surface, seems reasonable, but under this veneer hides a person determined to get his way, willing to use all the aforementioned tactics and more in the process. Useful confrontation or discussion is thwarted by these tactics at every turn.

Children often manipulate seductively by being nice and pleasing. Bill was a nice manipulator. He worked all situations by pouring on the sweetness and light. Over the years, he underperformed dramatically in school, but his teachers always commented about what a nice boy he was despite his poor performance. In junior high school, his math teacher showed his mother a test done just before Christmas break. Bill had done only about a third of the test, and that, inaccurately. On the bottom of the test, he had written, "Have a Wonderful Christmas, Mr. Olson." Below this he had drawn a happy face and signed his name. Mr. Olson said to Bill's mother, "How can I flunk a child who's this nice?"

Bill did not really have a friend in the world. He tried to nice his way along with other kids, but he could not earn their respect. Others saw him as an easy mark and just took advantage of him. Often he would fail to study for a test "because" he had lent his books to others. As he got older and his style of manipulation worked less well, he became depressed, angry, and resentful. People just didn't do things right (in other words, his way). In therapy, he talked about how he often imagined himself obtaining a gun and blowing away those he felt were "against him." Bill could not own any responsibility for his situation—it was all the responsibility of someone else. How often have we heard of a teenager who has murdered his whole family, but neighbors and acquaintances report, "He seemed like such a nice boy."

Judy is like Bill in some ways. When she wants something, she flashes a glorious smile, and her eyes sparkle. Her dad melts, and when the inevitable request comes, he complies. On the few occasions when he refused, Judy's wonderful attention was instantly withdrawn and replaced by whiny argument, petulance, and guilting. Judy's dad has learned to avoid her wrath because his self-esteem is not great enough to stand up to her petulant tantrum. He "needs" her attention, phony as it is.

Judy has now learned to use the same technique on boys at school, and dominates one boy after another, at least until they get wise to her. She can't understand why her romances never last, and she always blames the boy for the failure, saying things like "He's such a jerk, I don't know why I ever went out with him in the first place." Judy's emotional life is a roller coaster, and the boys she's been dating lately really aren't so wonderful—emotionally independent guys won't have a thing to do with her. We fear that her life will be one long saga of failed and abusive relationships because she has no idea how to relate to males without using seductive control tactics. Judy is trapped by her skill at seduction and coercion, and probably won't find a way out of this dead end until her life crashes and she has no alternatives.

Seductions are also commonly used by individuals suffering eating disorders: Anorexics are commonly perfect, pleasing, and nice children; bulimics tend to be outgoing, talkative, and sometimes sexually seductive. These kids learn to manage their world by using these tactics, but it all collapses in adolescence, and the symptomatic result is an eating disorder.

Flexible Standards/Adoption of a Subculture

Failing, manipulative teenagers will often adopt a tailored set of "values" that allow them to do what they decide to do. These values often come from an adolescent subculture (punk, hippie, and so forth). When confronted about their behavior or lack of performance, they offer the explanation "I don't believe in that, it's against my standards."

Sherry had a wide-open party at her parents' home while they were away for the weekend. The house was torn apart, the police were involved, and Sherry, drunk and abusive, spent the night in an adolescent psychiatric unit. When her parents asked why she didn't stop the party when it was getting out of hand, she angrily responded, "Because that's against my principles—I would never ask someone to leave my house!" Sherry uses the same gambit to explain her school failure and her loss of numerous jobs. When the situation is examined more closely, it seems that Sherry can always come up with a "principle" to fit the occasion. Her parents have lectured her about values, and she's learned this is their Achilles' heel.

Open, Planned Dishonesty

When people think of manipulation, this is what they generally imagine is happening. They believe the manipulator is consciously aware of his manipulations, of the lies that support his con. Some people operate this way, but most manipulators are only vaguely aware of the untruths and reality distortions underlying what they are trying to do, or they have convinced themselves that their lies are all right, using a "means justifies the end" rationalization.

Planned dishonesty is institutionalized by some unscrupulous lawyers, businessmen, politicians, salesmen, religious evangelists, cult leaders, and other deal makers to suit their own ends. Their dishonesty may be by commission or omission, and they often rely on the facts not being available to the person they wish to manipulate. The manipulated person cooperates with them by not taking responsibility to ask enough questions or find out the facts before acceding to their wishes.

Targets of this kind of manipulation generally wish to believe they are being told the truth; they want to have faith in the manipulator. The manipulator must be skilled in his pitch; smoke and mirrors are his stock in trade. A third party, observing the con in action, will be amazed at the gullibility of the victim—not remembering, of course, when he himself bought that set of encyclopedias or gave money to a "worthy" cause. We're all subject to this kind of manipulation at some time in our lives; skepticism and experience are our only defenses.

Honest Manipulations

Honest manipulations are commmon situations in life where the parties involved know that deception is part of the game being played. The winner discovers the loser's hidden position first. Poker is the classic example of this kind of manipulative game, but other examples abound: Many business deals, buying a house or car, organizational politics, bargaining of all kinds, jokes, and good storytelling—any situation in which all the cards are not on the table and everyone knows it—are examples of honest manipulations. These are often "healthy" interactions; life is full of them, and children should be encouraged to learn about them. Perhaps every kid should learn to play poker!

Characteristics of the Manipulative Interaction

Some characteristics are common to all manipulative interactions. These help us understand manipulation and discover when a manipulative game is taking place.

Mutual avoidance is almost always present. The manipulated person may be avoiding guilt, unpleasantness, struggle, perceived risk, loss of face, embarrassment, loss of control, anxiety, or damage to property or person. The manipulator wants control of the situation and avoids the anxiety associated with its loss. The manipulator commonly wants something tangible from the manipulated, but persists not because of this want but because s/he will experience anxiety if they are not in control.

We commonly see parents who are up a lot at night with a child. Treatment for this problem is simple to explain, but very difficult for many parents to do. It involves putting the child back to bed with no interaction as many times as it takes for the child to stay put. Often the first night of treatment goes on all night—the record so far is 136 trips back to bed during an eight-hour period! The parents took turns hauling the child back through the night. The next night they had to take him back to bed fifty times, the following night twenty-three times, then eleven, then once, and on the fifth night, the child slept through the night.

We always warn people to expect that the child will try every tactic to defeat the parental agenda—from asking for a drink of water to throwing the worst temper-tantrum they've ever seen. Children try to maintain their sense of control over the situation and its predictability, and not until they have exhausted every trick in the book will they stop trying.

Fears in the night are a common reason for preschoolers to get up and join mommy and daddy in their bed. Sean was just such a child. A bright and precocious four-year-old, he had been sleeping with his parents for two and a half years. Recently monsters had come to reside among the dust motes and discarded toys beneath his bed, but that was only the latest in a long series of ploys he used to gain access to his parents' bed. When his parents brought him to us for help, they were exhausted and tense, and commented that there was a good reason why Sean did not have a younger sibling. Sean's father was tired of being interrupted every night, and had tried everything he could think of to keep his son in his own bed at night. He had even lost his temper a few times and spanked Sean, but always felt guilty afterwards. Sean's mother was in a quandary. She wanted to be with her husband alone at night, but related to Sean's fears and felt she must do something about them—who knows what damage they could do if he were left to deal with them himself?

We gave them our standard program and warned them that Sean, and they, would have an awful few nights. We suggested that they prepare Sean for what was going to happen and tell him he could draw pictures the next day of the monsters he saw in the night. We assured them that Sean could deal with his own emotions with their support and loving guidance. We told them to prepare themselves because Sean would try everything he could imagine to get them to allow him to leave his bed.

They started on a Friday night. Sean behaved as expected, whining and crying, screaming and kicking, as he was put back in his bed over and over again. Everyone was up all night. The next night went much better, and four nights into the program, Sean made a half-hearted attempt to leave his bed, but then went to sleep. One week later, he and his family returned to our office, looking refreshed and happy, to report on their success. Sean, they noted, seemed happier during the day and had become more likely to comply with parental requests than ever before.

Sean is an anxious, controlling child. He wanted to remain dependent and continue sleeping with his parents. And he had mastered all sorts of ways to achieve this goal. He feared the independent alternative—sleeping in his own room. His parents feared for his well-being if they said no to his demands and were, as a result, unable to ask him to deal with his own problems.

Both Sean and his parents had secret agendas. Parents who are easily manipulated may be convinced that negative emotional experiences are risky for their child. The child doesn't know this, but learns, through trial and error, that his parents will capitulate when he displays certain emotions. He learns to employ these emotions in response to situations he would like to control, rather than experience these emotions through a rational, cognitive process. As he gets older, he may become aware of the cause of his parent's vulnerability, but he learned and perfected the pattern without conscious awareness and will have a very hard time breaking it.

Manipulators maintain their sense of security in the world (avoiding anxiety) through control of others. While a particular manipulation may have an ostensible objective (in Sean's case, sleeping with his parents), the energy put into the manipulative game comes from a fear of a loss of control of (or change in) the situation, not the ostensible objective. The person being manipulated will be unaware of this and see the struggle as having to do with the stated objective. Sean's parents believed he really was afraid of the monsters under his bed, despite the fact that this explanation was only the latest in a long series of justifications they accepted to allow him to continue to sleep with them. They worried that he would not be able to deal with his fear if they refused his behavior. Other manipulators offer deals, make promises for the future, cajole, or seduce with suggestive language or behavior.

It is important to remember that children learn to operate in the systems in which they exist, by the rules that function in these systems. Children are not conniving little psychopaths, but they are motivated to serve their own wants and will learn quickly to use big people to satisfy their desires if there is a way. Any child will try to manipulate, most will find occasional success, and a few will discover that certain tactics work reliably on certain individuals to bring about the wanted outcome. These last are the children we're concerned with.

The reality of Sean's situation is skewed. Standing back and taking an honest look, most anyone can see that things don't seem quite right, but in the midst of the situation, as avoidance takes over, dishonesty and deception gain a life of their own.

Accomplished manipulators often keep a scorecard. They bitterly remember defeats and use them in future interactions to gain advantage. The presence of this scorecard is a red flag that a manipulation is being attempted. Often, when they have been roundly defeated, bitterness is all that remains.

Accomplished manipulators also see their world in polar terms. You're either for 'em or agin' 'em. Others are viewed as good guys or bad guys, depending on their cooperation with the efforts of the manipulator, who often demonstrates little appreciation for the depth and breadth of the human qualities of others. Extreme, judgmental statements (for example, "I hate . . . ," "The best . . . ," "The most . . . ") are common. These gross generalizations and stereotypical statements about others or about situations suggest lack of honest, thoughtful consideration and, unfortunately, characterize the world view of the manipulator.

Threats are almost always manipulative. They involve one person trying to coerce another into doing it his way, and they are often dishonest. Parents who threaten their children to control behavior are themselves manipulating. These parents will be rewarded with countermanipulation from their children rather than compliance. Children who use threats to get their way may eventually learn to use the big guns in their arsenal—violence or the threat of suicide.

When a manipulation fails, the manipulator is angry and bitter. There is little room for forgiveness and understanding in this scene. The anger and bitterness may become vengeful, and retribution may follow. At the same time, little expression of real feelings happens: The manipulator does not say "I'm angry because I feel so out of control, so powerless." It is unlikely that the manipulator will have the insight that the feeling of powerlessness derives from his failure to control another person.

Many parents try to manipulate their children to behave well: We see parents trying to control behavior by using incentives and promises, punishments and retribution, bargains and bribes, threats, and nagging. These tactics rarely succeed in producing desirable results, but often teach the child how to "play the game." And by using these misguided techniques, parents unwittingly damage the ability of the child to become independent. We'll talk more about this later.

When manipulation is occurring, confusion reigns. If you can't figure out what's going on, stop and examine the situation. When you're arguing about nonsensical things, when the discussion is going nowhere, when you're baffled or buffaloed, think manipulation. The distortion of reality is a fundamental characteristic of a manipulation, confusion and bafflement the byproduct. A common way to handle this confusion is to suspect a "deeper" problem—something mysterious that only a competent, trained therapist can understand. Children are commonly referred for therapy on this pretext. Unfortunately, the outcome rarely justifies the trouble and expense. Worse, the therapist may actually concoct a fanciful and creative explanation for what's going on, and others will uncritically buy into it, leaving the child saddled with a reason for misbehavior that removes any pressure for change. Thomas Szasz, a psychiatrist and critic of our current psychotherapuetic culture, states that psychotherapy "conquered what is, in effect, the human condition by annexing it in its entirety to the medical profession." Psychology, pop or professional, is rife with convenient explanations for inappropriate behavior that allow individuals to deny responsibility for their own life, mistakes, happiness, or behavior.

Why can't I do it? Why can't I wear it? Why won't you let me? The great question "why?" heralds the start of a reasoning/negotiation session. Reasoning with another may seem okay, but it is a common form of manipulation used by bright and verbal children, and responded to by their bright and well-educated parents. Some experience with negotiation is very useful in life, but much of life is non-negotiable and being able to tell the difference is paramount to long-term success and happiness. The child who routinely gets the world to come around to his terms through reasoning and negotiating with those in power (parents, teachers, and so on) is being poorly prepared for healthy and independent functioning. Parents can help teach healthy coping skills by clearly identifying what is negotiable and what is not. When a child attempts to negotiate at every turn, when the question Why? comes up frequently, when all attempts at guidance and limit setting are met with a counter-argument, manipulation is occurring.

Procrastination commonly identifies a manipulative interaction. "I'll do it as soon as my TV show is over," or, "I'm busy right now; I'll do it later." By appealing to reason, these statements allow the child to avoid doing what is asked. The reasonable parent allows this to happen despite the fact that the child has not taken responsibility for duties that are supposed to be completed. The child learns, systematically, to put off the unpleasant, and this is poor preparation for most of life. The parent learns to avoid the child's displeasure at being made to do what s/he is asked. But later, the child's poor school performance tells the story. Procrastination should alert us to a subtle manipulation that can be devastating in the long term.

Some children are wonderful in one setting and horrible in another. Preschool reports are glowing, but home behavior is unbearable; Dad and the child get along just fine, but Mom's hair is graying quickly. What's going on? Children learn quickly where manipulation works, and who they can manipulate. This Jekyll/Hyde scenario tells us where the child is adapting well and where the child has learned to make the world behave the way s/he would like. The model of behavior centers around the child learning to take advantage, push around, cheat, lie to, abuse those closest to him. If you love me, you'll give in to my whims, you'll do it my way. You'll put up with my abuse and give me what I want. Think of the future consequences of this sort of arrangement!

"That teacher has it in for me"; "I hate Mr . . . "; "I hate English"; "It's boring." These statements suggest a manipulator who can't get things to go his way in the situation he doesn't like. When a person's comfort in the world is vested in the ability to manipulate specific situations, he will strongly dislike and fear situations that he can't control. Usually the statements made will not be mild and thoughtful but extreme—not "I don't really care for math; it's not my strong suit," but "I hate math; it's boring." Likewise, when someone is the best, the world's greatest, the only, you may be hearing about someone who is cooperating with a manipulation. Suspect manipulation when you hear these strong statements. Linda Kellogg, a psychologist we respect highly, says, "Even if the teacher is boring, even if the teacher has it in for you, that's how life is. Deal with it."

Secrets are often the cornerstone of a manipulation. Open, honest communication is often the best preventive medicine a family can take against manipulation. (But beware: Open, honest communication does not mean permission to put down others aggressively; it does not mean that the invasion of personal boundaries is okay.) If you are asked to keep a secret, be a little wary of agreeing to the condition. Some secrets are delicious fun ("I've got a crush on . . . ," or "Guess what I'm giving Mom for her birthday?"), but others are the beginning of a manipulative gambit ("Promise not to tell Dad—I flunked English" or "What I do in my room is my business, so stay out"). If you agree to the conditions, you may have just colluded in a manipulation. As an adult and a parent, you need to make the distinction, and announce it up front ("If you want to tell me about your grades and want me to keep it secret from Dad, you had better keep it to yourself").

Kim is a pretty, twenty-year-old woman who came to us because of depression that started after she entered college. She had done well in high school with little effort. When she got to college, she tried to get along just like she had in the past, which yielded terrible grades. She became depressed, dropped out, and got a job during the semester before she came to see us, but didn't tell her parents. We spent time discussing her lack of effort in college at the start and the cycle of failure that resulted. Together we decided that she had not been working up to her own internal standards. She had made lots of excuses for her failure to perform but evaded the real issue—hard work. She felt terrible about herself. As a first step, we encouraged her to face her parents, to 'fess up. It took three months for her to work up the courage, but she finally did it. At the next visit, she seemed like a new person. She had acted in a fashion consistent with what she believed was right. She felt good about herself for the first time in two years. She started school again, ready to face the hard work of studying, and is doing much better. We think she learned something about facing up to life's hard work.

Finally, manipulations are characterized by lack of adherence to values, or by the creation of new "values" to fit the situation. Some manipulators seem to have no consistent set of values; others have the ability to edit their values to fit their particular momentary needs. Integrity describes a person whose behavior is largely consistent with their value system; manipulators do not have integrity because their value systems don't reliably govern their behavior.

Modifying Reality—The Essential Step

The very essence of manipulation is deception—both of others and self. The deceptions of a manipulator are rarely planned. Rather, they just happen, just turn out that way: The manipulator takes advantage of the opportunity. Consider the following story:

Tom was a twelve-year-old sixth grader attending a public junior high school recommended by his sixth-grade learning-disabilities teacher. His school performance throughout the fall had been miserable, despite a program that considerably reduced his workload and provided one-to-one help in his learning-disabilities classroom. Historically, we learned that Tom had been identified as learning disabled in second grade because he had difficulty learning to read. From then on, he received daily special help with his studies, but, even with this extra attention, his performance was never more than marginal. We weren't surprised to learn that he never seemed to have much homework and that what he did have was done only with the assistance of his parents. Further investigation showed that Tom was way behind in all his classes, with lots of undone school and homework.

Throughout our initial interview, Tom was withdrawn and angry; this was characteristic of his attitude at home as well. We found that while Tom claimed he had friends, he rarely had phone calls and was never invited to other kids' houses. At school he seemed to exist on the fringes, uninvolved with anything or anybody. He had dropped out of sports at the beginning of the school year. We learned that he believed all his problems were the fault of someone else: His teachers expected too much of him; the other kids were mean; his coaches were "dorks"; his parents didn't provide enough help.

Because of his long history of lack of effort, we were skeptical about Tom's learning-disability designation. It was clear to us that he had learned to work only with help; he wouldn't even try without adult supervision. After some thought and discussion, we proposed a program to be instituted with the help of his LD teacher: Tom's parents would be told what work was assigned to him; they would not help Tom do his homework, but they would ensure that it was of reasonable quality; he would not be allowed to do anything else until he finished each day's assignments; and he was to study in his bedroom, not at the kitchen table. Tom hated us, our program, his parents, and his LD teacher, but he grudgingly began to do the work that was assigned—or so it seemed. Tom's math teacher had refused to go along with the plan, believing that kids must "sink or swim." (We wanted to point out that Tom had never learned to swim in the first place and needed some lessons before being dumped in the water, but we never got the opportunity.) Just before spring break, Tom's parents found out he had done practically no work in math. He had been telling them that he did it all in school. They consulted with us, and we recommended that he make up all his work over spring break.

Tom's parents confronted Tom on the first day of spring break and told him he was going nowhere, doing nothing else, until he made up all the math homework. Tom threw a fit. His parents stood firm, and his temper-tantrum escalated and became physical. His father was forced to hold him for some time to prevent him from hurting someone. In the midst of this altercation, Tom's mother called us and asked us what they should do. We asked whether they could see it through, and they replied that they thought they could. We told them to "hang in there." Finally, exhausted and defeated, Tom sat down to start his homework. He spent days working on it. His parents would not accept sloppy or inaccurate work, insisting he redo any work that was substandard. He complained bitterly, but continued to work. He claimed that he had already done some of the work, that his teacher had lost it, that his parents weren't fair in making him spend his whole spring vacation doing homework. His parents wouldn't relent; they didn't buy his arguments. Tom finally got all his homework done and even had a couple of vacation days left. When school began again, he turned in his work, to his math teacher's amazement. After that, there was math homework to do most nights, and by the end of the year, Tom's grades had improved.

The following year, Tom was put in more difficult classes and his LD time reduced. His parents and LD teacher continued to monitor his work performance carefully, and occasionally would have to intervene to keep Tom on the straight and narrow. Tom began to do well in school. By eighth grade, Tom was put in regular classes and accelerated in math, which had become his favorite subject. He checked in periodically with his LD teacher, but needed only her encouragement, not her supervision, to do his work. He started playing basketball, found some friends, and even ran for school office. Since then he has done well, with a few ups and downs, and next year he will go to college.

Early on in his school career, Tom had become convinced he could not do the work presented in school. His teachers and parents validated his doubt about his abilities by assisting him in his performance, rather than insisting upon his performance. Everyone concerned began to believe that Tom could not perform without help, and this belief provided the opportunity Tom needed to avoid schoolwork. Until his junior high LD teacher blew the whistle, this belief, based on nothing more than his lack of effort, lived a life of its own and dominated everyone's approach to Tom. He learned to manipulate the adults around him within the framework of this belief. Inadvertently, Tom, his parents, his teachers, and the special-education staff had created a false reality that allowed Tom to underperform dramatically. We now see Tom as an anxious person with above-average abilities and no learning disability, who learned very early on how to be dependent on the adults around him. It took years to repair the damage done, but Tom is finally on his way to an independent future.

Tom represents an example of what all manipulative people do. Reality, in one way or another, is perceived erroneously because all persons involved want to avoid the truth.

The Essence of Manipulation: Editing Reality

To manipulate, one must take advantage of another's willingness to see things in a distorted fashion. To be manipulated, one must conveniently forget some of what one knows, believe blindly in a falsehood, or suspend one's healthy skepticism. The manipulator may convince his target of the falsehood, or his target may come already equipped with assumptions or beliefs that the manipulator discovers and puts to use. Here are some common examples:

- *The job of parents is to ensure the happiness of their children, to protect them from the damaging effects of unpleasant emotions.* If you believe this, you may be manipulated by anger, sadness, crying, whining, pleading, pouting, and other demonstrations of displeasure. We believe that the job of parents is to provide those things children cannot supply for themselves: food, shelter, loving interest, concern, unconditional love, and guidance based on values. Within this framework, it is children's responsibility to find their own happiness. We wouldn't suggest for a moment that children's happiness should not be a concern of parents, but parents should ask why unhappy children cannot generate their own happiness.

- *The job of parents is to work hard to provide material wealth and financial security for their children.* Certainly security is, to some extent, a responsibility of any parent. But when it becomes the sole duty of a parent, when tangible goods supplant love and attention, parents may be manipulated into endlessly supplying the material wants of their children. One depressed teenage boy asked us, "Why should I bother with school or a job when I can get anything I want just by asking? The other day I told my parents I wanted a keyboard and we went right out and bought one—for

$3,000." We can just imagine what went through his parents' heads when he expressed interest in something.

- Some parents value social standing very highly. Their children may quickly learn that any threat to public appearance carries a lot of weight and can be employed to get their way, or they may find that being perfect in social situations is very effective in keeping parental attention focused on them.

- If academic or other types of achievement are very important to parents, children may learn to excel in school, not for themselves but for parental attention and goodies. One woman we know studied piano throughout her childhood, went to college to study music, and was headed toward a performance career when she suddenly realized she had pursued music only to please her mother, not herself. She became resentful of all the time she had spent doing this, and quit piano and music altogether. Today, she realizes that playing the piano was her way to ensure her mother's continued attention, to garner favor from her mother.

As an example, consider this: Our society generally holds the belief that psychologically malformed adults result from individual traumatic events during childhood (a belief inherited from Freudian Theory). Many parents become afraid to confront their children, to place limits on their behavior, because they know a major emotional ordeal will result. Unpleasant emotions, such as anger and frustration, are seen as potentially traumatic; therefore, children should be protected from experiencing these emotions. Following this logic to its natural conclusion, parents are led to believe that the essence of good parenting is to ensure the happiness of their children. Children quickly discover this pervasive mindset in their parents (or teachers or others) through experience and soon learn how to get what they want merely by threatening or displaying negative emotions. This method works until, as teenagers, they can no longer claim the protected status of children. With little prior preparation, they are suddenly asked to take responsibility for their own lives and happiness, and they crash.

There are other parent-held beliefs or practices that make it difficult to see reality clearly, and these have similar effects on childrearing. Parents who put everything into work, parents who distort their own reality with drugs, parents who adhere to the latest popular explanation for their children's troubles, or parents who have listened to too much conflicting childrearing advice without heeding their own value system—these types of parents raise children who learn to manipulate their way through life until they reach an age when their manipulations no longer work. We see this happen frequently, and our predictions about outcome run true. Sadly, the outcome is always blamed on somebody else.

Yesterday, I received a phone call from a mother enraged because a pediatric dentist felt he needed to use sedation and restraint to do some dental work on her enormously uncooperative three-and-a-half-year-old son, Mark. She wanted to take Mark elsewhere to get the work done, believing that there must be another dentist who could do better with Mark. Though I've developed a good relationship with Mark over the years, it's still a major struggle to examine him—and I don't have to do the delicate work of a dentist. I'm reasonably certain nobody's going to accomplish anything in his mouth without means approaching general anesthesia.

Trouble is, Mark runs his family. His mother, in her candid moments, knows it, but keeps hoping things will change. She has never had the will-power or strength to change things. At this point she sees the dentist as the bad guy because he cannot reason with three-and-a-half-year-old Mark; she has convinced herself that there must be a more persuasive dentist out there. I can predict what will happen when Mark is in school—his difficulties will be the fault of the teacher. It's likely that things will only get worse for this poor child unless his parents make a major course change in parenting.

Children who've learned to get by through manipulation of their world learn to see reality in a highly edited and embellished fashion. The reality they see conveniently supports their current manipulative ploy, and changes as conditions warrant. The hallmark of this is confusion, endless argument, anger, fault-finding, blame, and guilt. Stopping it requires steadfast and persistent confrontation from a very secure footing. With our patients, when we begin to hear reality-based statements, we know that progress is being made.

Distortion of reality takes many forms. Margie (in chapter 1) distorts reality by attempting to rearrange her body image; Mark has been led to believe he's in charge of his world and vigorously combats any attempt that threatens this belief. Other manipulative children may employ distortions along a spectrum that extends from Margie's single-minded perspective to views that are completely opportunistic. Here are some other examples:

Ben was adopted. Both parents wanted children but were unable to conceive. They doted on Ben from the start. He was a fearful and sensitive baby. He reacted to change poorly, and his mother catered to this characteristic so that his life would go along smoothly. Ben's sometimes unbridled emotions were agony for her. Ben's father disagreed with this approach, and Ben learned, early in his life, to run to his protective mother when he didn't like what the world, and especially his father, had to offer. When Ben was two, he became ill with a serious illness from which he eventually recovered. During his hospitalization, Ben's mother was at his bedside night and day while his father continued to go to work and care for the household. Ben's mother believed he might die, and after he recovered, she protected him even more.

Ben's parents did not have a strong marriage in the first place, but all this caused a rift between them that widened as Ben got older. They finally separated and divorced. At the beginning of the separation, Ben spent half his time with each parent, but every time he was asked to do something he didn't want to do at his father's house, he would get angry and resentful and call his mother. She would drive over, pick him up, and console him. As time went on, Ben began to say that he hated his father, and spent less and less time with him. His father coached his soccer team, so Ben became reluctant to play. His father tried to make things better by taking a trip with Ben to attend a World Cup soccer match, but as soon as they came back, the old pattern reemerged. One day, Ben refused to go to a game, but his father insisted that he had a commitment to the team and had to go. Ben called his mother to come and get him, then delivered his coup de grace: He quit soccer.

Finally, in a dispute over yardwork, Ben's father lost his temper and lightly cuffed him on the arm. Ben called his mother, and she arrived quickly to remove him. Ben and his mother claimed child abuse, and Ben no longer saw his dad. Ben became depressed, withdrew from other kids and activities, and suggested that he wanted to kill himself. Therapists with the same protective approach as Ben's mom tried to help, further extending his protective cocoon. Ben is now an isolated, depressed teenager who is estranged from his father, trapped by his own fragile control of the world, and unable to find his way out of his predicament.

Ben doesn't really hate his dad, but he fears the experience of loss of control over his world when he's with his dad. His control is, in reality, only over others, principally his mother. It is fragile, tenuous, inflexible, and maladaptive; it is useless in the real world. His stories sound like child abuse, but in reality they are merely the conflicts that most parents and children experience as children grow up. Ben enjoyed soccer, but he could not deal with any suggestion of compliance with his father's values, so he quit. And nobody was ever able to insist that Ben deal with reality—he could always call mom and tell a story of abuse and anguish, and she would facilitate his escape. Ben faces a tough road ahead even if people stop cooperating with his version of reality.

How often have you heard the parent of a small child say, "I can't wait till he's old enough to reason with"? Kristin is a pretty, pouty thirteen-year-old. Her parents are articulate people who have always tried to manage her by using reason. Kristin has learned to counter every argument by using her own considerable verbal talents, and she generally gets her way. As Kristin entered her teenage years, she became increasingly sullen and angry—life wasn't going her way like before. School and friends wouldn't cooperate with her, no matter how hard she tried to convince them of the correctness of her positions. Her friendships changed, and soon the only kids who would interact with her were other children like herself.

Kristin and her parents came to see us when they were at a stalemate over Kristin's demands to hang around with her friends in an area of town that had become the local hangout for dissatisfied and dispossessed youngsters. Kristin was angry because her parents "would not listen to reason." During the first session with us, Kristen and her parents spent most of an hour in a convoluted, angry, and tedious argument about their restrictions on her. In private sessions with Kristin, she stated she planned to move out with her boyfriend as soon as she (and he) were sixteen years old. We asked how they would support themselves; she figured their parents would pay for it.

Kristin has always been able to make the world be the way she wants it. She has always found a way around the "no's" in her life. When confronted with her parents firm stance about her comings and goings, her ultimate response was to create another false reality, the idea that she could move out of her parents' house and they would actually pick up the tab for her to do this! We tried to convince her parents to stop arguing with her, to stop the endless and bitter verbal battles. We tried to teach them another approach, which is outlined later in this book, but they were so committed to this course of management—they had had thirteen years of training after all—that this proved impossible for them. They finally quit coming to see us, but we predict they'll be back when things get bad enough.

For each of these people—parents and children alike—a little self-deception became a belief, and each was trapped in the end because they could not see the reality of their situation. We could continue with examples indefinitely: In order to manipulate, the manipulator must distort reality. While some manipulative children may be quite conscious of their deception, most are not actively aware; when challenged, they will defend their perceptions vigorously and often become angry and hateful when challenged.

In order for the distortion of reality to work, those being manipulated must accept and go along with the deception (enable it). Ben's mother had to believe he might be hurt by the emotions resulting from conflict with his father. Tom's parents and teachers had to believe he was learning disabled. Margie's parents had to believe that a perfect little girl who never ventured off to satisfy her own needs was somehow ideal. In each of these situations, the adults involved were not able to pull back and take stock of the situation. Fears and insecurities distorted their perception of reality, paralyzing them and rendering them ineffective in promoting independence in their children. In a later chapter, "Becoming Manipulation-Proof," we address this problem.

Outcomes

Since manipulation is based on avoidance, the manipulator feels relief at the successful conclusion of his action. He has worked his way around something he fears, though he may have achieved little else. Other emotions may also be felt, like happiness or glee, but they will be short-lived. Contentment, accomplishment, or competence are foreign emotions for the manipulator. If the game has been unsuccessful, he will experience anger, anxiety, and vengefulness. He will assign blame, and he often will direct strong emotions such as hate towards his target. He will amply demonstrate his intense displeasure, and he will redouble his manipulative efforts at the next opportunity.

Since manipulators work through others to control the situations they face, they avoid any situation in which their control is challenged. They run away from situations in which they must comply with the wishes and rules of others. Unfortunately, facing this sort of situation could offer another healthier approach to life, one that could lead to a sense of self-control within situations rather than control over situations. Healthy, well-adapted people gain self-confidence from this sense of self-control within diverse situations; their focus stays on their own behavior, not the behavior of others. They have learned that they can survive, that they are competent, and that they can manage themselves within the boundaries and rules of life's situations.

From the viewpoint of an outside observer, there may be no clear benefit to the participants in a manipulative interaction. Often, manipulations end in a stalemate, and an observer may wonder why the behavior persists. Many manipulations are just an exercise in control. The outcome for the manipulator may be maintenance of the status quo, in which his sense of security is vested in his control of the world. Manipulators find change threatening, not challenging, and want to avoid it.

Manipulative interactions are rarely goal-directed beyond the maintenance of control over others. Few manipulations achieve progress toward some long-term objective; as a result, manipulators commonly have difficulty with extended effort. An outside observer will see failure, but the manipulator experiences relief and calls it success. Long term, the manipulator fails miserably because, in the end, the world is not under his control.

Rather than being consistently governed by higher values (that is, having integrity), manipulative behavior is opportunistic. When advantage has been taken, outcomes are neither fair nor win-win. Others will come to resent what has happened to them; relationships will eventually suffer. Friendship and commitment to shared purpose become impossible; the manipulator often finds himself moving on to new relationships, all the while blaming others for problems experienced in the past.

Manipulators rarely experience a sense of competency and self-worth, which we call self-esteem. They may be happy when things are going their way, but their understanding of their own value will be subject to the cooperation of others. Many manipulators may see themselves as the center of the universe. When this turns out to be false, their anger, resentment, and despair will be overwhelming.

Finally, as this manipulative approach to life fails, symptoms will appear: alcoholism and drug abuse, eating disorders, depression, suicide, promiscuity, dropping out, inappropriate and antisocial behavior, pervasive anxiety, irresponsibility, and unreliability. Luckily, treatment of these problems is sometimes successful and the manipulator is resurrected, often with a new approach. If we look at treatment programs, such as the twelve-step program of Alcoholics Anonymous, we see that they often teach self-control, eschewing other control—by design, these programs teach antimanipulative behavior.

Conclusion

Here is the definition of manipulation we have found useful:

Manipulation is behavior that, through dishonesty, threat, or subterfuge directed toward other persons, allows the manipulator to delay, avoid, or escape aversive or uncomfortable circumstances. Manipulation may serve some desired additional result, but its existence is not dependent on this added outcome.

We've observed that manipulations seem to follow a set of rules:

1. Manipulations are complex avoidance behaviors. They may achieve some positive end, but they exist because they avoid something else: change, work, pain, angry confrontation, or loss of control of a situation.

2. Manipulations are reciprocal: A manipulator's ploy is enabled by a complementary avoidance behavior on the part of those being manipulated. In order to be successful, a manipulator must discover and use what the person he is interacting with wishes to avoid.

3. If a manipulation fails, a manipulator will usually resort to a cruder and more coercive ploy.

4. People who use manipulation to adapt to life often see the world in black and white terms: Others are seen as good or nice (that is, susceptible to the manipulator's game) or bad, jerks, or mean (unmanipulable). Little appreciation for the depth, breadth, or independence of human qualities exists. Strong judgmental, stereotyped labels pepper their speech when describing others or situations ("He's the best," "What a dweeb," "English is the worst").

5. Most manipulation is not consciously planned or executed, but is a learned pattern of behavioral adaptation. A manipulator commonly doesn't recognize the dishonesty inherent to his manipulations. The earlier in life the manipulative behavior was learned, the less aware the manipulator will be of his behavior.

6. More complex learning environments produce more complex manipulative behavior. Bright and learned manipulators are more difficult to discover and treat because of their subtlety and social sophistication.

7. Manipulative styles are determined in large part by the inborn temperamental characteristics of both the manipulator and those being manipulated.

To Do List:

1. Make a list of the manipulative interactions you observe both between yourself and others and between your spouse and others,

particularly your children. It is important not to assess blame or be judgmental, just report your observations objectively. Ask your spouse or partner to do the same. If you are a single parent, ask a close friend to help.

2. Try to identify the hidden agendas that allow the manipulation to take place: What is it the parties are trying to avoid? What are you trying to avoid?

3. Write down alternative ways to handle the interactions honestly without regard to the difficulty or fears the alternatives present.

4. Now openly analyze the trouble you foresee if you were to proceed with your alternate method for handling the situation. Compared to the long-term destruction of self-esteem, do your fears make sense?

5. Try some of your alternates—but expect to have to work at it.

The Critical Factor: Temperament

Any parent with more than one child can describe the differences among their offspring. Their description will most likely include physical characteristics, like hair color and texture, eye color, and body size and shape. Parents will also describe features of each child's personality that have been present from birth. These will often be seen as differences between children, rather than starkly described attributes, because pure characteristics of personality and temperament are difficult to define without comparison.

Scientists interested in human and child development have long argued the issue of nature vs. nurture: Are we who we are because of our inborn characteristics or because the environment in which we were raised affected us in certain ways? Like many other arguments in theoretical science, this debate has wavered back and forth because reliable basic information about human development is incomplete. Often the arguments are posited as an either-or question: Either we are genetically determined or environmentally trained. Neither extreme position accurately represents the truth. Recently, numerous twin studies have shed some light on this issue. These studies try to quantitate the genetic contribution (often expressed as a percentage) to the individual outcome: It seems clear that identical twins, separated early and with no contact with one another in the interim, often share many similarities in personality, physique, general interests, career choice, and even spouse selection, but they are not identical in every way. Taken as a whole, it is clear that neither genes alone nor environmental influence alone can explain how we develop.

Each person is born with many genetically determined temperamental attributes. Each of us starts life with a unique collection of inborn proclivities, natural skills and gifts, mannerisms, and operating styles. How these inborn factors actually play out in life depends, in large part, on characteristics of the environment that nurtures and trains us. Who we become is the result of this unique interaction and is virtually never the result of just one factor, genetic or environmental. Furthermore, not only does our environment affect us, but we affect our environment in return. The either/or question is moot: Living is an interactive process in which both nature and nurture are important; each of us is a unique product of the extraordinarily complex interaction between the two.

The study of inborn temperamental characteristics is, at best, rudimentary. There is not a generally accepted list of attributes, let alone an understanding of their inheritance. We have, however, identified some traits that we have found to be clinically useful in understanding the people with whom we deal. They seem to have predictive value: When we know these attributes are present, we can draw conclusions about how a person will behave and interact with others with surprising accuracy. To demonstrate, we want you to do a little exercise: Place yourself, your spouse (or the child's other biological parent), and your children on each of the following temperamental spectrums. Try to be as realistic as possible, avoiding behavior patterns you aspire to or have learned (for example, "I really want to act immediately on my feelings, but I've learned to control my impulses" or "Sitting quietly during long meetings is no fun, but I've learned to do it"). Ask your spouse or someone else who knows you and your family well to cross-check your answers.

FAMILY TEMPERAMENT EXERCISE

	1	2	3	4	5	6	7

I. Activity
Restful, calm, able to sit still for long periods of time   *Restless, Ants in the Pants, busy, active, can't sit still*

	1	2	3	4	5	6	7
Mother	____	____	____	____	____	____	____
Father	____	____	____	____	____	____	____
Child 1	____	____	____	____	____	____	____
Child 2	____	____	____	____	____	____	____
Child 3	____	____	____	____	____	____	____

FAMILY TEMPERAMENT EXERCISE (continued)

	1	2	3	4	5	6	7

II. Decision Style
Ponders, thinks about thoughts, feelings, desires, ideas: indecisive, deliberate, patient

Must act on thoughts, feelings, desires, ideas: decisive, impulsive, impatient, hurried

	1	2	3	4	5	6	7
Mother	___	___	___	___	___	___	___
Father	___	___	___	___	___	___	___
Child 1	___	___	___	___	___	___	___
Child 2	___	___	___	___	___	___	___
Child 3	___	___	___	___	___	___	___

III. Focus/Vigilance
When doing something, undisturbed by or unaware of surroundings

When doing something, always aware of surroundings and easily disturbed

	1	2	3	4	5	6	7
Mother	___	___	___	___	___	___	___
Father	___	___	___	___	___	___	___
Child 1	___	___	___	___	___	___	___
Child 2	___	___	___	___	___	___	___
Child 3	___	___	___	___	___	___	___

IV. Physical Orientation
Gives precise directions, uses landmarks to navigate, gets lost easily

Gives general directions, finds way without landmarks, never really lost

	1	2	3	4	5	6	7
Mother	___	___	___	___	___	___	___
Father	___	___	___	___	___	___	___
Child 1	___	___	___	___	___	___	___
Child 2	___	___	___	___	___	___	___
Child 3	___	___	___	___	___	___	___

FAMILY TEMPERAMENT EXERCISE (continued)

	1	2	3	4	5	6	7

V. Anxiety

Goes with the flow; easygoing, not bothered by change or unpredictability

Wants control; upset by unpredictability, disorganization, change; likes order

Mother ....

Father ....

Child 1 ....

Child 2 ....

Child 3 ....

VI. Musicality

Musically adept; singing or playing an instrument comes easily.

Music is nice, but making music is not easy at all.

Mother ....

Father ....

Child 1 ....

Child 2 ....

Child 3 ....

VII. Regularity

Inner clock reliable; tends to wake, eat, retire, and do work at the same times each day

Schedule varies most days; unpredictable sleep-wake cycles, work productivity, and appetite cycles

Mother ....

Father ....

Child 1 ....

Child 2 ....

Child 3 ....

FAMILY TEMPERAMENT EXERCISE (continued)

	1	2	3	4	5	6	7

VIII. Social Orientation

Enjoys solitude, quiet. Avoids or just tolerates groups or social activities

Loves a party, gravitates toward a group of people, finds solitude boring

	1	2	3	4	5	6	7
Mother	____	____	____	____	____	____	____
Father	____	____	____	____	____	____	____
Child 1	____	____	____	____	____	____	____
Child 2	____	____	____	____	____	____	____
Child 3	____	____	____	____	____	____	____

Now examine your results. You will most likely find that traits present in a child are also present in at least one of the parents. We believe each of these traits to be inherited, though each may be modified and accommodated to by environment. This is just a sampling of some of the many possible temperamental trait-spectrums. We can't say for sure whether these are pure traits or derivatives of other, more basic traits—knowledge in the area is still in its infancy. We can say that knowledge of where a person fits on these spectrums can predict behavior accurately in a clinical setting, that each of these can been seen and characterized in a small baby or young child, and that each seems to persist in an individual over the years.

As children grow up, they learn to accommodate many of their inherited traits, emphasizing some, restraining others, and understanding that different situations often call for a different mix. Each child will find that some life situations fit comfortably like favorite old clothes but that others are always like wearing a new outfit that just doesn't hang right or has too much starch in the collar. The comfort of a situation has much to do with genetically determined predilections—inborn temperamental characteristics—although practice and experience will often make an uncomfortable situation somewhat easier.

Some temperamental characteristics can usefully predict relationships between people. For instance, two people who score high on the decision style spectrum (II) will often have great fun together, but if they get into a conflict, their disagreement will escalate quickly into a major battle. A combination of a high and a low scorer on this scale will make fights uncommon; while the quick-to-act person is reacting, the pensive person will withdraw to think things over and the fight will fizzle. Two people who score high on the anxiety scale (V) may struggle for control incessantly, but the complementary combination (a low scorer and a high scorer) may result in the high scorer taking charge with relatively smooth results (though the high scorer may get quite distressed that his or her counterpart doesn't worry about having everything "just so"). A person who scores high on both scale II and V will be subject to fits of temper, while a person who scores low on II and high on V will tend to withdraw and ruminate when upset, vacillating interminably at times about his or her worries and concerns. A person who scores low on both scales will often be very easy to get along with but will not be a self-starter or leader.

Persons scoring high on scales I (restless), II (quick to act), and III (highly vigilant of surroundings) fit the clinical description of Attention Deficit-Hyperactive Disorder, which is probably not a disorder—in the sense of something wrong with the person's brain functioning—at all, but just a collection of traits that make it very difficult for such people to sit quietly at a desk, pay attention to a teacher, or complete the paperwork in front of them. Put the person with these traits in a different setting—selling something, hunting out in the woods, or functioning as a well-trained decision maker faced with a crisis—and you'll find they perform admirably, whereas others may find themselves at a loss.

You should notice a strong relationship between scale III and IV (physical orientation). People who are highly and continually vigilant of their surroundings record the sequence of everything that goes by as they move about, fit it all into a model of the world carried in their head and navigate using that model. The mental model they construct is of the whole; specific landmarks—such as street names, buildings, and so on—are not particularly important, but fitting the sequences together into the larger structure is. On the other hand, people who are usually focused typically identify specific landmarks and navigate from one landmark to another in a connect-the-dots fashion. These people do not construct an overall spatial model of the world in their minds, though they may be quite adept at using maps. They will find that without identifiable landmarks, they have little general idea where they are in relation to the rest of the world.

Implications for Parents

Since each child is a unique blend of temperamental qualities, our parenting must take these qualities into account. For instance, some children require only minimal parental input for behavioral limits to be set, while others repeatedly challenge every limit or rule, exhausting and exasperating their parents. Some children love to organize and keep their things neat and tidy; others leave a trail wherever they go. Some babies love to sit and observe; others begin exploring their world very early, crawling before six months of age and never stopping after that. Some babies become quickly bored, constantly seeking new experiences; others are content playing with the same thing for hours on end.

Many parents, in a valiant attempt to be fair, try to make everything the same with each of their children, but the differences among their children thwart this noble effort at every turn. Parents often are uncomfortable when comparing one child to another, not realizing that making comparisons is essential to identifying, understanding, and celebrating the uniqueness of each child. We often see parents who come to us dismayed and frustrated by a challenging child because they had a much easier time teaching the limits to a previous child, and the parents can't understand why things aren't going as smoothly this time. We hear people gossiping and clucking at the difficulties some other parent is having with a particular child, never understanding how large a role temperament plays.

While our approach to each child needs individualization, rules and expectations for behavior should not be tailored to each child within a family. When we alter our expectations according to a child's nature or perceived delicacy, we invite manipulation. Parents must learn, however, what kind of approach works best with each of their children—endurance and persistence; humor and patience; a clear, consistent, and firm hand; or only occasional reminders to keep the rules well-defined.

The rules and decisions parents make should be based in their beliefs and values. Most of the rules we deal with in life are arbitrary or customary, or derive from ethical principles that comprise the basis of our culture. These rules don't generally derive from infallible reason based on proven truths or even statistical probabilities and, as such, can be argued against just as easily as for. Verbal (probably another temperamental trait) children have a field day when we try to teach them to behave by trying to teach them the reasoning behind the rules—they learn to master reasoning around rules, justifying their misbehavior and infractions. We wouldn't suggest that parents be arbitrary and capricious dictators with their children, but if a rule or decision is arbitrary, don't try to justify it with reason. If a rule derives from your belief system, say so, rather than trying to justify it with reason. If a rule comes purely from a reasoned exercise, explain the reasoning if you like, but prepare yourself for a debate. And remember that despite popular belief to the contrary, what children learn when we reason with them about rules we're trying to establish may be only that if they can reason around a rule, then the rule doesn't apply to them. We see this several times a day in children who are failing, sad, and maladapted because the world won't yield to their reason.

The temperamental characteristics both of parents and child, taken individually or in combination, strongly influence whether a child will learn to manipulate. For instance, an anxious child may try to manage anxiety by trying to control his surroundings through his parents, beginning at a very young age. If his parents, because of their temperamental makeup, are inclined to cooperate, this child will discover his parent's susceptibilities and work hard to develop ways to accomplish his end. By the end of his preschool years, his ability to control his environment may be finely honed. (Sadly, though, as he enters the outside world, he will attempt to do the same with others but will find less success and finally face failure when neither teachers nor friends are able or willing to adjust the world to suit his desires.)

The specific manipulative style adopted by a child depends, to a great extent, on temperament. For instance, highly verbal children working with their equally verbal parents are likely to find themselves in a continuous negotiation, a battle of wits that never ends. His parents may remember when they said, "I can't wait 'til he can talk so we can reason with him." Now they wish he would just button his lip. Finally, exasperated, these parents may become autocratic and dogmatic, even sarcastic and abusive, when the child won't see things their way.

The quick-to-act child may learn to become angry and abusive to others until they capitulate. While most children have some temper outbursts in their second year of life, these children may have many tantrums a day. If these tantrums are successful, or if the threat of a tantrum gets them what they want, angry piques may become a way of life—the method of choice in getting one's way. The long-term implications of this pattern of manipulation are frightening. We generally suggest that parents merely walk away from the one-year-old who is throwing a fit. Older children can be quietly and quickly removed to their room until their tantrum has passed. Welcome them back to the fold when they have recovered. It is essential that children who are subject to temper-tantrums learn to remove themselves from situations when they get angry. Other methods of managing anger just don't work well in the long run, and children who use abusive anger to get their way will do this with others, a very unsuccessful style in the larger world.

A pensive child may sadly withdraw until others accede to his wishes. This child may learn that withdrawal will always get the undivided attention of adults, and may use it whenever he feels anxious. We remember Mary, a pretty, quiet four-year-old who had been doted on by her mother and grandmother since birth. The family lived in an area of large homes and few other children, and Mary had experienced little contact with other kids. Her mother enrolled her in a preschool, but within a week, her preschool teachers were very concerned because, despite their best efforts, Mary consistently withdrew, refusing to play with the other children. Mary's teachers coaxed, cajoled, and demanded, but soon they would find Mary back on the sidelines, isolated and sad. We were consulted. Mary was charming, and her charm dominated the initial interview. But it was immediately obvious to us that Mary was used to and loved undivided adult attention. We suggested the following intervention: Ask the preschool teachers to let Mary sit by herself and be sad, steadfastly ignoring her withdrawal. We encouraged them to be patient, waiting for Mary to approach the other children, and then to attend to her sparingly. If she came to the teachers for attention, they were quickly to divert their attention to the rest of the children. Within three days, Mary was playing with the other children and having a great time—and she no longer seemed as interested in adult attention.

This same temperamental setup produces sad, poor-me manipulators who control adult attention and favors through obvious demonstrations of unhappiness. Adults who feel they bear responsibility for a child's emotions are perfect targets for this sort of manipulation. Unfortunately, when adults intervene, the immediate unhappiness may go away, but it will soon recur, the pattern repeating itself. We've stated this lesson before, but it bears repeating because it is so important: Children, like adults, own their own feelings and must learn to take responsibility for them. We can offer them comfort, solace, and support when appropriate, but if we fix their problems for them, we do them a great disservice. Children get ready to solve the big problems in life by learning to solve the little ones they face while growing up—and we mustn't interfere. Give them the ball (the responsibility) and cheer them on. Comfort their fumbles and celebrate their successes.

The anxious, neat, well-organized child will receive kudos from her parents and may learn to do everything perfectly. She is a parent's dream, and parents may do everything in their power to keep the dream alive. This child may learn to use perfect behavior to arrange the world the way she wants through their parents, but, as she gets older, she may become dismayed with situations and activities that won't respond to her perfectionism. Soon her dismay will turn to anger, directed at her parents, who can no longer provide what she wants. She will withdraw from "risky" activities, doing only those things that she can do perfectly. She may focus on one area of her life over which she can exert exclusive control and become symptomatic with this obsession. If this area concerns weight, then eating disorders, like anorexia nervosa, may develop. If schoolwork is the focus, straight A's may result at the expense of other areas like sports and social activities. When this rigid control doesn't work, depression and despondency often follow. We once took care of a boy who spent months building a perfect, radio-controlled model airplane. During its construction, he had become a hermit, avoiding contact with friends and family. His grades in school suffered. The product of his efforts was a huge, magnificent contraption. One calm winter day, he took it out on the ice of Lake Minnetonka for its maiden flight and fired it up, and off it flew. Unfortunately, it flew so well and so fast that it quickly flew out of range of his radio control transmitter. Eventually, it ran out of gas and crashed spectacularly on the ice, thoroughly destroyed. Having nothing to fall back on, he became depressed, more withdrawn, and even suicidal. He lacked the resiliency to survive this loss—his brittleness evoked great concern in his parents and others. We were more concerned that he had vested everything in this one perfectionistic project; we knew that we could not help him unless we could gain access to his perfectionism, learned as a young, manipulative child. He would remain brittle until he was able to take life as it is, demanding not perfection of himself (and others), but only the best he could do.

Parental temperament is critical, too. The anxious, quick-to-react parent will be easily baited into a fit of anger, stalemating any effective action. The pensive parent will often not respond to a child's temper-tantrum, and though this child may always be subject to quick anger, the child will not learn to use angry outbursts to control others. But this same parent may be easily guilted into agreement with the child's wishes by sad or withdrawn behavior. The focused parent may miss behavior that needs attention, while the vigilant parent may attend to all the wrong behavior. The anxious parent will want things to be perfect and be subject to manipulation by a perfectionistic child. As we can see, there are as many ways to manipulate as there are temperamental types and combinations.

Each of us have many inborn temperamental characteristics that don't change with time. We can, however, learn to live with and accommodate our individual characteristics as we mature, emphasizing those that are to our advantage and reining in those that give us trouble. We can learn to read situations and act accordingly. For instance, anxious people who want things to be just so can learn to restrict their perfectionistic demands to areas they have decided are their own responsibility, rather than every area that impacts their lives. They can learn to do their best where it counts, but not allow their perfectionism to overflow onto other people, trying to control the behavior of others. Successful business and professional people often show this pattern. Our goal for children is to help them do the same, to learn to accommodate best who they are, to live in the world as it is rather than trying to create artificial worlds that suit their needs. We hope to help children learn self-control rather than other control so that they can function independently, dealing well with the life situations in which they find themselves.

Temperamental characteristics are not the only variables that determine manipulative style, but they are certainly the most important. We hope you can understand better how a manipulation develops and works by understanding both your own temperament and those of your other family members.

To Do List:

1. Go back and review the exercise in this chapter. Look at the parent and child temperaments carefully.

2. Look at the manipulative behavior that occurs in your family and see whether you can explain what's happening purely on the basis of the temperaments involved.

3. See whether you can define what you might do to change your behavior so that manipulation stops. For instance, if you are pensive and focused, you may find that your child does lots of things he shouldn't when you're not looking. It may be necessary for you to work at being aware of his misbehavior so that you can stop it when it's happening.

CHAPTER 4

Healthy Kids:
A Pediatrician's Perspective

I n deciding the scope and direction of this book, we decided that the special viewpoint of a pediatrician, so useful to us, would be helpful to the reader. Because of what they do, pediatricians have the opportunity to watch, from a very intimate vantage point, many children grow from infancy to adulthood. No other professional has this opportunity—not even nonmedical experts in the field of child development. Given the requisite time, an abiding interest, and the appropriate background, pediatricians can begin to define what goes into the rearing of healthy, well-adapted, resilient people. One of us is a pediatrician who has practiced long enough for a generation to have grown up in his care, indeed, long enough to have begun to see the recycles—children born of parents who were his patients as children. The information in this chapter is based on his years of observation of children who've become successful adults, of their families and parents, rather than on the myopic view of professionals whose view is limited to a small age range or children with problems. We believe that possession of a context of knowledge about the development of well-adapted children is essential if we are to understand why a particular approach to child-raising succeeds or fails.

Over his years as a pediatrician, Dr. Swihart has been amazed—and distressed—at the fads in childrearing that have come and gone. He's seen well-meaning parents labor away, following, to the best of their ability, the tenets of some contemporary child-raising fad. He's watched while they read everything they can get their hands on, first trying one method, then another, and becoming more confused with each successive tome they plow through. Over the years it has become apparent that most childrearing fads are based on some theoretical notion about parenting and child development or on the results of limited scientific research rather than on careful, empiric observation of successful families. The best advice we can give parents is this: Be skeptical about what you read and hear; to judge the merit of someone's pronouncements about childrearing, use what you see in families that are doing well. Often the best resource for information is successful parents, people who've truly been where you are and survived to tell about it. This chapter should help you get the lay of the land and provide some guidance about what you should be looking for.

First, a few caveats about popular childrearing advice. Much of the available advice contains assumptions—rarely made explicit—that don't wash. Some of these assumptions can render parents impotent to do what's necessary to empower their children to adapt independently, set their own goals, discover their own values, and generate their own self-esteem. The sources of these assumptions include cultural beliefs mixed in with theory expounded by past and present experts. These assumptions are woven into the fabric of what is said or written, commonly hidden from view, but, nonetheless, profoundly influential in how we see children. Here are some common assumptions that we think are important for parents to be aware of:

1. It is easy to damage a child psychologically.

2. Trauma to the developing psyche is the principle cause of later maladjustment.

3. Trauma is "emotional"; therefore some emotions can be dangerous to the developing psyche.

4. Undesirable behavior is caused by bad emotions.

5. Because bad feelings may be traumatic, good parents will go to great lengths to prevent them and will work diligently to ensure the happiness of their children, avoiding the difficulties remembered from their own childhood.

6. Likewise, as a society, we must protect children from emotional trauma and struggle; otherwise, children will grow up damaged.

7. As a corollary to the above, self-esteem is damaged by bad emotions. Since bad emotions often result from criticism or denial of a child's wants, to say no, to allow struggle, frustration, anger,

disappointment, sadness, and failure to happen to a child, is risky to self-esteem.

8. Self-esteem can be given to a child (by being positive).

9. Persons with healthy self-esteem show it by being happy virtually all the time—anxiety, frustration, anger, and sadness are all evidence of poor self-esteem.

10. Children are all basically the same; the differences we see are mostly due to environmental (parenting) effects, not genetically determined temperamental differences.

11. Our behavior is cognitively controlled; we consciously decide and guide almost everything we do.

We wouldn't argue for a moment that some traumatic experiences have very damaging effects, that deplorable, hopeless conditions breed the view that any obstacle is impossible, any struggle fruitless. But emotional "traumas" are not the source of most of our children's ills, nor are they the source of most adult problems. Trauma has become a scapegoat for people who want easy answers, who want to assign blame for their own personal difficulties, who want to shift responsibility for their problems elsewhere: "Gee, it's not my fault, I was abused as a child." Nonsense. But becoming a victim, assuming victim status, will certainly perpetuate the problems people have.

The opposite approach—eliminating all difficulty and struggle—doesn't work either. The answer is somewhere in the middle—allowing children to deal with their real-world difficulties in an environment of support, acceptance, love, and clear guidance. Given these conditions, children can develop their own self-esteem and find their own happiness.

Looking at other cultures or our own society at a different time lends support to this point of view. Further, the individual stories told by elderly persons about the difficulties they had to overcome in their youth, about the stern upbringing they were subject to, but who harbor no resentment for all they've experienced, argues our point well. Our society's current approach doesn't work very well. We need to—must—reevaluate the fundamental underpinnings of our approach to children.

Healthy Children

One of the authors likes to tell the following story: I have a philosopher/barber. Bill cuts hair in a one-chair hole-in-the-wall littered with the detritus of a hobby intellectual. I don't know any other barber shop where one finds stacks of *The Economist* next to dense philosophical treatises piled on top of a collection of *Woodenboat* magazine. For nine dollars, I get a good haircut and thirty minutes of insightful, probing conversation. Sports is the only subject that's off limits.

One day several years ago I was at Bill's for a haircut—a euphemism we've tacitly applied to a little repair work around the perimeter of a sizable patch of epidermis devoid of follicular activity—when an appealing, enthusiastic young woman popped into the shop. She asked Bill when he'd be done; he told her, and she said gaily, "Bye, see you at 6:00."

I was intrigued, so I asked Bill who she was. "Oh," he replied, "Haven't you ever met my daughter?" I told him I hadn't, and pointed out his obvious lack of social grace in not introducing us. As we joked, I watched through the window as she got into a jazzy little red car and drove off. "Nice wheels for a kid, Bill," I commented. "Don't look at me," he replied. "She bought them herself!"

I was even more intrigued, so I asked Bill to tell me more. With obvious pride and no little amazement in his voice and manner, he told me about his daughter.

"She's had some sort of job since she was fourteen, telephone marketing, waitressing, and now jobs at college as a research assistant. She got her first job by convincing someone she was actually sixteen. When she was a freshman in high school, she got accepted by the options program, and started taking courses at the U. When she graduated from high school, she had enough credits to become a junior at the University. She's now a senior majoring in French and international relations, and she's nineteen years old. She just told us she's going to France next year to attend a year of college there. She knew her mother and I would have a problem with this idea, so she worked out all the details before she told us about it—she's even got a place to live and a job lined up. We couldn't say no!"

I had never heard any of this before, and now I was really interested. I asked Bill whether he thought there was anything about the way he and his wife parented their daughter that contributed to her becoming such a self-sufficient and independent young woman. Bill thought for a few moments and then replied, "When she was about five, we decided that we couldn't protect her from the world. We could love her, support her, but she had to learn to deal with the world on its terms; we couldn't do it for her. She just took the ball and ran."

In some ways, maybe that's the whole story. Obviously, at age five she was already primed to go out into the world and succeed. She also has innate gifts of intellect and temperament. But her parents allowed her to try, they got out of her way, and they supported her progress. Most importantly, they didn't try to protect her from experiencing life on its own terms.

Bill's daughter is a stunning example of a healthy, well-adapted person. Her future is bright because she is well-equipped for the world and well-equipped to pursue her own course in life.

What Are Healthy Kids?

Healthy kids are not hard to spot. But before describing what healthy kids *are,* we'd like to point out certain things that healthy children *are not:*

- They are not "perfect" kids. They struggle with limits and test the rules. They challenge authority on occasion. They don't always keep their room clean, pick up after themselves, or show perfect consideration for others.

- They don't necessarily do what we think they should do. Their goals, interests, and standards may differ significantly from those imposed on them by the adults around them; this often results in friction.

- They are not always happy. They don't like to fail any more than anyone else. They do experience anger, frustration, disappointment, and sadness.

- They don't talk about everything to their parents. They don't necessarily express all their feelings to others.

- They are not perfect students, though they are often very good students.

- They don't always behave within the rules. They may do things they know are forbidden. When reprimanded, they may not be terribly upset.

The following seventeen cardinal features describe what healthy kids *are.* They are not universally present nor consistently present (it is unlikely you'll ever meet a child who has all of these features), but they sort of make up a shopping list that we should look for in our own children. These are characteristics worthy of our support and attention when we become aware of their presence:

- They want to take care of themselves. They resist the efforts of others to do things for them that they feel competent to do themselves.

Because they insist on taking care of themselves, they learn how to solve the problems they face, adding to their knowledge of their own competence.

- They have a distinct self-identity. They know who they are, what they want and like, what skills and interests they possess. Along with the desire to take care of themselves, they develop responsibility for self.

- They are resilient. If they fail, they pick themselves up and try again. They have learned that persistence in the face of failure is an inherent part of achieving goals. They need not explain failure to others, shift responsibility and blame, or find fault outside themselves. They profit from their mistakes and accept that there will be more. Healthy kids learn that they can only change themselves, not others, and immediately look at their own behavior when problems occur.

- They are proactive—they don't wait to be swept along in the course of events, reacting to the bumps and lumps along the way. They can initiate the actions necessary to achieve their goals; they don't wait around for others to make things happen; they are not put off by the risk inherent in pursuing their goals. We are repeatedly distressed, despite years of experience, at the frequent answer of young teenagers when asked what they've thought about being when they grow up: "I don't know." No maybes, no dreams, no interests, no hobbies—just a blank. Healthy kids often have some idea, some dreams about the possibilities; some even believe they know for sure at a tender age.

- They are assertive. They've learned to stick up for themselves without becoming aggressive. When they assert themselves and are denied, they can usually accept the denial without trying to force someone else. They go after what they want, accepting the responsibility to get it themselves.

- They can have fun. They like to play; they enjoy learning the rules of games and honing their skills. They don't shy away from competition; rather, they relish it and are motivated by it, and they aren't crushed by failure. If fun sometimes involves breaking a rule, they can accept the consequences of their actions.

- They can accept new challenges. Their sense of competence allows them to try new things. They know that any new challenge is risky, that they might not do well at first, but this doesn't dissuade them from trying. New activities and skills are usually learned through trial and error, so they may experience considerable frustration in the process. We may notice them feeling anger, sadness, and disappointment more commonly than their less healthy counterparts simply because they take on challenges more often.

- They require discipline. They are often spirited; they commonly test the rules and limits of each situation. They are far from perfectly behaved, but can accept limits and rules once they are established. They require guidance from strong, secure adults. They give weak adults headaches.

- They know about personal boundaries. Though capable of intimacy, they respect the privacy of others. They are not naively candid; they keep their own counsel and resent invasion of their personal boundaries, especially by an overly interested adult. They don't tell all to their parents, but reserve their privacy of mind. We always worry when the parent of a pre- or early teen tells us, "We are so close. We talk about everything." Over the years, this statement has indicated some striking problems. This parent has abdicated parenthood in favor of friendship. Boundaries, roles, and relationships have become confused, and the child will have a rocky time establishing his/her independence.

- They assume that others are responsible for themselves. Since they take responsibility for their own lives, happiness, failures, and successes, they may not be very understanding of another's inability to accept responsibility for self. They don't operate as mini-social workers: Instead of taking on the problems of others, they may empathize and provide comfort during another's struggle. At times, they may seem distant, uninvolved, even self-centered, and unconcerned with others. In fact, they just refuse to participate in dependency; they eschew caretaking of others.

- They are self-controlled. They strive to play the game well, to function well in life, and they have discovered that this is done best by control of self. When things don't go well, they are unlikely to have a tantrum in an attempt to force others to take responsibility for them. Instead of trying to control their world, they are self-controlled within their world.

- They are usually honest with themselves. They don't reinterpret reality for their convenience, but assess reality accurately and do their best to deal with it.

- They are not easily manipulated. When they've been taken in by somebody, they learn from the experience. They are not incurably naive; they can accept reality as it is without putting a "spin" on it.

- They are optimistic and humorous. They believe in their competence; this belief feeds optimism. They see the humorous side of the human condition and can laugh at themselves or others when appropriate. They will often handle failure with humor rather than with anger.

- They may not be persistent in doing what someone else wants them to do. They don't necessarily perform for someone else's benefit, trying to please parents, teachers, coaches, or friends. Instead, they are motivated to meet their own expectations, not those of others. When they don't live up to their own standards, they may be quite upset—just as they should be.

- They can lead without controlling. They can accept compromise, work with others, cooperate with a team or group. They don't always have to be in charge; things don't always have to be done their way. They are also good followers and teammates.

- They are value-guided. When younger, they learn to live within the values of their family; as they get older, they develop their own morals and ethics. They develop the ability to live within a value system despite temptations and difficulties that come along: They have integrity.

What Produces a Healthy, Well-Adapted Child?

Just as you might expect, the families of these children share characteristics that produce a good environment for their children. In the last chapter of the book, we discuss how to work toward building the following characteristics into your family. For now, we want to describe what we've learned over the years by watching families that produce healthy, well-adapted children.

Value-Guided Parenting

We'll start with the single most important characteristic, the one that gives rise to all others: These families are uniformly value-guided. We hear a lot about family values these days, especially from politicians, as if there is some universally agreed upon standard collection of family values everyone should follow. In fact, the values that families hold differ dramatically within our own potpourri culture, not to mention cultures outside of the United States. Your family values are what counts, not the notions of some political hack who would like to define them for you. If your values differ from what are perceived as the American mainstream, more power to you.

The values held by a family are the most essential piece to the childrearing puzzle—they are the only thing that provide guidance and ensure long-term consistency in childrearing. They allow parents to do all the things they do in a way that is additive and makes sense during their children's time with them. Nonmanipulative, well-adapted children come from families in which a family belief system prevails. Nothing else will suffice—not reason, nor negotiation nor compromise, nor emotional sensitivity, nor loving attention—to ensure that today's lessons add to and extend the lessons of yesterday.

The parents in these families have well-defined values, and their values guide their actions; they have integrity. There is general agreement between the parents about what they believe, and they teach their children to live within the family beliefs. Opportunity, convenience, feelings, desires, and public embarrassment never supersede family values. No family member, least of all a parent, is excused from following family beliefs.

Beliefs and values tend not to change over the years. They are the gold standard from which rules and decisions arise. They ensure long-term consistency, so what children learned last year or last week fits with and adds to today's learning. A long-term, congruent pattern emerges, yielding, in the end, non-dependent young adults with a well-established personal value system. No other method of parental guidance will do this; many will interfere.

Thirty-some years ago researchers at the University of California at Berkeley began a study of a group of families with young children. They studied the parenting style of each family extensively and categorized it.

The children have been followed up to the present and evaluated as to how they did as teenagers and adults.

For this study, parenting approaches were categorized in the following ways: *passive* (parents were highly permissive in parenting; conflict and unhappiness in the family were avoided at all cost); *authoritarian* (parents ran the show; their arbitrary decisions and rules were absolute and determined by momentary expediency, emotion, or convenience); and *authoritative* (parents were clearly in charge, but decisions and rules were guided by something higher—the family belief system). You can probably predict the outcome: Children reared in the authoritative families have done much better over the years in their lives and careers than children from the other two groups.

Family Vision and Goals

Like any human organization, families don't function very well if they don't have a good idea of where they're going. Successful families have goals, and these goals taken together become the family's vision for itself. Some goals may be short term, practical, and readily attainable. Others may be long term and lofty, attainable only in generations to come. Goals give family members, especially children, a sense of what they're about, where they're going. More to the point, goals tend to keep everyone working in the same general direction when things get difficult.

You might be asking, "Did the parents in highly functional families just sit down one day and write out a set of goals?" "Are the goals generally written down and hung over the front door for all to see?" "Who defines the family goals?" "Do they ever change, or are they carved in stone?" Few families have written goals, but they exist, nonetheless. Family goals start from the parents' shared vision of what they want in life, but they are not static and unchanging. Instead, they evolve as families grow, as children have more input and develop their own interests and pursuits.

A useful exercise is to write down answers to the following questions, then share the answers with your spouse:

1. What do I want for myself over the next year, and over the next ten years?

2. What do I want for my family over the next year and ten years?

3. What do I want for my children in the same time frames?

4. What sort of adults would I like my children to become?

5. If I died, how would I like my family to remember me?

6. When my children are adults, what contributions to their development would I like them to remember?

7. In my answers to the preceding questions, are there conflicts? Are they reconcilable?

After you've answered these questions, construct a personal set of goal statements for short-term and long-term goals. After you've done this to your satisfaction, sit down with your spouse and compare your lists. Are they compatible? Can you reconcile differences? Now construct a set of family goals from your two lists. If your children are old enough, convene a family meeting for their input and education. Post the family goals somewhere, and redo the whole process on the anniversary of the first attempt. As your children become more mature, they will want to have input—but remember, these are family goals, not individual goals, and you are the parents.

This process has many benefits for you and your children. It makes clear for the parents what is really important. It gives children the opportunity to see where things are headed, that there is long-term direction, that things are not random. It allows parents to assess progress toward goals, and modify goals to fit the reality of their situation better.

This is not a process to be entered into lightly. It is hard work and takes time. The first attempt may be superficial, but persistence will pay off in the end.

Caring Rather Than Caretaking

Effective parents care for their children, but they do not caretake. The difference is subtle but very significant. Caring means loving your children and being concerned about what happens to them. Caring is taking the time and effort to work out and enunciate family values and goals carefully and thoughtfully, and then live by them, even when it's not easy or convenient. Sometimes, caring means having the strength and wherewithal to stand by while your child is grappling with one of life's problems. Caring means supporting your children through the rough spots rather than repaving the road for them.

Caretaking is a subtly but profoundly different approach. It is doing for your child what your child is capable of doing for herself. It is modifying the rules for your child's immediate comfort, trying to manage your child's emotions, or running interference so that she doesn't have to deal with the world. Caretaking inevitably leads to dependence and poor self-esteem.

Setting Boundaries

Families that produce healthy children have well-defined personal boundaries. Who each individual is, what individual roles and responsibilities are, is clear to everyone in the family. Parents are parents, not their children's friends, playmates, co-conspirators, or slaves. Parents have their own lives, interests, and activities to pursue—allowing children to develop their own. While children are very important family members, these families are not child-centered—they are family-centered. Parents have integrity; they are good role models as well as steady and consistent limit setters. These parents love their children tremendously, but well-defined boundaries foster independent problem solving.

Family Leadership

All social animals share some common characteristics. Of particular note is hierarchy; we know of no example in which a stable social group exists without establishment of a hierarchy. Scientists who study the behavior of animals, from bees to elephants, readily accept this observation and often focus on the manner in which hierarchy is established within the group of animals being investigated. The rituals higher animals use to determine dominance are often elaborate and risky—but the survival of the social group seems dependent upon them. When lead (dominant) animals lose the ability to maintain their leadership, a social upheaval ensues until a new social order emerges and the group can function smoothly. Read anthropologist Elizabeth Marshall Thomas' *The Hidden Life of Dogs* for a fascinating account of this process among canines, which she observed for many years.

The history of humankind reveals the exact same process. In order to survive and thrive, human societies appear to require leadership and hierarchy. The types of hierarchies and their ongoing maintenance and renewal are exceedingly complex, providing grist for the mill of thousands of students of history, political science, sociologists, anthropologists, and philosophers. Human social behavior, from elegant political debate to the cruelest of wars, is all about establishing and maintaining hierarchy. Hierarchies are established at every social level, from government to neighborhood groups of kids. Human social organizations suffering a disruption of hierarchy, a loss of leadership, will go through a predictable sequence of events leading to the reestablishment of social order. Humankind differs from other animals in the complexity and creativity of the process used, not in the outcome or necessity of the process to attain social stability. The continued function of a social group is absolutely dependent on the successful conclusion of this process.

Human families are no exception to this rule. The stability of a family depends on the clear establishment of hierarchy. Parents who cannot establish or maintain a dominant position cannot function as parents, instead functioning more like controlling peers to their children; the result is interminable and destructive conflict. In effective families, leadership stays with parents. Parents in these families understand the necessity for leadership and are therefore willing to resolve quickly, in their favor, struggles over who's in charge. Parents in these families are not arbitrary and capricious dictators, but rather more like limited, benevolent monarchs. They willingly listen and allow great freedom of action, but they hold to the principles on which the family is founded. Well-run families are not true democracies; you can't vote out the president when you don't like what s/he does.

Leadership may be matriarchal, patriarchal, or, as is common today, shared in some fashion. Parents support one another, and they resolve their differences out of earshot of the children. One mother of four wonderful young adults told me: "Whenever Peter (the father) was going to be late for dinner, as he often was, I did whatever I had to do to hold the kids off until he got home. It was always very important that we all sit down and eat together with him." This father was an essential part of the family; everyone admired him and relished his presence and patiently waited until he got home to eat. Interestingly, this was not a patriarchal family, but one led by two parents who shared leadership and supported one another's roles steadfastly.

Parents plagued by constant marital strife over leadership need to take stock of what they're doing. Shared leadership, in any circumstance, is difficult to achieve, but a very worthwhile goal. Some methods of achieving a harmonious marital outcome include clear division of areas of responsibility; frequent, regular parent alone time (such as a weekly night out); written definition of goals and values; and clear boundary definition between parents and children. Parents who first take care of themselves and, second, take care of the integrity of their marriage will find raising children easier and more satisfying than parents who put children first in these priorities. Children must still rank in the priorities, but children will surely suffer if a parent becomes personally unhappy and dissatisfied or the marriage falls apart. Obviously, this all assumes that both parents in a family are willing to and capable of thinking beyond their own personal needs and demands; it assumes the marriage itself is not founded on manipulation but on love and respect.

Honoring Differences

These families accept and revel in the differences between each individual in the family. They do not dwell upon negative aspects of their children or behavior, instead focusing on the positive. Parental optimism is infectious; they sit back, amazed at what they have produced. The emphasis in parenting differs for each child according to their nature and temperament. There are no bad children, just different children. These parents don't fear making comparisons of their children; any judgments are made in a context of unconditional acceptance and an understanding of human differences.

Nonmanipulative Parenting

The parents in these families don't try to manipulate their children into behaving well. There is little uncertainty in their minds about their values and beliefs. The rules and decisions follow the belief system. Children are expected, like it or not, to follow the rules. Parents expect they will have to teach the rules. Limits are clearly, quickly, and consistently defined. Incentives, rewards, reasoning, rationalization, and retributive punishment are eschewed in favor of guidance, clear correction, and immediate interference with unwanted behavior. They don't spend time reasoning with or cajoling their children to behave well—as a matter of fact, they spend very little time discussing behavior at all. Since the family's rules are founded on beliefs and values, they are customary and procedural; they are non-negotiable. Little time and effort are spent arguing and explaining the why of rules. Instead, parental attention is directed toward ensuring that children learn to follow the rules.

Inventive consequences for misbehavior are not used; rather, children are always expected to do whatever the family values call for when they've misbehaved (that is, apologize, clean up their mess, or return something they've taken without permission). While these moral consequences are used, parents don't necessarily expect a "lesson to be learned." Instead, they insist upon the correct action because they cannot conceive of not doing so.

Family Identity

These families have identity. Family history, goals, and beliefs make up this identity, and it is celebrated and illustrated through family traditions and stories. The children in these families are proud of belonging; they go out into the world as representatives of their families and usually behave accordingly. Parents in these families have worked hard to create this identity—a lot of thought and effort have gone into the process.

When we were children, before TV dominated people's lives, there was little that was as much fun as sitting around telling stories, especially stories from our parents' youth. We can both remember hearing our parents or other family members tell stories and begging to hear the favorite family tales again. Nothing they could have done would have told us more about who they were, what they valued, and where we came from than those stories. The stories themselves became family lore and sometimes family jokes—but they identified the uniqueness of each of our family heritages.

Families do this less than they once did, yet it is one of the best ways to transmit to children a sense of identity, of belonging to an entity with meaning. Take a vacation from the tube, and start telling stories—your kids will love it and gain a sense of family from it.

Family traditions do the same thing. Religious families generally have some traditions at holiday time, but many other traditions can be started if we see the need and use. Valentine's Day, Mother's and Father's Day, the day after school is out, or the day after Thanksgiving are all days that lend themselves to traditions. Some families pray before dinner, and dinner becomes a ceremonial occasion, a celebration of each family member. Take time to create these traditions; they carry far more impact and meaning than we sometimes realize.

Child-to-Child Bonds

Because parent-child boundaries are clearly defined, children tend to bond to one another strongly. Parents do not involve themselves in sibling squabbles, though they may set clear upper limits on what may be done to resolve conflict. "You'll have to settle it yourselves" is their standard refrain. They don't referee, and they don't participate in the resolution. They don't protect one sibling from another. They understand that the differences siblings have with one another are the children's differences, not the parents.

One family we knew had a Saturday job jar. On Saturday morning the children divided up the jobs on their own, out of earshot of the parents. They were told they could argue and squabble all they wanted, but the jobs were to be done before anyone had free time, and the resolution of who got which job was entirely the domain of the children. Interestingly, all the children learned to fend for themselves in the process. Another mother told us, "My kids don't sleep in their bedrooms much in the summer. They sleep in

the family room together because they enjoy being together in the evenings."
The second-oldest daughter in this family told Dr. Swihart, at her precollege
physical, that her biggest regret at leaving home was leaving her two younger
brothers—not her parents or friends! When parents are overinvolved, when
parent-child boundaries are indistinct, children vie and compete for parental attention, destroying the close bonds they might have with one another.

Family Play and Activities

There is truth in the adage that families that play together, stay together. Family
vacations, especially vacations for shared recreation like camping, skiing, sail-
ing, sightseeing, and fishing, profoundly impact the sense of family identity.

Routine activities, such as eating dinner, cleaning up the house, or attending events together, become focal points for family interaction. These
times have high priority; they are rarely sacrificed to some other agenda.
There is an air of tradition about these times, a celebration of the family and
each of its individuals.

Some families love to camp and explore the world around them; others
participate in sports or attend sporting events featuring a family member.
Here in Minnesota, families fish together, canoe in the Boundary Waters
Wilderness, race sailboats, water-ski, or just lounge around at the beach.
For some families, like farm families or families who run small businesses,
work may be a central shared activity. The specifics of the family activity
don't seem to matter much; participation together is the critical element.

Family vacations give a sense of togetherness that no other activity can
provide, and the details are often fondly remembered and recounted for years.
Dr. Swihart ran into a seventeen-year old-patient at a local store. They started
talking about Montana, and he told this young woman the story of a horrible
backpacking trip in the Beartooth Wilderness during which everyone in his
family got sick. She asked whether his family went backpacking together very
often. He told her that they did as often as they could. Her face became
wistful as she said, "Our family never does anything like that." He was
struck with her longing to do something adventurous with her family, and her
realization that, at her age, it would never happen.

Chores and Family Responsibilities

These families have well-defined chores and responsibilities for all family
members. Children are not on a free ride. This is started young and continues as long as the child resides in the family household. Grandma's rule

presides: Do what you have to do before doing what you want to do. There is rarely a reason to shirk your responsibility, but there may be plenty of reasons to plan ahead and do your chores early so that you can do something you want.

Effective Parenting Techniques

Parenting techniques vary from family to family, but certain characteristics are common: Incentives and rewards are not used; deals are not made; threats are not used; negotiation is saved for the truly negotiable; punishment is not seen as helpful and is not the final ploy to try to get a child to behave; limits are defined nonpunitively, quickly, quietly, briefly, and without prior warnings or threats; once a limit is set, it is not dwelled upon further but is quickly and consistently reestablished whenever necessary. After misbehavior has been interrupted, the child is promptly welcomed back into the fold with no further ado. Any discussions about rules and limits tend to be rather one-sided—parents informing the child of the rule transgressed and the expectation they have for future behavior. The child is not invited to comment or, especially, to try to explain her behavior. Very little time is spent at this, strengthening its impact.

There are two approaches to parenting commonly seen in our experience. The first, which we like to call incentive-punishment parenting, assumes that the way to get where we want to go with our children involves establishing incentives and rewards for good behavior and punishing consequences for undesirable or unwanted behavior—so-called positive parenting. This approach to childraising is, at its core, manipulative; it destroys a child's ability to become independent. Incentives and rewards change behavior only so long as they're in place and desired; punishments change behavior in unpredictable ways, rarely yielding the desirable behavior intended. Sadly, this is by far the most common form of parenting out there today.

The other parenting approach we'll call guidance and limit-setting. It is commonly seen in families that produce healthy children. This form teaches children skills they'll need to adapt to the real world, and, with long-term attention to the family value system for guidance, produces independent, self-reliant children. It is up-front, nonmanipulative, and nonjudgmental. It assumes that children must be trained to behave properly, that they will need continued input as they grow up and face new challenges, and that they will periodically retest limits. The parent in this model does not carry the burden of keeping the child happy or finding incentive to promote good behavior. The child is on her own to try out lots of behavior, and the parent limits the unacceptable. This method is described in greater detail later in the book and is summarized in the appendix.

Conclusion

Healthy children don't just happen. They come from families in which optimism prevails, from families that believe in their children. You can create this kind of family, but you must focus clearly on the elements and process that make an optimistic family possible. Start first with a "mission statement" (a la Stephen Covey in *The 7 Habits of Highly Effective People*) for yourself, and then one for your family. Include the characteristics described in this chapter and others specific to you. Then put your mission statement into effect—you'll be pleased with the outcome.

CHAPTER 5

Independence and Dependence: Development

E ric Olsen is a busy, blue-eyed, towheaded, happy three-year-old, but he's also dominant, noisy, and often demanding. One day, his thirty-four-year-old-mother, Alison, took him grocery shopping at the local Super Valu. Eric is the youngest of three children, so Alison is wise to the ways of three-year-olds; she's been there before. Squirming in the cart as his mother was picking up ingredients to bake some cookies, Eric spied a jumbo bag of his favorite food: M&M's.

"Get me M&M's!" he commanded.

"We don't need M&M's," replied Alison.

"But I love M&M's! I want M&M's."

"No, Eric. No M&M's."

Whereupon Eric began to howl at the top of his lungs: "Want M&M's! M&M's! M&Mmmmmms!" Alison realized she had two choices: either give in and get the M&M's to quiet Eric, or refuse, which would mean finding a way to give the angry, disappointed Eric time to deal with his frustration. Now, Alison is conscientious about feeding her children healthy foods and limiting sugary snacks, but more important, she knew that if she caved in, Eric would learn to believe that throwing screaming, raging fits gets him junk food and perhaps many other things in the world.

Moreover, she realized that the next trip to the grocery store might become Buy Me-Buy Me Hell: A tantrum over M&M's would lead to screaming for Starbursts or fits over Fritos.

So Alison left her shopping cart smack in the middle of the aisle. She picked up her son, who was by this point wailing and flailing, and walked

83

out of the store. She sat Eric down on the sidewalk and waited patiently, ignoring the stares of fellow Super Valu shoppers. Some glared, but others smiled knowingly.

Eric's attempt to force his mother to do his bidding lasted about a minute. When he calmed down and had been quiet for about twenty seconds, Alison asked, "Eric, are you ready to go back to the store now?" Eric, looking slightly chagrined, replied, "Yes, Mommy." So they trundled back inside, found their cart, and resumed shopping. Three aisles later, Eric's mother asked, "Eric, which cereal would you like? Here are your choices . . . " Eric picked his favorite without argument and hugged it all the way to the checkout.

Never before had Eric behaved like this in a grocery store, and this experience gave him the opportunity to learn several lessons. He learned first that throwing a fit at the supermarket did not get him what he wanted, but only got him bounced from the store. Second, he got a small lesson in learning how to calm himself down when he was furious about not getting his way (experiencing many such moments during his childhood will result in his acquiring a pervasive sense of self-control). But, as Eric processed his disappointment at not being able to control the situation, he learned the most important lesson—a little about adapting to the limits set by his parents.

Often, parents simply give in to a child in order to avoid the nagging, the negotiating, and the embarrassing emotional displays that will predictably come if they refuse. But if a three-year-old is routinely successful in forcing others to do his bidding, his tantrums may later evolve into much more subtle and complex manipulations. No one will be exempt—parents, teachers, coaches, and friends will all experience being forced into compromising situations by this young tyrant. As he grows up, the difficulties he gets into may no longer be limited to the domestic or educational arena, but spread into the community to become legal and major.

Over the course of our clinical experience, we've noticed that most of the distressed parents we see experience difficulty establishing behavioral boundaries for their children and that these same parents have difficulty empowering their children to generate and maintain their own self-esteem. This, plus the observations we outlined in chapter 4, lead us to our basic premise, born of years of helping people to parent more effectively: Children must learn and be taught how to adapt to the world. Training a child in the skills needed is the central, essential job of parenting. No matter how much we love and care for our children, we do them no good by screening and shaping their surroundings to shield them from the difficulties and distresses of real life. To approach childrearing this way will only lead to low self-esteem and incurable dependence. Real life has a plethora of rules and conditions that we all must observe in order to find success. The more skilled children are at navigating these rules and conditions, the better they will do. We must send this message to children in everything we do with them.

Children will not automatically grow into resourceful, resilient, independent adults just because their parents feed them, clothe them, and give them lots of love. Children require much more than this—most importantly, the parents' steadfast guidance, which takes a lot of energy and forethought. It would have been far easier, and certainly less embarrassing, had Alison caved into Eric's hysterical demands for M&M's. But by not doing so, she provided essential guidance about behavior in a public place, one of many small lessons that will equip Eric for the larger world.

The vast majority of the parents we see are committed to doing the best job of parenting they can—despite the difficulty they're having when they come to see us. It is clear that they want to raise their children to be independent, ethical, resourceful, and successful adults. But the means to achieve this admirable goal is not so clear to them. Childrearing was once a much simpler business. Decisions were made more easily, values were shared and understood throughout a community, transgressions were handled quickly and decisively. But over the past forty or fifty years, the picture has become considerably muddied—parents find themselves awash in an ocean of conflicting opinion, values, and methods. All around them lie the flotsam and jetsam of failed attempts, making parents all the more timid and insecure in their efforts.

Two Styles of Adaptation to Life

For clarity in this discussion, we will contrast two fundamentally different ways of adapting to life, dependent or independent, as if they existed in black and white. In real people, there are many shades of gray—the most independent people may, for instance, at times operate quite dependently, and vice versa.

When our adaptation is dependent (or indirect), we look to others to manage our lives for us. We learn to establish control of others in order to get them to do the things we don't want to do ourselves. We see examples, subtle and blatant, every day: the boisterous child like Eric who attempts to bully and badger a parent into buying candy by threat or tantrum; the family that spends all its time trying to pacify a volatile mother who might get upset; a handsome and powerful man who uses his looks and charms to manipulate women into supplying his needs; the academic underachiever who gets away with doing very little schoolwork because the insecure adults around him are afraid to ask more of him.

Dependent people tend to:

- manipulate others to supply their immediate wants

- avoid difficult or unpleasant tasks

- shift blame and responsibility for mishaps

- explain and justify their failures

- feel good only when they are in control of others

- feel anxious or angry when they have lost control of others

- ignore their values when following them is inconvenient

- arrange modification of the rules in situations to suit their own interests

- control situations rather than participate or lead

- interpret reality selectively

Independent adaptation (or direct adaptation) is seen in people who readily accept responsibility for their lives and eschew the use of others to attempt to adjust the world to suit their needs.

Independent people tend to:

- function within well-developed sets of ethical standards

- observe the rules and values of their parents, schools, teams clubs, and even informal peer relationships

- take responsibility for their own actions

- perceive the rules of a situation quickly and operate within them

- accept the rules of a situation without imposing their personal modifications or reinterpreting those rules for their personal convenience

- be capable of leadership as well as participation

Independent children are not perfect; they test limits and rules. But they quickly learn to comply with the rules they discover and, therefore, are able to participate in a wide variety of situations. They don't blame others when something goes wrong and, if they break a rule, they can accept the consequences. The most independent individuals own up to their mistakes with dignity. These individuals show reliability; they can be trusted. They do what they say they are going to do. They are not egotistical or arrogant, but are capable of individual thought and assertiveness. They are not controlling of others; instead, they are most capable of participating with others.

The qualities of independent adaptation are what we, as parents, all wish for our children. What is the connection to manipulative behavior?

Independence—A Definition

At first blush, the definition of independence seems paradoxical. To many people, independence means freedom to do whatever you want, anywhere, anytime, anyplace. But under close scrutiny, we discover that just the reverse is true. Independence is the ability to set and pursue personal goals without requiring the help of others. It is the ability to function effectively within the rules that govern situations. It is not complete freedom of action or will; its existence presupposes situations, all of which have governing rules. Independence is a necessary condition for the establishment of interdependence.

The most independent among us have learned to function most skillfully within the rules of our life situations. A simple metaphor may illustrate this crucial point: If a child decides to play a game like soccer, he must first play by the official game rules or he won't even be allowed to play. If he does play within the rules, he is then afforded the chance to develop his skills at the subtleties (rules, again, but at a different level) of the game. In this metaphor, the most independent soccer player is the most skilled player. An athletically gifted player who repeatedly breaks the rules of play, arguing with coach and referee, won't get to play, and his abilities will never be expressed or refined. Though more complex than soccer, the metaphor holds for life. The most independent person plays the "games" of life with the most skill. He does not expend much energy trying to change, skirt, or employ someone else to bend the rules. Instead, he accepts and participates in life's activities as he chooses, but directly and skillfully, within the rules.

This is not to suggest, we hasten to add, that the independent person is incapable of deciding against participation. He may choose to break from an accepted pattern of behavior. He may opt out of a situation. But when he does, it is with forethought and understanding of his responsibility for the consequences of his decision.

What we have described here is a vision of an adult who plays "life's games" exceptionally well, who consciously and carefully chooses which game to play, knows when he's running afoul of the rules of the game, and accepts the consequences of that transgression. He willingly accepts responsibility for his decisions and refuses to blame others for mistakes he's made. This person does not expect others to make his life okay. Instead, he sees that as his job. He owns his life, his emotions, and his past, present, and future.

Development of Children into Independent Adults

No theory of child development is all-inclusive; none exclusively describes the specific sequence of development leading to adult independence. We would like briefly to offer a scheme of development that we have found useful in understanding how children become self-reliant, resourceful adults.

Learning

Most human behavior is learned through practice and experience; we learn by doing. Though we may consciously initiate, guide, and evaluate new behavior we are trying to learn, the actual learning occurs only through practice. Development consists of modifying, improving, and customizing behavior already learned and adding new behavior. We store behavior learned in the past and call upon it automatically, as needed. For instance, remember when you learned to ride a bicycle: You watched others, and you received verbal instruction, but in order to ride successfully, you got on, fell off, and got on again until you refined the basic movements, through practice. Very little of this was dependent upon a conscious analysis of bicycle riding and, when you got good at it, it became automatic and easy. Conscious guidance and analysis may foster the initial acquisition of new behavior, but refinement of the behavior occurs only with practice. Even intellectual disciplines, like algebra or musical performance, are acquired and sophisticated through trials, feedback, subtle modification, and retrial until a satisfying result is obtained. And, interestingly, if we consciously guide our performance of something well-learned, we become clumsy and inefficient. The best saxophone player or downhill skier will tell you about being "in the groove," a state of performance in which the conscious mind is empty of thought and the person's whole being is given over to the activity. The athlete or public speaker who loses focus on the performance at hand, who becomes conscious of his own activity or tries to direct his behavior, invariably falters.

The Developmental Process

How is it that children learn to be independent, adaptive adults? The process can be broken down into three stages that correspond roughly to the three stages of a child's life: infancy/preschool, school age, and adolescence. Here's what happens:

A. Infancy and Preschool

Before the ages of five or six, children learn the fundamentals of living. They learn the rudiments of communication with others and the basics of getting along in the physical world. They learn to play and be playful. They learn to think and reason. During these early years, children are discovering the most fundamental rules of how the world works.

For instance, babies find out during the first few weeks of life that certain sounds they make in the presence of another person, reliably elicit a response. After practicing this rudimentary interaction for awhile, babies learn that certain sounds made by another indicate a willingness to participate in a reciprocal exchange of sounds. At that point, a parent can initiate a preverbal interchange with a baby and verbal interaction is born. What remains is a complicated process of attachment of meaning to sound collections we call words. Part of how a baby's world works involves verbal interaction, so babies adapt by learning, through trial and feedback, the rules that govern communication between persons. This has little to do with linguistics, but with interaction which is based on unwritten rules that most people in a particular culture will learn, without conscious analysis, at a very young age.

During this period, children are also learning the unforgiving rules of the physical environment: They learn about gravity and their own mobility (to crawl, stand, walk, run, or ride), and the rules that govern objects outside of them, such as a thrown ball or a dropped object. In both these examples, children are incorporating rules about the world into their behavioral storage for immediate use in the future. Each accomplishment becomes the basis for the next learning step, and each is essential to the next. The rules are neither learned nor expressed cognitively (through the use of conscious thought and analysis); not even an adult could do that without extensive study. Instead, they are learned subcognitively (without thought and analysis) and incorporated into the child's "behavioral repertoire." (We mean subcognitively—not to be confused with Freud's subconscious. The learning may be quite aware, but not dependent on conscious thought and analysis. If it were, we wouldn't have time to do anything else.)

These learning steps will not occur in a vacuum nor in a world that is highly unpredictable. Developmental steps depend upon practice in a world that operates by consistent rules. A child, for instance, reared solely by a deaf parent, will not learn effective verbal communication. In some cultures, babies are kept bundled on a papoose board until around one year of age, not allowed to crawl about, stand, or cruise. When finally released, they quickly learn all the developmental steps that lead to bipedal mobility. Some babies learn certain behaviors easily, while for others the same behaviors are more difficult to develop. Speech development may differ greatly due to innate differences between individuals and may also be affected by the specifics of responses from others. For instance, since play between young siblings is not verbally dependent like interaction with Mom or Dad, children with a slightly older sibling often learn to talk later than their sibling simply because much of their interaction and practice time is spent playing with the older child (our observation). On the other hand, a child with a somewhat older sibling may learn to talk a patois intelligible only to that older sibling who acts as the child's interpreter. A first child who spends much of her time interacting with a verbal adult usually learns verbal communication quickly.

Children also learn, by experimentation, how their social environment works. They learn the rules here just as they learn the rules about their physical environment. They learn what they are allowed to do and what is forbidden. They may learn that from early on they are responsible for their own happiness, or they may learn that others serve that function. They may learn to accept "no," or they may find out how to work around a "no" to make a "yes." They may learn that problems they encounter are largely theirs to solve, or they may learn who can be recruited to solve their problems, and how to do the recruiting. To us, it is this arena of development that is most fascinating: It has a lot to do with determining a child's style of adaptation to the world.

There are two patterns of adaptation that emerge during this early period. Which pattern arises depends upon the way the social/family environment works. Physical skills develop in response to nature's unyielding and absolute laws, but families are more flexible and operate in at least two different modes. These modes are determined by the basic assumptions about people held by the adults governing these environments.

Dependent Pattern

When we see children developing a dependent pattern of adaptation, it is commonly because the people (parents, other adults, siblings) around the child operate as if the child needs their protection from stress, trauma, mistakes, and unhappiness. They often believe that the associated emotions will wreak irreparable damage, so they act to eliminate the source of the bad feelings. More rarely, parents are disinterested or preoccupied enough that only noisy, unpleasant displays of emotion attract their parents' attention. The rules and limits made by these parents are predicated on this internal agenda. They believe children should always be happy and strive to achieve this goal, feeling like failures when their child is not happy. The child's emotional state becomes their responsibility, not the child's. Imagine the crazy quilt of limits and rules thus produced, when every moment's decision is tailor-made.

Since the child cannot understand his parents' agendas nor make sense of the rule structure in which he finds himself, he adapts by doing the only thing possible: He exerts control over the supposed rule-makers. This makes the situation more predictable and, thus, less anxiety-provoking. His mode of control will be determined by his temperament and that of his parents. He may learn to use whining and angry outbursts with his mother and sweet talk with dad. Just by looking sad, put-upon, and withdrawn, he may control the actions of his nursery school teacher. No matter the style, this child has become dependent upon adult co-conspirators to adjust the world to his liking.

By age six, the dependent child is adept at controlling those around him and, as he enters the second stage, he will expand this pattern into the larger world of school and community. His manipulation of the people around him is not a conscious, cognitive process any more than learning to throw a ball is—it is just a learned pattern of response to his world. When another person fails to cooperate with this learned pattern, the child becomes anxious, fearful, angry and attempts, by any available means, to alter the other's posture. When we intervene to change this pattern of dependency, this becomes a critical therapeutic juncture: Dependent children will not learn self-reliance unless the adults they are manipulating can weather the storm created when they suddenly start refusing to participate with their dependent and manipulative ways.

Independent Pattern

Independent children are reared by parents who have confidence in their children's innate competency. They seem to know that their children will survive, so they are quite comfortable making clear and enduring rules and consistently setting limits according to these rules. They don't see themselves as emotional protectors of their children, so they regard a child's emotional state as the private, exclusive property of that child. They do not feel responsible to fix or alleviate the anger and distress a child experiences over a limit, decision, or rule, other than to provide respectful human comfort. If a child is upset over something, they view it as a learning experience for the child, not as a potential threat to the psyche. As a result, the child learns resilience and self-reliance. He can survive a disappointment and adapt, just like a toddler who stumbles while learning to walk. He arrives at school with the resolve to figure out how school works, and the self-confidence to survive and persist, despite difficulty. He has emerged from his first five years of life with experience that has taught him how to get along, make himself happy, and pursue his own goals. An independent six-year-old is well on his way to becoming an independent, self-sufficient adult.

B. School Age

During grade school, children hone and polish patterns of behavior they've learned in the first six years. They apply the lessons of their first six years to new situations.

Dependent Pattern

The dependent child learns to control teachers, friends, coaches, or others by whatever means he's learned at home. He may become more skilled at being sad and depressed, "forgetting" his responsibilities, charming his way, negotiating compromise, or abusing others into following his demands, or he may strive to be "perfect." As his world gets bigger, he will begin to find situations in which his manipulative skills don't work so well, and he will withdraw, finding these situations not suitable to him. The dependent child will make a career out of finding his way around rules and expectations placed upon him and, sadly, many adults will cooperate to avoid his distress and unhappiness. He will make a profession of getting school work adjusted or playing only with kids that do it his way, or pushing parents and relatives into buying or doing what he wants. As he gets more and more ensconced in this pattern of behavior, he becomes completely unable to adapt himself to a set of conditions—always expecting the world should adapt to him. His world becomes a small house of cards contingent solely upon the willingness of others to adjust to him, and ready to collapse during the next stage. This child has learned to control others rather than to adapt.

Independent Pattern

The independent child, on the other hand, is a wonder to behold. He soaks up the rules of new situations like a sponge. He quickly learns to play by the rules and then vigorously pursues sharpening his skills in the subtleties of the game. New situations, new games intrigue him: He eagerly pursues learning the way to succeed in every possible environment. His self-confidence soars. He makes mistakes, breaks rules, and learns from his mistakes. He is not particularly fearful of the possibility of failure—he's had his share and survived and has learned that failure is an unavoidable part of life. Above all, he has learned to understand and adapt to the workings of a life situation quickly and accurately. He has become self-controlled.

C. Adolescence

Adolescence—the time most parents dread. The myth, in our culture, is that the teenage years are a time of universal rebellion, a time of great difficulty. But this legend is simply not true for all children, or even most. When adolescence is truly awful, there is usually good reason.

Dependent Pattern

The dependent child can no longer keep his house of cards standing. Life will no longer do his bidding, and he is left bereft of skills to adapt. The legacy of this collapse is angry rebellion; depression and despondency; suicide; eating disorders; school failure; social troubles; delinquency; slavelike adherence to adolescent subcultures; disrespect of parents, teachers, property, and law; drug involvement; and so on. The child who has never been required to adapt often can't. He goes on trying to make the world the way he wants it, by whatever means. Until he is completely defeated, he will not begin to experience adaptation, and then, it will be a slow and painful process to develop adaptive skills, often requiring years. A dependent adolescent possessed of some special qualities—like the beautiful girl or the accomplished athlete—may make it through, avoiding immediate disaster. But this serves only to delay the crisis that will almost certainly come later in life. This is strong stuff. Many people would like to make up simple explanations for the ills of adolescence, the most popular of late being labels that cast our children as victims (such as those of abuse or neglect.) We don't deny that these are real problems. But manipulative behavior isn't born of these adverse circumstances. It is born of the youth's inability to adapt adequately to his or her life circumstances. For the adolescent who is dependent, the inevitable crash with reality—that he can't control the world around him—can be devastating. This, to our minds, is as critical a problem as any form of abuse or neglect. And addressing it forces us to respect our children and resist labeling them as victims.

Independent Pattern

The independent adolescent arrives self-confident of his ability to survive. He continues to perform and produce, he disdains dope, and he respects parents, property, and law. He has goals and pursues them persistently. He knows that he has the ability to function in most situations. Life is fun, and he's glad to be alive. All things are possible, and he chooses to go after those that are consistent with his identity and goals.

During this period, he goes from guidance based on parental morals, values, and rules to self-guidance. He develops, using the rich background of his own experience, his own unique code of ethics. By his early twenties, he is characterized by self-defined goals and by the ability to adapt and operate in the world effectively. His self-esteem is strong, he possesses his own set of ethics, and he demonstrates integrity, following his own standards. He becomes a competent, self-confident young adult.

Limits and Independence

Daily, we can observe examples of the two developmental sequences we've described here. Children will follow one or the other, based on the consistency and effectiveness of the limit-setting they've received from their parents. The child whose parents have never set secure limits and boundaries needs only to learn the job of controlling her parents and others. She doesn't have to practice adaptation to the larger world. Her view of the world, her experience with the world, is indirect and false. Thus, she starts down a pathway that will inevitably result in self-hate, anger, chronic disappointment, and despondency. The child who has had excellent limit-setting during her early years will learn the skills of independent adaptation. She will develop resiliency; she will be prepared to deal with the larger world effectively. Early parental guidance is the key to eventual self-guidance, and early parental guidance is built on a foundation of effective limit-setting.

Limit-Setting, Discipline, and Punishment

Limit-setting is not based on punishment. We see, daily, parents who try to manage an unruly child by using some sort of punishment or threat. When we teach these parents to use a completely different approach, to guide their children first by the establishment of boundaries on behavior, they come back amazed and gratified. Stop thinking, *now,* that punishment will "teach them a lesson they'll remember." They won't "think twice before doing it again." Forget the idea that to set limits you must punish wrongdoing. Drop the notion that if you could just find the right punishment, everything would work out fine—this approach just doesn't work! By now, the reader is probably getting impatient to have some suggestions about methods that will work. This is the topic of the last three chapters.

Independent people have the skills to develop and maintain their own self-esteem. Independence develops in children when they learn to adapt to and function within the rules of various situations. Our contribution to their adaptation consists of defining the rules at home clearly, consistently, and nonpunitively over time so that they acquire the skills necessary to adapt in the real world.

We like to use the following metaphor for childrearing: Life is much like a collection of playing fields. Parents choose some of these fields for their children, transport them there, and allow the child to explore the field and its activities. Parents teach the basic rules of play by setting limits and insisting on practice of the appropriate skills. From there on, the child is free to learn to play well, to perfect skills through trial and error. When the child is headed for the brambles at the edge of the field, parents intervene and send their child back into the action. If the child chooses not to play, wants another field, parents must decide whether this is okay, whether to allow it. When the child fails in her efforts on the field, parents can comfort her with the message, "I know you can do it; keep trying." Parents must not intervene to change the rules of play to suit their child. When the child finally achieves success, parents can congratulate, cheer, and admire, but remember whose success it was.

Children must find their own way on the fields of life; if we interfere, we limit their learning, their responsibility and, ultimately, their freedom to become independent.

CHAPTER 6

Becoming Manipulation-Proof

I n the last chapter, we focused on the relationship of manipulative behavior to the development of dependency. We showed how manipulative behavior was antithetical to both independence and self-esteem. Conversely, behaviors contributing to the development of self-esteem and independence are inherently nonmanipulative.

Now, we would like to help you to become manipulation-proof. This requires that you learn to recognize both the manipulative behaviors your child uses to control situations through you, and the blind sides that open the door to this kind of exploitation. By blind sides, we mean those thoughts, biases, feelings, and beliefs you possess—hidden agendas, really—that your child discovers and uses to manipulate you. Unless you can identify and alter your blind sides, you cannot become manipulation-proof.

While reading, think about similar situations and behaviors involving your child. Consider also what you do, feel, think, and believe when confronted by these situations and behaviors. As part of this presentation, we will guide you through some necessary observations of your own child, using the framework shown in the chart on the next page. When you have completed and recorded these observations, you will have identified your child's unique manipulative behaviors and your own blind sides. With these insights in hand, you can begin to make the adjustments necessary to prevent manipulative behavior, a powerful avoidance process that can turn the joys of parenthood into emotional turmoil.

MANIPULATIVE INTERACTIONS OBSERVATION CHART

Problem Situation	What My Child Did	My Response	What I Was Avoiding (Thoughts, Feelings, Beliefs)
Daniel, age 6, was asked to take out the recycling.	He stalled and walked slowly.	I told him several times to get moving. He didn't. So, I helped him.	I was in danger of being late.
Maggie, in third grade, was to read 10 pages in her reader to me.	She stumbled over the words, got upset, and tears welled-up in her eyes.	I helped her, gave her hints, broke down the words, and praised her a lot.	She broke my heart. I was afraid that if she got frustrated, she would never learn to enjoy reading.
Shopping at Target with Jonathan, age 6. He wanted a toy and I said "no." We didn't have enough money.	He began a tantrum. He fell to the floor and began to scream, "I have to have it!"	I made a deal with him. I would reward him with a cheaper toy if he behaved in the store.	His tantrums have been awful in the store. What will people think? Besides, I could reward him for good behavior.
Annette, age 4 won't go to bed at night. She is afraid of the dark.	She got out of bed, cried, trembled. She begged me to lie down with her.	I lay down with her in her bed until she fell asleep.	Her crying was getting to me. I felt so bad for her. How could I force her to stay in bed alone when she is so afraid? Her dad was starting to get upset with all the noise.
Phillip, age 13 and an "A" student, complained that his assignments are boring.	He said he knew the material and would not do the work.	I looked at his work and tested him on it. He really knew it. I told him he didn't have to do it. I would call his teacher and explain.	If I push it, he argues forever. I was also afraid that if I had him do boring work, it might get him turned off by school.

Problem Situations and Your Child's Response

Look at the above table. The first two categories are entitled "Problem Situation" and "What My Child Did." To use this format, first write down recurrent problem situations. When a problem comes up, observe your child's actions and record them. Pay particular attention to the categories of problem situations listed below.

Compliance

Compliance becomes an issue whenever a child is asked to do something. Examples include asking the child to take out the garbage, put his dishes in the sink, or come in for dinner. Any behavior other than what is asked is noncompliant and worthy of recording. For instance, your child might argue, request a delay, or ignore your request completely. You might also be asking your child to stop doing something, like roughhousing, teasing a sibling, or playing with the TV remote. If your child fails to honor your request, he is noncompliant. If a child cannot accept "no" for an answer but acts to try to change the "no" to a "yes" by arguing, pleading, crying, throwing a tantrum, or just blatantly disregarding your decision, he's noncompliant. Most noncompliant behavior is manipulative.

Persistence

Persistence is sticking with a task until it's completed. Persistence becomes an issue only after the child has initially complied. For example, suppose that you ask your child to clean her bedroom. She seems willing and goes to her room to clean. But once there, she gets as far as the Legos strewn across the floor and the cleanup job suddenly becomes a construction project, with dirty underwear and socks ignored or quickly swept into the closet or under the bed. In children who lack persistence, there are usually numerous examples: Homework isn't completed, dressing for school involves nagging and reminders, or shoveling snow off the sidewalk requires more involvement from you than if you did it yourself.

Obeying Household Rules, Responsibilities, and Values

There are two ways children disobey recognized household rules and responsibilities: A child may not do what is expected or may do things that are forbidden. Examples are failing to flush the toilet after using it, not doing homework, lying when confronted, using the phone during forbidden times, making noise when someone is asleep, roughhousing on the furniture, and taking too long to shower.

Emotion-Provoking Situations

Emotions frequently expressed by your child, such as anxiety, fear, apprehension, sadness, despair, anger, and guilt, should alert you. Frequently expressed emotions are commonly manipulative; your anticipation or observation of your child experiencing an unpleasant emotion may set you up to take care of the emotion-provoking situation for your child. For instance, if you know that your child will likely become anxious or fearful in response to a new situation, you may try to prepare him thoroughly beforehand, offering inducements and promises in exchange for his cooperation rather than merely supporting him through the experience, fully confident in his ability to cope. Children who are perfectly behaved or people pleasers often replace assertiveness with their perfect or pleasing ways, preferring to "nice" the people around them into complying with their wishes, avoiding any risk of failure or disapproval.

Sadness, frustration, and anger work the same way, evoking vigorous responses from adults who have a hard time allowing a child to experience these emotions. The adult's guilt sets him up to be manipulated, and the child gets what he wants.

The following lists review the behaviors that children commonly use in response to problem situations, to avoid or delay compliance in the situation. It should be noted that, even though a behavior is listed under a particular situation, it may also serve just as well in other circumstances. For example, listed under noncompliant behaviors is arguing. A child may argue to avoid an anxiety-provoking situation or any other situation.

BEHAVIORS THAT CAN BE USED FOR AVOIDANCE

Non-Compliant Behaviors

Whining and crying

Temper-tantrums

Arguing

Ignores the request

Refuses to do as requested

Does as she pleases

Puts task off until later

Refuses to stop a behavior

Seductive

Physical aggression

Does not take no for an answer

Demanding Behaviors

Do it now, Dad!

Keeps nagging when told no

Whining, crying, and temper outbursts

Threatening

BEHAVIORS THAT CAN BE USED FOR AVOIDANCE (continued)

GENERAL EXAMPLES/SITUATIONS

Family Value	*Child's Response*
Do your best	Gives up easily
Respect others	Makes disrespectful remarks
Be honest	Steals or lies

Family Rules	*Child's Response*
Don't use the phone after 9:00 PM	Calls a friend after 10:00 PM
Flush the toilet	Doesn't flush

Nonpersistent Behaviors

Starts with homework and quits to watch television

Gets distracted by other activities

Gives up easily when fully capable

Angry, Agressive Behaviors

Hits, punches, kicks, bites

Threatens physical harm

Anxious, Fearful, Apprehensive Behaviors

Withdraws from emotional-provoking situation

Pleading, begging "Please don't leave me alone!"

Physical complaints

Makes excuses

Hysterical crying

Panics

Shyness

Trembles

Runs away from feared stimulus

Seductive (for example, a wiggle in the walk)

Repeatedly seeking reassurance (for instance, "Will I be okay?")

Perfect behavior

BEHAVIORS THAT CAN BE USED FOR AVOIDANCE (continued)

Sad Behaviors

Doesn't smile

Mopes

Pouts

Cries

Listlessness

Tired

Passive Aggressive Behaviors

Willingly agrees, but does as he pleases

Charming or overly affectionate

"I forgot"

Guilty Behaviors

Tries to get others to remove guilty feelings

Blames others for his mistakes

Your Avoidance Behaviors

With this summary of what children will do to avoid situations, you are ready to identify what you do to allow (enable) your child's manipulative behavior. List how you responded to your child's behavior under the appropriate heading. Generally, parental enabling behaviors fall into three categories:

1. The parent's action facilitates a reduction in what the child perceives as noxious or upsetting. For example, after hearing complaints about how much work it will take to clean the bedroom, the child's parent helps clean the room or decreases expectations for thoroughness.

2. The parent's action permits a child to delay starting what the child perceives as unpleasant. For example, after missing three days of school already, John promises his mother that if allowed to stay

home for just one more day, he will go to school tomorrow without fail. John's mother allows him to stay home.

3. A parent's action allows a child to eliminate, altogether, the noxious situation. For example, rather than ignite a predictable battle by asking the child to do a job, the parent does it for him.

Finally, write down what you were trying to avoid in the situation. It is likely that any parental response that results in the child manipulating the situation is based on something you were trying to avoid. When observing interactions between you and your child, ask yourself: "Am I doing something merely to get out of or head off an unpleasant circumstance?" "What is it I'm trying to avoid?" By identifying the fears, distress, and guilt that cause you to enable your child's manipulative behavior, you will begin to understand your blind sides.

Your Blind Sides

Your blind sides are those thoughts, feelings, beliefs, and behaviors that permit your child to manipulate. Blind sides are the hot buttons a child presses, allowing a manipulation to proceed. When a child starts to avoid something, parents may experience an emotional response. The emotions experienced are accompanied by a stream of thoughts and beliefs that, like the emotions themselves, may serve to justify either the child's behavior or the parent's response. Once the emotion is experienced, the process of justification, rationalization, and self-deception begins. Some blind sides are a result of a belief system. Belief systems arise from experience: events in childhood, what was learned from parents, education, things seen and heard in the media, and what children have taught us. Whatever the origin, beliefs can allow parents to be blindsided by their children. Beliefs compounded with emotional responses are particularly powerful in this regard.

For example, Albert, a nine-year-old, is asked to take out the garbage. He protests bitterly that he does all the work around this house and his brother never has to do anything. Theresa, his mother, thinks to herself, "He is pretty tired and grumpy tonight." She says, "Albert, you have had a long, hard day. I guess I can take it out for you." Based on her emotional response to his anger, she has rationalized a justification for his actions.

Other times, feelings, thoughts, and beliefs may be used to justify a knowing parent's actions that allow a child to manipulate. Sarah, age three, has been put to bed. She has been read to, given a hug and a kiss, and tucked in for the night. Ten minutes later, Sarah is out of her bedroom complaining tearfully that there are giant ants in her bedroom. Sarah's mother, a bit annoyed with her fears, thinks to herself, "I better go lie down with her. If I don't, she will be up all night long and I'm beat. I can't put up with her fears tonight." She lies down with Sarah until the child falls asleep. Sarah's mother has justified her actions, and Sarah is allowed to manipulate. With just a little experience, children develop a keen awareness of what it will take to manipulate a parent.

Common Blind Sides

Following are summaries of nine common feelings and beliefs that parents have shared with us, insights into how they have been blindsided by their children and hooked into being manipulated. We hope that these summaries will help you examine what characteristics make you vulnerable to your child's manipulations. We don't presume to know exactly what you experience, nor do we believe that what has been identified here is all-inclusive. Following each of the blindsides are some suggested antidotes.

1. Fear of Losing a Child's Love

Some parents will justify allowing their child to manipulate because they fear the loss of the child's love and affection. This fear becomes a powerful lever in the hands of a child who finds that even a gentle tug at it will send his parents scrambling to ease his burdens, all the while justifying both their actions and the child's behavior: "If I don't do as he asks, he won't love me." "What harm could there be if I give him what he wants?" "He looks so unhappy with me. I can't stand it!" "Oh, well, rules are made to be broken— better to break a rule than a heart." Or "It makes no sense to jeopardize our relationship over something so arbitrary." All this to avoid the imagined possibility of losing the child's love and affection.

The parent who is divorced or separated is especially susceptible to this fear, particularly the noncustodial parent. The result is "Disneyland" fathers or mothers, parents who do everything possible to ensure that their children have a great time, avoiding unpopular rules or conflicts during their limited times together.

Fear of losing your child's love is generally ill-founded. Any child, however well-parented, may, on occasion, be mightily displeased with you. Parental decisions are not always popular. But when manipulative behavior becomes a way of life, you will ultimately lose your child's respect and, very possibly, love, permanently. First strive to earn your child's respect, and love will usually follow—not the other way around. While there are no guarantees that elimination of manipulative behavior will result in your child loving you, the odds run strongly in that direction.

Melanie, a young woman we know, went through a horrible adolescence of drugs, alcohol, sexual escapades, and scrapes with the law. Her divorced and single mother adopted a tough-love approach, despite her fear of losing her daughter forever and misgivings over the very real risks to Melanie's physical person. For seven years, she didn't try to make things okay for her daughter; she wouldn't even allow Melanie in the door if she wasn't "straight." She loved Melanie unconditionally, but refused steadfastly to participate in Melanie's self-destructive behavior. She built a support group around her and never yielded to the temptation to try to make her daughter love her. She knew that her daughter wasn't even capable of loving, just using. After these long years, Melanie finally pulled herself together and, three years later, is now an honors student at a prestigious local college. Melanie told us, "I always knew my mother would be there, that her rules wouldn't change despite how awful I had been. I know that the cause of my problems had a lot to do with my parents' divorce, a father who didn't seem to care, and the way I had been raised. But the only thing that got me through all of it was my mother hanging in there year after year." Over and over, we hear a common refrain from young adults who got away with manipulation as children and adolescents and must now deal with the consequences, "I wish my parents had made me follow the rules when I was younger. I wouldn't be in this fix now."

Divorced or separated parents fearing the loss of their child's love can take comfort in knowing that parents who place limits on their children are the ones who, long-term, are able to achieve and maintain a loving relationship with them. There is no question that a hostile former spouse can create a rough road for the relationship between you and the child—but nowhere nearly as rough as the one created when you allow your child to manipulate. When you lose your child's respect, love cannot flourish. Bottom line: Treat children lovingly and with respect, and don't allow them to manipulate you. Teach them to respect your strength and character, and love will take care of itself.

2. Inconvenient Times and Places

Children come well-equipped to inconvenience their parents—particularly when you are the least prepared to handle the problem. They will misbehave in public places, when you are on the phone or trying to communicate with others, or when you're in a time crunch. Any inopportune time is ripe for manipulative behavior. At some point you have probably been embarrassed, perhaps to the point of tears, while your child loudly misbehaves in public. If so, you have likely developed multiple strategies for dealing with future outbursts. Your answer may be to give them what they want, perhaps negotiating, but saying "yes" when you should say "no." Children learn early that time is on their side when dealing with their parents. You may have found yourself in this kind of situation: Your eight-year-old daughter is dawdling watching cartoons when she should be getting dressed for school, so you nag her to hurry up, make the bed for her, or threaten dire consequences if she doesn't get a move on. Justification for your actions might be, "What else am I supposed to do, there just isn't enough time to teach her to do things the right way." Or perhaps your strategy is to offer rewards to entice good behavior, always equipped with a bag of goodies to distract your child from squirming and running around.

Daniel and his family were clients of ours and serve as excellent examples. Daniel had just turned three and had all the skills necessary to dress himself, indeed had been able to accomplish this for some time. One morning, his dad went to Daniel's bedroom and found him playing instead of getting dressed. He said, "Daniel, you need to get dressed, and you have to be done before I get out of the shower." Daniel was ready before his dad even got into the shower. He was completely dressed except for tying his shoes. Over the course of the next two weeks, this scene repeated itself, and Daniel began to dawdle more each day. Over the next month, several trips into his bedroom each morning became routine. Daniel's father justified his actions by saying to himself, "I have two boys to get dressed, and I have to get them out of the house on time! I have appointments, and I can't be late!" or "That T-shirt has a tight neck, and it's difficult for him to pull over his head." Daniel's dawdling worsened, requiring more and louder reminders to him to get dressed in the morning. Finally, one morning his dad went into Daniel's room to discover Daniel with his pajamas off and one leg in his underwear—and that had taken twenty-five minutes! He lay there naked, investigating the springs of his bunk bed. Then and there, Daniel's dad realized that he could no longer justify Daniel's behavior or his own. He decided that he was going to need to do what he felt was the right thing all along. It took some planning at first; everyone had to get up earlier. But with a liberal application of Stop, Pause, and Redirect (a procedure that we discuss in depth in chapter 7) and no more justifications, Daniel quickly became efficient and punctual.

Parents who find themselves trapped by inconvenience will only make things worse by changing what they would ordinarily do because of the inconvenience. Suffering a few minutes of embarrassment in the supermarket, telling someone you'll call them back, or being late to work are excellent investments that pay incredible dividends over the time you are raising your children.

If you're having problems like these, it is always possible to deal with them effectively if you do a little planning. If your child is a dawdler, start out your day fifteen minutes early. If you have problems in public, practice by taking a few trial runs to the store when there's no time pressure. Set up a dummy phone call, and every time your child interrupts, put down the phone and carry out the procedure described in chapter 7. Establishing a good and consistent base of management with your child now will definitely save you uncounted hours in the future.

3. Parental Feelings Triggered by the Child's Emotions

A child's tears, panicked withdrawal, or angry outburst will cause a parent to feel badly, often making them available to manipulate. Rationalizations come easily to hand: "I did a lot of the same kinds of things when I was young," "I remember how badly I felt when my parents made me go to swimming lessons, so I'm not going to do that to my child," or "I can't have my child go through that; it is just too awful." Guilt, fear, anxiety, and remorse all set a parent up to change the rules and be manipulated. A parent's rationalization might go something like this: "Taking the garbage out can't be all that important when it is such a battle. What is the effect on him when I insist and he gets so angry? It can't be good for his sister to see him so totally out of control." When a child is facing a feared situation, parents may feel they have abandoned their child or are not providing their child with enough security. They may think that the momentary loss of security threatens self-esteem. Faced with this, parents may become the child's coping mechanism rather than supporting the child while he finds his own coping strategies.

If you find yourself feeling, angry, sad, guilty, irritated, or anxious over your child's reaction to something, ask yourself: If I fail to deal with this problem now, if I bail my child out of the situation, what will be the long-term effect? In general, things will only get worse. Better that you deal with problems early because later they will become bigger and sometimes impossible for you to manage. Remember, though, that when a manipulative behavior is interrupted, an intense outpouring of emotions will likely result. It is rarely easy to stop manipulative behavior, but the earlier you start, the less difficult it is. If you feel guilty when your child is unhappy and avoid dealing with your child's behavior, you will provide your child with more opportunities to elicit your guilt. Don't sacrifice what you know to be right and proper for the sake of the child's momentary happiness.

4. Fear of Angrily Losing Control

Parents are sometimes anxious that they will lose control of themselves, feeling they may become too angry and do something harmful to their child. This causes them to become tentative, and they fail to deal with the problem, often deceiving themselves. Robert's father had a hot temper, often barely controlled. He had received a few thrashings from his father as a child and feared he might do the same to his son. Robert had a fiery temperament as well, and other children soon discovered he was easy to bait with teasing, causing difficulty at school. After the third call from school about his son's aggressive behavior, Robert's father began to criticize the school for a lack of supervision, "I would do the same thing if I were teased by those kids, wouldn't you?" Unfortunately, Robert's father didn't know any other way to teach his son to contain his angry responses and was afraid of what would happen if he confronted his son. We taught him to remove Robert quietly when he was just becoming angry, and eventually Robert learned to do this for himself. Once he was able to do this with other children, his aggressive behavior abated.

If you feel you are at risk of losing control and doing something to harm your child, please get someone to assist you. That may be someone from a mental health clinic, a psychologist, a psychiatrist, a religious counselor, or a close friend. Act now; don't put it off. Learn better ways to handle your own anger, and learn better ways to handle your children—this is the only way to reduce the risk of abuse. Besides, responding to manipulative behavior with anger works only for the short run. It will not teach the child to behave better. Worse, once in the habit, you set in motion a vicious cycle; the intensity of the anger required to set this type of scenario in motion always increases, and abuse eventually results. If you can't control your anger by telling yourself, "Cool your jets on this one," remove yourself until you cool off. Learn to act quickly before you've become angry—the longer you've put up with misbehavior, the more angry you'll become.

5. Lack of Confidence

Parents who lack confidence in their parenting skills are prime targets for being manipulated. They become anxious and fall prey to the their children's manipulative behavior. These parents feel they must do the "right thing" or the child will forever be "scarred." So they become immobilized with anxiety. They're convinced that doing nothing in response to their child's manipulative behavior is far better than doing the wrong thing.

If you lack confidence, you might find some reassurance in knowing that the business of rearing children is not easy for anybody. The two authors of this book can testify to that, both as professionals and as parents. Between the two of us, we have well over forty years of experience counseling parents and some thirty-five combined years in dealing with our children. Parenting isn't easy, and some children would be a challenge to the most experienced and confident parent. There is no one right way to parent, though there are a few principles that can help guide parents (see chapters 7 and 8). If you consistently do what you believe is right, if you refuse to be badgered, guilted, or argued into doing what you feel is wrong, and if you can support and comfort a child while she solves her own problems, then your confidence in yourself as a parent will soar. Good parenting does not require perfection. One small mistake will not scar your child for life. Individual mistakes don't cause significant damage, but allowing a child to manipulate freely over the years because you lack confidence does.

6. Parent Overload

Parents who are overwhelmed with work and difficult schedules may be quite daunted with the challenge of dealing with a child's manipulative behavior. We hear, "I would rather do the dishes myself than to put up with all the hassles"; "I just don't have the time to mess around with her tonight"; "I can get it done much faster or better if I do it myself." These parents are overestimating the effort and time required to correct behavior and underestimating their own capabilities for teaching their children appropriate behavior. Parents who are stressed by life's circumstances, or by financial or family difficulties, may give up, saying to themselves and others, "I can't do it," "I need time for myself," "I'm too exhausted," "I'm too upset to deal with this." Sometimes, parents have clinically identifiable problems like depression and become immobilized. Parental problems like these open the door for manipulation and worsen the parental situation. If you find yourself relating to these descriptions, you won't likely make progress with your children until you address your own problems and priorities.

7. Parental Beliefs

When a child's specific avoidance behavior plays into the parents' belief system, manipulation flourishes. If you, for instance, believe that it is your job to ensure the happiness of your child, s/he will play to this theme, becoming sad, withdrawn, or angry. Parents may believe that they must provide more for their children than they had when they were young. Parents who have vowed to do differently than their parents are at risk of getting blindsided. For example, a father who remembers bitterly the aloofness of his own father will tend to overcompensate, believing, "Unlike my father, I am going to spend lots of time with my children." This father may become his child's principal playmate, a decidedly unhealthy situation for the child who must learn to deal with peers. We see many children who misbehave in school simply because they are addicted to adult attention and cannot get along with peers.

Parents can become trapped because they believe that a particular behavior is a "stage." Children in their second year of life are allowed to misbehave because they are in the terrible twos; siblings are allowed to disrupt the entire household with their fighting because everyone knows sibling rivalry is normal; limits are not placed on a child's behavior because the young child doesn't understand the rule. Unfortunately, these children may not learn to behave adaptively because their parents have excused themselves from stopping misbehavior. Your child may be in a "stage," but that is an opportunity for you to teach the right way to behave. All won't be well just because a child gets older and grows out of the "stage." Parents and teachers often believe that learning must be fun, that if children don't enjoy the process of learning, they won't pursue learning in the future. Learning is often not fun; it is hard work. Discovery is exciting, and the use of well-learned basic skills to explore an interest or avocation may be fun, but learning basic skills is rarely fun. Phonics, basic math, and memorization of facts is tedious work, but life is full of tedious work that we must accept. The belief that learning must be fun has paralyzed our educational system and can paralyze your efforts to support your child's education.

Reevaluate your beliefs. If you want to give your children happiness, think about this: Happiness is not yours to give; your childrens' happiness is *their* job. All you can do as a parent is guide your children in learning the skills needed to adapt to the world in which they live. Once children have learned those skills, they are equipped to find their own happiness.

Reexamine the childhood experiences that were so difficult—why were they a problem for you? Did it have to do with your preparation for them?

Were your parents finally so frustrated with you that they lost control? Was it the harshness, arbitrariness, or dictatorial way in which you were dealt with as a child? Or was it truly a lack of attention and caring? Probably it was the former. Learn from your own experience, but don't permit yourself to be blindsided in an overcorrection for the deficiencies of your childhood.

Are we suddenly building an argument against parental control of manipulative behavior here? Not at all. What we are suggesting is simply that it's possible for parents to come up with a cure that's nearly as bad as the disease. Interrupting the occurrence of an avoidance behavior need not be handled in a harsh, arbitrary, or dictatorial fashion. In fact, we are suggesting quite the opposite. Interrupting a manipulative behavior must be done quietly, calmly, and without emotional blackmail. The rules should be consistent over time and applied to all members of the family.

Parents who feel guilty because part of their goal is to provide the child with more than what they have, might do well to sit down and examine what it is they have and how they got it. It is also important for them to identify their feelings of success and accomplishment. Most often, you got where you are because of hard work, persistence, and the belief that you could do it. The needs you experienced in childhood may have provided some of the inspiration for the skills to get you what you have today. It is the challenging experiences of childhood that teach you to utilize ingenuity and effort to overcome adversity.

If you get manipulated by a belief that a behavior is a stage or is normal, or that a child must have a complete verbal understanding of the rule, you may want to rethink that belief rather thoroughly. While it is true that children appear to go through stages of development, it is not true that they will grow out of their manipulative behavior. In fact, it is quite the opposite. The behaviors don't just go away with the passing of time, through development or developmental changes in the brain. The behaviors are changed by the child learning what is acceptable and what is not. They learn to adapt by having limits placed on them by parents. It is through experience in having to adjust to the rules that acceptable behavior is learned. Children don't need a complete verbal understanding to learn from experience. Learned behavior is not just verbal. Much of what we do on a daily basis is habit and not managed by verbal control. Knowing what to do does not mean that you will do it. The converse is also true. The terrible two-year-old can learn to be a terrific three-year-old by having to accommodate to her parents' expectations—without verbal input or understanding. Siblings who solve their conflicts with one another quietly and nonaggressively have learned by experience to do so because of their parents' insistence that it be done that way.

8. Guilt over Children's Stress

Guilty feelings may arise when there has been a stressful event in the child's life—for example, divorce, adoption, illness, diagnosis of a learning disability, death of a parent, remarriage, or financial hardship. Because the parent feels that the child has been traumatized or short-changed in life, the child's misbehavior is justified or is accepted as normal, given the circumstances. When an unacceptable behavior occurs, the parents begin to justify or rationalize the behavior: "My heart goes out to him. How can I expect him to behave any differently with all that he has had to deal with?" "How can I expect her to behave when she has been so sick?" "She is just acting that way because I don't have the money to give her the little extras that other children have." "If my jerk of an ex would only spend a little more time with him, he wouldn't feel so angry and act that way." Under the weight of guilty feelings about the child's stress, the rules are changed, expectations are lowered, and the child is ultimately permitted to manipulate.

Bert and his family are an excellent example. Ten-year-old Bert came to our attention a year and a half after he had been hospitalized for two weeks with a serious illness. After a month of recuperation, he was back in good health. But during his recuperation, he became depressed.

Bert was sad, irritable, and disrespectful to the members of his family. His grades in school had plummeted. He had become argumentative and noncompliant. Explaining that the problems first started when he was hospitalized, Bert's mother explained, "Both his dad and I felt so sorry for him, we didn't think it was a good idea to confront those behaviors when he was so sick. We felt that he needed more attention, and so we tried to spend as much time with him as possible." As long as everything went his way, Bert was content. When things were not the way he wanted them, he grew irritable and demanding. Bert's parents soon found themselves doing things for him that he was capable of doing for himself, including household chores and homework.

During his illness and recuperation, the rules were changed. Unacceptable behavior was accepted, and Bert did more of it. Bert's parents also got into the habit of justifying and excusing his misbehavior. They could always find a reason to justify Bert's actions. "He just seemed so out of sorts tonight," "He's had a hard day," or "Bert is special; we almost lost him."

In treating Bert's depression, we focused on confronting his parents' blind sides. They needed to stop justifying, rationalizing, and excusing Bert's behavior because he had been ill eighteen months ago. Allowing Bert to behave badly was doing him no favor; it only made matters worse. Fortunately, his parents took our advice and quit excusing his behavior. They effectively shut down his manipulations. After a remarkably short time, Bert's behavior and depression turned around. His grades improved, and he reestablished friendships. In describing the changes in Bert's behavior, his perceptive parents wrote: "It was like a heavy load had been lifted from his shoulders."

9. Conflict Between Parents

Another common and troubling setting for manipulative behavior emerges when the child falls in the middle of a conflict between parents. The mother may feel the father is nonsupportive and then say to herself, "What the hell. Why should I do it if he won't help?" Often, parents have sharp differences in their expectations about the child's behavior or in their opinions on how a behavior is to be handled. Such a rift between parents provides fertile ground for manipulation by the child. Sometimes the conflict centers on differing definitions of acceptable and unacceptable behavior: When is the bedroom called clean? When is the child's behavior called disrespectful? Sometimes the sharpest disagreement is over how to deal with a clear misbehavior. One parent considers the other to be too harsh, and vice versa. Both parents end up compensating for one another. One raises the ante while the other one decreases the requirements. Children, uncanny in their ability to spot conflicts, take advantage of the situation and manipulate. They side with the parent who makes things easier for them. The easier parent and the child form an alliance against the other parent. The child now has a partner in his avoidance behavior.

Children who manipulate because of conflicts between their parents must be stopped. Parenting is difficult enough as it is, and the lack of a united front will defeat your long-term efforts before you even start. Sit down and work out your differences. Start with a discussion of values and goals. If you can't make progress, get help from someone who is a professional. A chronic, pitched battle between parents is never helpful. If you cannot agree on management, even after reading chapter 7 of this book, agree to stay out of each others' business, treating one another with great respect. The specific nature of compromise that parents must make to work together is not terribly important in our point of view. Supporting one another's efforts is, on the other hand, essential. For example, if one parent has high expectations for room cleaning and the other parent believes that it is the child's bedroom and he ought to be free to have the room anyway he likes, short of having the house condemned by the Health Department, the parents might then split the difference. They might require, on a weekly basis, that the child put his dirty clothes into the laundry, do a little dusting, and take out the garbage from his bedroom. Even though the parents have individual preferences, their compromise becomes the household rule—and they stick by it.

One conversation will not be enough. There will always be situations that you don't anticipate. Huddle, don't sabotage. Maintain your united front. For example, Sarah's mother asked her to put the dishes in the dishwasher and sweep the kitchen floor. Sarah complained to her dad about the extra work. Though he believed that putting the dishes in the dishwasher was enough for one day, he knew he had to support his wife. So he avoided the temptation to reduce Sarah's workload. Once the child completes the job, the parents can huddle together, away from the child, and discuss what their agreed-upon expectations should be in the future.

Sometimes children will attempt to use one parent to intercede with the other over some rule or decision. You will demonstrate your respect for the other parent's decision and your united front by telling the child to deal with the parent who made the decision, no matter how you feel about it.

Often, parents will get into conflict about how a particular behavior is to be managed. One parent feels that the other parent's approach is harsh and excessive. Even in this set of circumstances, it is important that the parents maintain a united front with the child. If you feel that real abuse is happening, confront it and seek help. If the management technique is only harsh and somewhat excessive, do not interfere at the time, but once the crisis is over, sit down and work out your differences.

Ben's parents found themselves in just such a predicament. Ben had been sent to his room to clean it. After an hour and a half, his dad went to his room to see what was taking him so long. Once he got to Ben's room, he found that not a single Lego had been put away. What he found was a rather nice replica of the Sears Tower. This happened to have been the third day in a row that Ben had been sent to his room, and nothing, except for the building of the Sears Tower, had been accomplished. Ben's dad hit the roof. He yelled at the boy, threatening him with grounding for six months if the room didn't get cleaned up within the next hour. Ben's mom, hearing all the commotion, went to Ben's room to find Ben in a puddle of tears. She felt that what Ben's dad was doing was excessive and harsh. She was strongly tempted to interfere, but was able to thwart her desire. By this time, Ben's dad had said all he needed to say, left Ben's room, and headed for the kitchen. There, Ben's parents sat down and had a conversation about how misbehavior was going to be handled in the future. They realized that the ineffectualness of their approach had laid the groundwork for the explosion that followed and vowed to deal with problems earlier and effectively to prevent recurrences.

It is quite likely that parents will need several opportunities to talk and to give feedback to one another. We encourage you to make the feedback honest and encouraging. If one partner has had a difficult time setting limits on the child and is now doing so, a pat on the back while the limit-setting is going on can be quite beneficial. A wink or literal pat on the back will result in the other parent being more apt to set limits in the future. But remember, one pat on the back is not enough to create a persistent behavior—you will have to be vigilant and diligent in your joint efforts to establish sound rules of conduct.

Your Observations

At this point you are ready to do an observation of your child(ren).

Step One.   Familiarize yourself with the observation chart on page 98. Take note of the areas to observe, and look over the examples.

Step Two.   Observe your child for a day or two. In most instances one to two days of observation is enough, though, with some infrequently occurring behaviors, a week or more may be needed.

Step Three.   During your observations, make mental notes of the circumstances in which the problem behavior occurred, what your child did (the manipulative behavior), how you responded to your child's actions (your avoidance response), and what your were thinking and feeling that allowed the manipulation to be successful (your blind sides).

Step Four.   After each episode of problematic behavior, write down what you saw and heard by fitting them into the categories of the form. We strongly encourage you to write down your observations as soon as the interaction is over. With each passing moment, valuable information may get lost.

Protecting Your Blind Sides

As soon as you have completed your observation chart, you are ready to begin the manipulation-proofing process. Start with a careful review of the chart, paying especially close attention to the summaries of what you were avoiding in the interactions you recorded—the thoughts, feelings, and beliefs that caused you to justify the child's manipulative behavior or your acceptance of it. These are your own blind sides. Chapter 7 will discuss specific behavior management strategies for you to implement as a way of shutting down your child's avoidance behaviors. But first we want to help you build a permanent immunity to these behaviors. That means—above all else—learning to deal with your own anxiety, anger, and guilt, and changing some of your beliefs. Go back and reread the the section in this chapter on common blind sides, paying careful attention to the paragraphs supplying antidotes to being blindsided.

Looking Your Emotions in the Eye

As you may have noticed, several of the blind sides on our list involve parental emotions—feelings that children quickly learn to exploit to their advantage. Regardless of the emotion experienced, they all are powerful motivators of avoidance behaviors. Moreover, failure to manage your feelings or behavior simply compounds the problem. Your emotions grow stronger, and your desire to avoid grows more intense. All of this simply adds to your child's manipulative leverage. Successful manipulation breeds more manipulation, and the child becomes even more determined and skillful at controlling others. Save yourself and your children an immense amount of time, effort, and emotional turmoil—don't let them manipulate you!

Whether you are manipulation-proofing yourself or working to eliminate a manipulative behavior, you can count on the process being difficult in the early stages. For one thing, there's that matter of your emotions. There's no way around it: The best strategy for dealing with your emotional state is to face it—straight on. Each time you confront an emotionally charged situation and you resist avoiding it, the power of the feelings to foster being blindsided grow weaker. And ultimately the emotion will no longer produce an avoidance behavior.

A fundamental step is to make a firm resolve that you will not allow yourself to be manipulated. Once your decision is made, develop an action plan. That is, what are you going to do to keep your emotions from permitting an avoidance behavior? A suggestion is to decide to experience the emotions and not fear them. Rather, cope with the unpleasant feelings. Offer yourself some coping statements. "My emotions are not toxic; they only feel that way." "His misbehavior is manageable, if handled right." "Her screaming won't last forever." Suggest to yourself that you and your child can get through the episode and both of you will be better for it. Say to yourself: "I can handle it"; "I will hang in there"; "If I respond correctly, it will get better." Repeat to yourself that if you give in, it will get worse and you will have to do this all over again. Encourage yourself to do what is right. When attempted manipulation is in progress, remind yourself to be calm, relaxed, and in control. You might jot down several coping statements on a three-by-five card and carry it with you for those intense moments. During an emotionally charged time, pull out your card and use it as a reminder of how you are going to cope.

Some parents have found it useful, after experiencing their emotions, to do something to distract themselves during the intense moments while their child rails against them. They will put on their headphones and listen to music or a radio program. The advantage with headphones is that it masks outside sounds—a desirable feature when your eight-year-old is loudly complaining that you are unfair and unreasonable. Turning on the television also works. Others have found reading a valuable distraction. They will pick up a magazine or a good book and read until the crisis has ended.

When the crisis is over and if you are still emotionally charged, do something to relieve the tension. Do something physical. Take a walk, chop wood, clean the bathroom, or wash the car until you have discharged the emotions. Parents have also found it useful to go to a quiet place, take a few deep breaths, and relax for a few minutes. Taking a hot bath or reading until settled down has possibilities for some parents. We encourage you to find some adaptive way to reduce your tension.

When you have kept your emotions in check (at least outwardly), give yourself a pat on the back. You deserve some positive words: "I thought I was too tired, but I got the job done"; "I did it"; "I'm glad that's over"; "It wasn't as bad a I thought it would be"; "Handling this difficult situation has made both myself and my child stronger."

If your belief system or the assumptions you have about children cause you to justify your own or your child's behavior, refute those beliefs and assumptions. Substitute statements that will not allow avoidance behavior. By altering your thinking, you can effectively work through your blind sides, empower your child, foster independence, and set a parenting course that leads to building self-esteem—both yours and your child's. We have identified three assumptions that, if substituted for debilitating beliefs, will prevent you from being blindsided and will foster self-esteem.

Empowering Assumptions

A. Children are innately and fundamentally competent.

At birth, children come into the world having all the necessary equipment and potential for learning that will allow them to grow into independent adults. Babies only a few hours old are able to communicate their needs. When they are hungry, wet, or tired, they let us know. Parents and baby alike learn rapidly about one another. Babies go about teaching parents what their communications mean and what actions need to be performed. In turn, babies are also learning about parents and how they will handle their communications. From the very beginning, children are learning how to adapt—that's what child development is. They are equipped to solve problems. They may experience stress, anxiety, or other unpleasant feelings just like anyone else, but they are competent to deal with these emotions. Most important, they will survive the process and become stronger for it.

John and Julie were first-time parents, and Jeffrey, their two-month-old, was up to nurse every two hours through the night. Not only that, but he was wide awake, cooing like crazy between 2:00 and 3:00 AM. His parents were exhausted, but couldn't bear to hear him cry in the night. During the day, he woke only to nurse, but Julie couldn't get enough rest to ever catch up. She had been told to feed him on demand in the hospital, and she doggedly followed these instructions despite her failing enthusiasm for the whole program. Finally, Julie called a friend, the experienced mother of three, for advice. After hearing her story, her friend advised Julie that Jeff wouldn't break. She suggested that Jeff be awakened and fed frequently during the day and be placed on a strict nighttime schedule—one feeding at 3:00 AM. When it was not time to eat, Jeff should be allowed to exercise his lungs a bit. Julie was reassured that he would be okay and that he would turn his nights and days back around. Julie did as her friend advised, and within a few nights, Jeff was waking only once at night. John and Julie's mental and emotional states improved immeasurably.

Julie's experienced friend was right. Children don't break; they can adapt. As a matter of fact, one of the worst things we can do to children is to ask them never to adapt.

Believing that your children are innately and fundamentally competent alters profoundly the way in which you deal with them. If you believe children are not quite competent, you will interact with them as if they were incompetent. You will do for them what they are capable of learning to do for themselves. You will protect them from the very challenges that will equip them to deal with the world, thereby compromising their adaptation routinely and systematically. A childhood filled with this approach produces a weak, dependent person.

This past year, we met with an extremely depressed and frightened eight-year-old boy, Nicholas. Nick came in with a list of things he worried about and feared. He was afraid someone might break into his house and harm him or his family. He could not go about the house freely without someone walking with him. He was afraid that his mother might die in a car accident, even though she was a careful driver. Nick's grandmother was aging, and he was afraid she would die of old age. He worried about being kidnapped. He was fearful of going to school. He was afraid that while he was at school, his parents might die. During the height of Nick's depression, he could be found in the classroom not doing his work, but crying. When asked why he was crying, he would recite several of his fears.

Nick's concerned and loving parents did their best to reassure and reduce his worries and fears. Nick's mother would call Nick to let him know that she had arrived safely at the grocery store. Nick would have his sister, a three-year-old and hardly a protector, come with him to the bathroom to provide reassurance and to reduce his anxiety. When a scary show such as *Rescue 911* or *Cops* came on the air, the channel was quickly changed by Nick's parents so that Nick would not be exposed to anything that might be frightening. Nick's parents were always careful to watch the news when Nick was not around so that nothing in the news might trigger additional fears.

Nick's problems result from two factors. First, Nick is, by nature, an anxious child. He comes by this characteristic honestly—his father is a big-time worrier as well. But the second reason for these problems, and just as important, is that his parents believed he was incapable of handling his fears. They believed that Nick might be damaged by his emotions unless adults intervened protectively. They believed Nick could not handle anything that might provoke fear. When Nick became frightened, they felt it was their responsibility to rid him of this unpleasant feeling; Nick, as a result, became incapable of handling his own fears. Had his parents believed, from the beginning, that he was competent to handle his own emotions, Nick would have learned, even with his inborn anxious temperament, that he could take care of himself and handle his own fears.

Our treatment focus was directed to assist Nick's parents in changing their assumptions about him. We taught them that rather than view Nick as incompetent, they had to believe that he was competent and capable of handling his own fears. They didn't realize that they believed Nick (and all children) was incompetent, and they understood how pervasive this assumption was in everything they did with Nick once we pointed this out. As their assumption changed, they began to respond to him in a different way. They began to allow Nick to own and take care of his fears and worries; they expressed their confidence that he was capable of doing this. It wasn't long before Nick responded. When he was unable to get anyone to participate with him in his worry fests and found he was responsible for his own fears and anxieties, he worried less and less. His tears dried up. He went to the bathroom by himself. He was now able to go to school. He was freed of the dependency that had trapped him.

B. A second assumption, corollary to the first, is that children are tough, adaptable survivors.

How did man get this far if this were not true? Think for a moment of the conditions children live in around the world. They grow, thrive, and adapt in conditions that would be intolerable to us adults. They see and hear things that most of us would see as traumatic, yet seem undamaged and healthy, well-adapted in their environment, and able to function in their own culture as adults. Erik Erikson pointed this out forty years ago in his book, *Childhood and Society*. Erikson showed how different cultures reared their children in dramatically different ways, yielding adults who had learned the specific skills necessary to function and contribute to their own unique cultures. Margaret Meade described activities in Samoa among children and between children and adults that any social worker in our society would see as horribly sexually abusive and harmful, yet these children grew up and functioned wonderfully in their culture. Children will survive, if we will only let them.

C. A third assumption is that children's emotions are their own.

A child's feelings and emotional state are private, not the purview of the child's parents or other concerned adults. Children are perfectly capable of handling their own emotions. While parents should be a source of comfort and support to their children during periods of emotional turmoil, crossing the boundary between themselves and their children to fiddle with a child's feelings is invasive and damaging. A child's feelings belong to that child. It must be the child's responsibility to deal with and manage his/her feelings. If we stay on our side of the boundary, if we can support and comfort without becoming invasive and taking over, children will learn to cope with the feelings experienced during trying episodes. Attempting to make a child feel better by diversionary tactics, cheering him up by solving his problem or changing the rules, or telling him he is really a wonderful person when he has acted rotten and self-centered—these tactics only teach dependency. When the next rousing emotional experience comes along, the child will try to handle it through someone else, and probably will find a willing and sympathetic adult to cooperate. Best of all, letting a child grapple with his emotions communicates a profound faith and belief in him.

Recently, we saw Suzanne in the clinic. Suzanne is eleven years old and in the fifth grade at a local elementary school, and she has been a patient here since birth. Suzanne's mother and father divorced when she was four, and he moved to Georgia, where his parents live. Suzanne saw her father infrequently, and then only when she went to visit her grandparents. Her father was a drug user, and about a year ago, he suddenly died. Afterwards, both she and her mother went through a period of mourning. We had the opportunity to visit with them during this difficult time on several occasions. Suzanne recovered well. Throughout the following year, school went well for her. She was, and is, involved in a swim club and dance. Suzanne is a lighthearted girl who is self-confident and fun to be around. She has lots of friends and a steadfast, interested, but noninvasive mother. On three occasions this year, Suzanne has asked to leave the class because she felt like crying—all three instances were triggered by something that reminded her of her father, and two occurred around her father's birthday.

Just before the visit to the clinic, the school social worker pulled her mother aside and said, "I'm very worried about Suzanne going on to middle school next year. It's a lot harder [she means less protective] over there, and with all her unresolved problems over her father's death, she may have a really hard time."

When Suzanne's mother asked to speak to us privately and related all this information, we were stunned! It was hard to decide whether to laugh, cry, or call the school principal. Suzanne's mother, luckily, has her head screwed on straight, and was asking for feedback to make sure she wasn't missing something. We reassured her that any normal human being who has suffered a significant loss will revisit that loss and reexperience the emotions associated with that loss periodically, sometimes for the rest of their lives. Children usually rehash something significant in their lives many times over in light of new experience and maturity. That's healthy! The school social worker appears to believe that grief, loss, and the associated emotions should be neatly packaged and tucked away in the far recesses of the brain, never to be thought of again, and that some sort of therapy can wrap it all up so that it's "resolved." Thank goodness Suzanne's mother knows otherwise. Loss of someone dear is not something that can be resolved or truly understood. It's part of the human condition, it will likely happen to all of us, and it is a purely emotional experience not subject to reason.

The social worker was implicitly saying, "You really don't know your daughter, and she is incapable of handling her emotions"; "I know her because I'm an expert"; "She's got big problems." Had Suzanne's mother taken this to heart, she would have become a less self-assured mother and Suzanne would have suffered. Suzanne would have been deprived of her mother's confidence and implicitly told she was incompetent to manage her emotions. She heard what we had to say and remarked, "That's just what I thought, but I wanted your reassurance—Thanks."

This sort of thing goes on everyday in countless schools around the country. Children are not supposed to have bad feelings, and if they do, an expert needs to be hired to take care of them. And in the process, very adequate and caring parents are undermined and made dependent. Children do experience bad feelings and suffer loss, disappointments, and failures. All we adults can really do for them is listen, support, and comfort—and that's plenty.

By being supportive and comforting to your child, your behavior communicates that you care and understand. Implicitly, you are saying to your child that you believe in her ability to handle her distress, that you are optimistic and positive about her strength and character, that you believe she will not be overcome by adversity. In marked contrast is the pessimistic view of those who must meddle in childrens's emotions. Their actions bear the implicit message that children cannot handle or manage unpleasant feelings or cope with the adversities of life.

Jim, the nine-year-old son of a good friend of ours, had been playing Nintendo for an hour on a Saturday morning a few years ago. He suddenly jumped up, threw the control to the floor, enraged and near tears with frustration. His mother, standing nearby in the kitchen, asked what was upsetting him. Jim sputtered, "I can't get past level three on this stupid game." His mother smiled warmly at him and said, "I know, Jimmy. Some days are just like that." Jim calmed down, went back to the game, and finished at level five.

Jim's mother operated beautifully here. She acknowledged his distress, then made a wise comment about life in general. She didn't suggest a solution, but allowed Jim to figure out what to do on his own. She didn't take on any responsibility for Jim's distress, instead allowing him to own it and deal with it. Jim, as he has many times before, recovered his composure quickly and went on to prove to himself that he could get beyond level three on the "stupid" game. Jim has very high expectations for himself. Frustration, which he feels when he can't do as well as he'd like, is not an unusual emotion for him. His mother understands this part of his character and knows he must learn to deal with it by himself; she can't do it for him. Many cumulative experiences like this have resulted, today, in a sixteen-year-old who is realistically self-confident and excels in most things he attempts. Because his parents have been careful to avoid intervention when he's having difficulty with something, failure and frustration have been part of his experience and he has learned how to survive and keep trying until he succeeds.

Viewing your child as a competent, emotionally independent person provides the opportunity for many experiences that teach the skills of adaptation to the world. Strong adults have learned to be strong. Surviving and thriving in the world comes from practice and exercise as a child. Becoming psychologically strong is not much different from becoming physically strong. Both are accomplished by exercise. The more exercise you get, the stronger you become. A child, watching his parent solving a problem for him, doesn't get stronger. Only solving the problem for himself builds the psychological muscle to survive and thrive in the world.

We frequently hear about a childrearing approach called "positive parenting." The goal of positive parenting seems to be to protect the child from damage and trauma so that the child can grow up to be a "whole" person. The idea is simple: The more positive we are with our children, the less negative we are, the better off our children will be. The smoother and easier life is for children, the stronger their self-esteem becomes. This style of parenting uses rewards and incentives for good behavior. By employing choices and reasoning, this method attempts to avoid both confrontation of unacceptable behavior and the unpleasant emotions confrontation brings. Minor misbehavior is ignored, fearing that too much discipline will harm the child's self-esteem. When minor misbehavior escalates inevitably to more major infractions, consequences (read punishment), intended to "teach a lesson," are employed. When that doesn't do it, the ante usually gets upped, the punishing consequences harsher and more prolonged.

Though they rarely realize it, parents using the "positive parenting" approach hold a set of assumptions that are thoroughly pessimistic. They believe that children cannot find their own happiness, hold their own with others, set their own goals, or live with the results of their mistakes. Worse yet, they fear that children cannot handle the emotions created when limits are set, that the word "no" will be harmful to the child's self-esteem. This approach charges parents with complete responsibility for their children's happiness. The beliefs held by these parents are precisely the beliefs that cause parents to be blindsided. They open the door for widespread manipulation. They operate on the belief that children are incompetent to handle the ordinary stresses and disappointments of life.

The model of parenting we are proposing is quite different from positive parenting. Rather than assume your child is incompetent, we suggest you view your child as competent or one who can learn to be competent. See your child as tough, strong, resilient, and able to deal with adversity. Seeing your child this way completely alters your approach and protects you from being blindsided. You will see emotional discomfort as an opportunity for the child to learn to do for herself; instead of running interference for your child, you will be able to provide succor and comfort because you believe she is competent and will survive.

A final antidote against being blindsided: Have a clear understanding of your primary role as a parent. It is your job to teach your child to adapt to the world, not the other way around.

As you prepare to shut down the manipulative behavior of your child and to end your own avoidance behavior, you must recognize that it will be difficult in the same way that learning something new is always difficult. You and your child have had a lot of experience together and have developed some strong patterns and habits. It is important to recognize that interrupting your child's manipulative behavior is likely, in the early stages at least, to produce anxiety, guilt, and perhaps some anger. You will be highly tempted to go back to the old habits and patterns of interaction. Don't let that happen.

A number of our parents have found it beneficial to write down their blind sides and how they plan to work with them. They have also written down some statements that they have used to encourage themselves while they were in the process of dealing with their child's behavior. Mary was one parent who found this helpful. She listed her blind sides, the ways to confront them, and the ways she was going to deal with her feelings. One of Mary's blind sides was being caught by time. She wrote, next to that entry, "I will save myself some time if I do the right thing now. Don't get trapped into nagging, threatening, or screaming at her." To deal with her feelings, she wrote: "Bite your tongue, be calm, and it will get better." Just before she was to get her daughter off to school, she would review her notes as an additional reminder.

It is useful to do some imagined rehearsal. Imagined rehearsal is the same process that many athletes use to prepare themselves for a contest. The hockey player will imagine being able to see the open spots at the net. Figure skaters will imagine themselves successfully completing a triple Axel, or tennis players will imagine the proper moves when serving and correcting errors they have made in the past. Parents can use this same process effectively to guard their blind sides. They find a quiet place, close their eyes, and imagine themselves dealing with the child's manipulative behavior. They try to see in their mind's eye what the child does and how they allow themselves to be blindsided. They confront their old beliefs, substituting beliefs that will inhibit the manipulative behavior. They imagine pitfalls that might occur and develop a plan to deal with them.

For example, suppose that you get blindsided by your child's passive/aggressive behavior when you are feeling exhausted in the evening. When asked to do a household chore, your child cheerfully agrees but then doesn't follow through. Because you're tired and because of the child's agreement to do the work, you assume the work is going to be done. You do not follow up. Only much later do you discover that your child's cheerful "yes" was a smokescreen for skipping out of the task. Find a quiet place, sit down, relax, and imagine future situations in which you feel tired and your child agrees to a job. Imagine that when your child says "yes" you stay away from the comfort of the couch for a few minutes to check that he actually does as requested. Visualize yourself fighting off the strong temptation to go lie down by reminding yourself that verifying your child's performance will take only a few short minutes. Confront your belief that you are too tired. Suggest to yourself that you can handle the additional effort. Consider what the effect of your child's sneaking off will do to the child in the long run, and how taking care of the problem later will take more effort—and that you're just as likely to be tired then. Now, see in your mind's eye the sense of accomplishment that you might experience in dealing with an adverse situation. Remind yourself that you have done what is best for your child.

Now that you have done your homework, you are ready to start. You have identified the child's manipulative behavior, and you have identified the emotions and thoughts that permit you to be manipulated. You have confronted those beliefs, and you have inoculated yourself. You are ready.

CHAPTER 7

Shutting Down Manipulation

If we are going to raise children who don't try to use manipulation to adapt the world to their desires, we must be able to shut down manipulation as it happens. When we close the door to manipulation, we open many other doors for children to explore, enriching their adaptive experience immeasurably. In this chapter, we will explore a method of shutting down manipulation that works well and is gentle, quiet, portable, and nonpunitive.

Avoidance behavior, if successful, serves to eliminate, delay, or reduce something the child finds unpleasant. When avoidance works, the behavior becomes persistent. Like it or not, you as a parent are part of the interaction, and what you do will determine whether the manipulative behavior will become more or less frequent. If you react in a way that helps your child succeed in avoiding, delaying, or escaping a situation he does not like, you will see more of the same behavior in the future. On the other hand, if you consistently react in a way that requires a child to deal with something he doesn't want to face, then his attempts to manipulate around the situation will fade and finally disappear. That said, what you have to do is not easy, though it is relatively easy to describe.

In the following pages, we describe how some parents in families from our clinical practices dealt with their children's firmly entrenched avoidance behaviors by using a simple technique, which we will describe in detail.

Attempts to manipulate situations are part of growing up. All children will, at some time or another, try to change a situation to their liking through someone else. Some, even in the face of excellent and highly consistent efforts by their parents, will try to control situations persistently throughout their childhood. The frequency and persistence of a child's manipulative efforts are largely a matter of temperament. Parents should never take lightly a child's attempts to manipulate, although a light-hearted approach to the problem is almost always helpful. The stakes are high: They involve how a child learns, over the long term, to adapt to life. When you notice your child giving manipulation a go, don't just dismiss it as a stage of her development, something she'll outgrow. Instead, regard her attempts to manipulate as an opportunity for you to teach some of the things you'd like her to learn. Some of the best things you'll ever do for your children involve saying no, eliminating the easy way out, asking them to call upon resources they might not have discovered otherwise. Treat avoidance behavior as an opportunity for learning—learning that goes far beyond simply learning how to push the right button on Mom or Dad. As Thomas Szasz said, "Give a man a fish, you feed him for a day; teach him to fish and he can feed himself for life." Take your children fishing.

We will describe two procedures that parents can use to stop manipulation, and then we will illustrate their use. One is Stop, Pause, and Redirect; and the other is Extinction of Negative Reinforcement. Stop, Pause, and Redirect appears to work best with noncompliance, lack of persistence, rule breaking, and arguing. Extinction of Negative Reinforcement seems to work best for anxiety, fears, and apprehensions.

Stop, Pause, and Redirect

We developed Stop, Pause, and Redirect (SPRd for short) explicitly for the purpose of interrupting avoidance behavior. It works well for noncompliance and lack of persistence, spontaneous and repeated misbehavior (rule breaking), arguing and negotiating, and aggressive and abusive behavior. It is not helpful, after the fact, with behavior that has already occurred. It is particularly effective with behavior that is maintained by the attention and the responses of people around the child. Many of the existing approaches parents try to use to discourage these sorts of behavior are unproductive or even counterproductive. These include, but are not limited to, techniques often intended to be punishments, such as withdrawal of privileges; most time-out procedures; and virtually all delayed consequences. Stop, Pause, and Redirect is, on the other hand, a system that works. It is quiet, effective, and gentle; it can be used instantaneously anywhere, without the awareness of others; and it can replace all other methods of setting limits for children. It can, with adaptation, be used with a child of any age. It is not punishment and should not be thought of as punishment; instead, it is limit setting, pure and simple.

That's the good news. But the bad news isn't really so bad: SPRd is powerful only if used consistently and correctly. In order for SPRd to succeed, a parent must go through a training period until its use becomes second nature and then use it consistently for years. If you tend to try something for a little while, then try something different, or if you are looking for the magic method that will make an instant difference and make your children behave thereafter just the way you want them to, SPRd is not for you. SPRd takes work, persistence, and an unwillingness to yield to the temptation to resort to punishing techniques to solve a problem.

Here's how you do it: Your child is misbehaving in some way. He is not doing what he's been asked to do, he's doing something that is not allowed, he's gotten too wild in his play or too noisy in a situation, he's acting in a disrespectful manner, he's trying to argue or negotiate the non-negotiable, and so on.

First, STOP your child's behavior.   For this to happen, you must, immediately, without further ado, "park" the child somewhere close, convenient, and unentertaining. To be effective, you must stop the behavior before you do or say anything else—this is the hard part.

PAUSE until quiet.   After you park the child, he stays parked without any further interaction with you until he has become quiet and settled for a brief period (fifteen to thirty seconds at most; guess, don't use a timer—longer is not better).

REDIRECT.   Send your child off to do what he should be doing—"Go play," "Go pick up your toys," etcetera. This is where you may explain what it was your child did to get stopped in the first place and what is expected of him in the future. If you feel you must comment on his behavior, do it clearly, briefly, and quietly. Save long discussions for another time. To be effective, the entire procedure is best done in a normal speaking voice or even a whisper. The more dramatic you are, the less effective the procedure becomes.

Your approach with this procedure must be matter-of-fact and businesslike. Your manner should clearly demonstrate firmness and commitment to the procedure and insistence that the child follow the rules. As you get more proficient, you will carry out the procedure in an almost offhand, though still serious, manner. This is difficult when you are teetering on the edge of exasperation, pushed by a screaming child who is telling you that she hates you and that you are unimaginably unfair or worse. The key to handling all of this adroitly is, quite simply, practice. The more practice you get, the more skilled you will become at shutting down manipulative behavior. As you become more proficient, the limits you place on your child's behavior will become more clearly defined. Success with this technique comes with consistency—consistency over a long period of time. Inconsistency in setting limits only teaches your child that there may be a way to continue to manipulate, guaranteeing a struggle.

Warnings, reminders, second chances, or threats will render this procedure ineffective. Any commentary—warnings included—that takes place between the occurrence of the offending behavior and the imposition of the PAUSE phase of the procedure dramatically reduces its effectiveness. If you are in the habit of giving warnings or threats, work on learning new behavior yourself. Continuously remind yourself of these rules, especially when things are not going so well. We cannot emphasize this point enough: If you carry out the procedure incorrectly, you may as well not do it—you're wasting your time and energy. You'll find it very difficult to retrain yourself, to get out of old habits, but you must if you are going to stop manipulative behavior.

As you implement this procedure, you can expect your child to do whatever is within her power to change things back to the way they were before. For instance, during the PAUSE, you can expect your child to complain, argue, ask why, ask to go to the bathroom, or perhaps cry, scream, or even laugh at you. You can anticipate accusations of unfairness or barbed statements like, "I'm sure glad you parked me over here because that way I'm not next to you!" Initially your child will not like the procedure, but most children get used to it quickly and learn to live with it amicably. This is not punishment; the technique's effectiveness is not dependent on your child's displeasure with it. The most effective SPRd is quiet, quick, undramatic—and frequent.

The test of success of SPRd is behavior change. You will know you are making progress if you see your child do what has been requested after the first time you ask or if the incidence of misbehavior decreases. If he cheerfully goes to sit on the couch and smiles broadly as he sits there waiting, are you making progress? Only if you also see compliance with what you've asked him to do. If your child goes to sit on the couch, growling about how unfair things are, about the unfeeling treatment you give for such a minor infraction, is the approach failing? If there is evidence of improved compliance or less misbehavior, have faith—you're making progress.

Particularly during PAUSE, be wary of your own emotions. You may be blindsided into interacting, and this instantly renders the procedure useless. Worse, it teaches your child that he can find a way out. During PAUSE, there cannot be interaction. Do something to keep yourself from interacting with your child. Talk to yourself. Plan your day. Count your blessings. Remind yourself of the advantage to your child of adapting to the rules. Do some housework or put on your portable stereo. Whatever you do, don't interact until your child is quiet; then quickly resume by redirecting him.

The Initial Training Phase

The initial training phase of SPRd can be rough, so expect it to be. Once it becomes clear that you are willing to go through the process every time for as long as it takes, the procedure will become brief and quiet. (See the sidebar, written by the mother of one of our patients who initiated SPRd with her four-year-old.) We generally ask parents to start this procedure when they have plenty of time, to devote as much time as is needed, and to do the procedure as frequently as possible for the first few days. This gets the initiation phase over with quickly. You are creating revolutionary change in the relationship between you and your child. Change like this won't happen with a half-hearted attempt.

At first, some children do not stay where their parents have parked them. They get up and run to their bedrooms, find a different spot, or wait until you are not looking and then disappear. Stand nearby and intercept, quietly returning your child to the assigned place. In the beginning, you may have to escort your child back many times (we've seen parents take a child back to a particular spot up to fifty times) until he's convinced you do mean business and won't give up. If you give up just once, you will destroy all the progress you've made. Once you start, do not stop until your child is settled and quiet. Plan ahead—if you have a time bind, don't even start—we guarantee you'll get other chances. It is far better to not do a SPRd than to give up partway through.

From yourself you can expect—at first—that you will have to think your way through each step of the procedure. Suppose that your child tosses you a verbal zinger from the corner and—oops!—you respond rather than ignore her. Your kneejerk response takes over, you remember too late that while she is parked, you are not to interact with her. You may find yourself being tempted to justify an interaction with your child. For example, when your child asks, "What did I do wrong?" you will have a strong urge to

Brooke

The following was written by a mother who we trained to institute SPRd with her 4-year-old child. It should help the reader get the idea of what it takes to implement this technique and what the rewards are when it is done well.

Brooke is almost 4 years old. She is the youngest of our three children and has been our biggest challenge. When we sought help with her, she was clearly running our family. Everybody rearranged what they did and how they did it to suit her, just to avoid Brooke's wrath. We asked for guidance from Dr. Swihart. He suggested that we implement "Stop-Pause-Redirect" with Brooke, but he also told us it wouldn't be easy. He recommended we start the process by crisis rather than trying to ease into it. The following recounts our first two days— two days that changed the lives of everyone in our family.

Our goal was to regain control of our household. It took two full days before we saw any change in Brooke's behavior; two full days of constantly following Brooke around, immediately stopping any be- havior that we felt was inappropriate, and waiting for her to settle down. This meant abruptly ending phone conversations, pulling off to the side of the road three times, and not answering the doorbell on one occasion even though the person at the door could clearly see us sitting in the kitchen. We knew, to be successful, Brooke could never get back control of the situation, no matter what she did nor what the surrounding circumstances were. This may sound simple, but it was extremely tiring and difficult to do over an extended period of time.

On the first day, we had to physically hold Brooke next to us 33 times for periods ranging from 4 to 7 minutes, though one tantrum lasted 22 minutes. The entire time she was trying her hardest to get away. She was screaming her worst "bad words," and at one point told me she wanted a new mom. Sometimes she would be quiet after just a couple of minutes, and would be redirected to something else, and within seconds turn around and repeat the behavior all over again (and again). She tested constantly. When dad came home, she started right over at the beginning and reenacted almost all of the same inap- propriate behaviors for which mom had stopped and redirected her earlier in the day. It was, to say the least, depressing. At that point I felt I had made absolutely no progress with her at all. Right then I viewed her as the most manipulative child I had ever seen. But Brooke realized, after several hours, that daddy was just as capable of holding her in one place and she had run into a united front that wouldn't budge.

The second morning was just as bad as the first. I endured appalling looks at the grocery store as she sat on the floor at my feet screaming for what seemed like hours, but in fact was only about two minutes. I ended phone conversations without explanations and I ignored our other two kids in order to keep on top of what Brooke was doing. Brook's grandfather baby-sat for two hours in the afternoon and spent 1 hour and 15 minutes with Brooke sitting at his feet screaming, hitting, kicking and threatening him. After she had tried everyone, even grandpa, she was magically changed. She learned that when someone said she had to sit until she was quiet, we meant it. She found when she quieted, then she could go on to something appropriate, but not until that criteria had been met.

The third morning, mom or dad could stop an inappropriate behavior by telling Brooke to come and stand quietly by mom or dad. Amazingly, she would stop what she was doing and come right over. There was no screaming or fighting. When she stood quietly for a few seconds, we would redirect her to do something else, giving her a specific alternative.

Please understand that there are still days she tests us and several encounters like these are necessary. There are always new situations eliciting new behaviors. Some of these behaviors are inappropriate, so this is an ongoing process. Some new behaviors are harder to stop than others, and we have had some trying episodes, but nothing like the first two days. The bottom line is we all know the rules of "Stop-Pause-Redirect," Brooke does not run the show, and any unwanted behavior is immediately stopped. Brooke is a much happier child as she knows what we expect from her. Mom and dad aren't spending most of their time negotiating with her or trying to determine age-appropriate punishments that don't work. "Stop-Pause-Redirect" definitely works if you are willing to stick with it through some tough times. You'll be doing yourself and your child a favor by doing it. It really makes life much easier and more fun.

explain—but your response should be silence. You can explain what she did wrong during the REDIRECT part of the procedure (though at that point, your child may not be so interested in what she did wrong).

Don't try to do this in a public place until it's working smoothly and quickly at home. Expect your child to try hard to nullify the procedure with Dad or Mom, who initially trained it in, or that your child will rechallenge SPRd when Grandma shows up to visit. Your child may exhaust every option, test every situation, before things begin to go along smoothly.

Portability of SPRd

SPRd should be portable. For this reason, don't use a designated spot in the house to park your child. Instead, use the nearest boring location you can find, a place that is conveniently out of traffic. A room corner, a spot in the middle of the floor, a wall, a chair, a step—any of these will do nicely. You can have your child put her head down and sit next to you or stand next to you. Where you place the child does not matter. What does matter is that all behavior comes to a standstill. To carry out the procedure while driving a car may seem to be an impossible challenge at first, but it's actually quite easy, once you have instituted the SPRd procedure at home consistently. Stop behavior by instructing the child to put her head down. Pause until quiet for thirty seconds or so. Redirect the child as usual. At first, you may want to pull off to the side of the road and park in a safe place before implementing the procedure. Later you will be able to handle it without pulling off the road. This same method works well at the dinner table or at a desk at home or school. In a public place, have your child sit or stand in an out-of-the-way place. You may ask her to sit next to you, stand next to the Campbell's soup, put her head down on the pew at church, or accompany you to the foyer if necessary. In restaurants, having the child put her head on the table is often quite effective, though removing a smaller child outside may be a better method at first.

In public places, parents are often tempted to put a hold on the procedure to avoid embarrassment. They find themselves walking on eggshells, avoiding confrontation to minimize the need to implement the SPRd. Remember that as you become more skilled in carrying out the procedure—and as your child's practice with the procedure improves—his ability to respond without fuss or bother, and the potential for an embarrassing scene, go away. In fact, SPRd is the only method that provides gentle, quiet, and efficient teaching of limits in any situation without resorting to manipulative tactics like anger, argument, threats, nagging, promises, incentives, or rewards. Your child can learn to adapt and function in an endless variety of life's situations.

SPRd is a guidance technique, not punishment or retribution for a crime. All you want to do with SPRd is stop the behavior, wait for recovery, and go on with life. Don't try to make it more—by adopting a "the punishment must fit the crime" attitude—because that will destroy its effectiveness!

What About "Consequences" (Punishment)?

Generally speaking, delayed consequences don't produce desirable or predictable behavior change, yet there is a widespread belief that if a parent or teacher can find the right consequence and deliver it in the right way, then a child's behavior will improve. "Consequences" are usually punitive in nature and usually produce more undesirable side effects than good effects. The continued presence of the potential to be punished for a misdeed may alter the behavior of people, but not in a predictable or lasting manner. As soon as the punisher is gone, the behavior returns. The punished learn stealth, become devious, explain and justify their behavior, disappear, or sometimes just bait the punisher. Arbitrary consequences like grounding, withdrawal of privileges, severe and prolonged reprimands, work, and fines just don't work well. Put yourself in the child's place: If your employer used these sorts of punishing consequences for mistakes in your performance at work, would he get the performance he wanted? Probably not, especially over the long haul. Instead, he would get a bunch of dispirited, devious employees who looked at the want ads every Sunday! *Delayed consequences are a manipulative tactic used by parents to avoid real confrontation; they routinely teach children to countermanipulate.*

Ethical Consequences

While we strongly recommend against the use of delayed consequences for the purpose of changing behavior, we just as strongly recommend the imposition of moral or ethical consequences. Moral or ethical consequences are those that are used to correct the problem, to right a wrong. When you make a mess, you clean it up. When you steal, you return what you have taken with an admission of your wrongdoing and an apology. If you've been rude to your teacher, you write a letter of apology and deliver it in person. When you have hit the high, hard one and it goes through the neighbor's window, you own up to it and pay for it. These consequences will not change behavior reliably over the short term. They are simply the right thing to do, nothing more. The larger, value-based message will be perceived by your child at some point, but don't expect that it will necessarily happen right away or with only a few experiences. And when your child has to do something hard, to face someone he's wronged and apologize, remind him that this is not the end of life, that there is a future after asking someone's forgiveness. This was, after all, only a mistake and it won't be the last one.

After the Fact

SPRd is not meant to be used if there is a delay in implementing it. After a delay has occurred, there is not much that can be done that will alter the course of future behavior. Again, delayed consequences do not work, especially not a delayed SPRd. If more than a few seconds have gone by after a behavior has occurred, don't bother with SPRd. The only approach you can use then is to restate the rules. For example, Rachael's teacher calls to say that Rachael has been chasing Bob with a frog again and scaring him. Doing an SPRd when Rachael gets home from school is useless. What can be done is to restate the rule to Rachael. "Rachael, it is not okay for you to be scaring other children at school. You may not do that anymore. It must stop now. Tomorrow I want you to go tell Bob that you are sorry and that you will not frighten him again." If, in fact, you want to do something to change the child's behavior, contact the people who are there when the child's behaviors occur. Enlist the help of the school's playground supervisor. The supervisor could be instructed in the use of SPRd and asked to do it with Rachael in the event that she witnesses Rachael's frog antics.

Persistence

Parents who start using the technique will often see dramatic changes in behavior within a short time. They find that their child is more compliant, following the rules more comfortably and reliably. With the newly found improved behavior, many parents start to back off with the procedure. Because the child's parents are quite pleased with the improved behavior, they allow little minor misbehaviors to go unnoticed and unstopped. Gradually, over time, little bits and pieces of the child's misbehavior start to reemerge, and suddenly, things are back where they started, with lots of misbehavior and all the conflict that was going on when SPRd was first initiated. Correct your behavior, and your child will come along nicely.

Use in Adolescents

With some modification, SPRd can be used with adolescents, though introducing SPRd to difficult middle and older adolescents may not work. The modifications for adolescents are in the PAUSE part of SPRd. Rather than send your fifteen-year-old son to the corner or have him sit right where he is standing, you can ask him to go sit on the couch, stand still where he is, or go to the kitchen and wait for you. Quietly asking an adolescent to come to your side, waiting a moment for him to calm down, and then very softly, but firmly, stating your redirection often works surprisingly well. If your adolescent at first refuses to come to you when asked, look at him and wait him out. If he runs off to his bedroom, calmly walk into his bedroom and look at him, patiently waiting until he comes over to you. If he baits you, wait him out until he complies. Remind yourself that it isn't really his bedroom but that you've agreed to let him use it until he's old enough to move out on his own. Another modification of SPRd that is useful with adolescents who like to bait parents into arguments and negotiations is simply to give the wrong response: "I can't talk about that now" will often deflate and defuse a gathering harangue if you can hang in with it.

Use in Very Young Children

It is best to begin using SPRd in the second year of a child's life, preferably before the age of eighteen months. Children who have become used to being parked momentarily at a young age, who have had limits clearly and tirelessly set, are far happier, more self-confident, and independent than their counterparts who spend their lives probing the weaknesses in their parents system of behavior management. Parents who learn early to stop misbehavior routinely instead of reacting to it are not burdened with bad habits they need to unlearn when they finally decide they have to do something about their child's behavior.

With a small child, start by teaching her to sit or stand where you place her, until quiet, using a verbal command such as "sit and be quiet." At first, of course, you'll have to devote a fair bit of effort and time to this enterprise. Place her where you want her, stand next to her, and put her back in the spot quickly when she tries to run away. As soon as she stays in place quietly for fifteen seconds or so, let her go. Soon she will learn to sit or stand until you say it's okay to leave—most children will learn this within a day or two if you put in the effort. If she throws a fit, just wait it out without interacting. Very quickly she'll learn that the fit doesn't work and give up trying. The more repetitions, the quicker she will learn. Don't bother with the REDIRECT other than to invite the child to come with you or to go play. You can add the REDIRECT when your child's verbal abilities are developed.

Setting the Stage

When you use SPRd early in the course of misbehavior, you may be surprised at how easily your child handles the procedure. If you resort to its use after struggling to redirect the child, trying to head off confrontation, SPRd will not work very well and will more likely result in a major struggle. Use SPRd early and often.

Ignoring Behavior

Ignoring unwanted attention-seeking behavior is commonly recommended and may work if two conditions are satisfied: if you can really ignore it until it goes away, and if the behavior doesn't get a response from someone else. Most children seeking attention through misbehavior will either escalate the misbehavior or get very inventive with their misbehavior when they are ignored, until you break down and pay attention. For this reason, we don't recommend ignoring misbehavior as a general approach.

There is a modification of ignoring behavior that does work well in some situations, however: the wrong (or null) response. For instance, the child who says something that usually elicits an argumentative response from an adult but gets only a smiling, humorous response for his efforts, will often end up laughing instead of arguing; his attempt to bait his parents has fizzled. This technique is especially helpful with the child who says, "I can't" or who is afraid of something. Watch people who are very good with children, who lead them naturally—you'll see this technique in action. When parents use humor, it is very important that they not become sarcastic or put the child down. Just turn the tables on the child's worries and they will often magically evaporate. Parents who offer to help pack a suitcase for the child who says she is running away, who tell children to draw pictures of the monsters in their bedroom, or who quickly offer a toothbrush to clean the kitchen floor in response to complaints of boredom are using this technique. It is not true ignoring, but it doesn't provide a satisfying response to the child and so the behavior disappears.

Extinction of Negative Reinforcement

To use this technique, parents must remove negative reinforcement. (Remember what negative reinforcement is: Faced with an unpleasant situation, a person acts in a way that stops the unpleasantness. Negative reinforcement is not punishment.) If parents block a child's escape from or avoidance of an unpleasant situation or task, requiring that she face what she fears or despises, the parents are eliminating negative reinforcement. With avoidance or escape prevented, a child must then cope with the unpleasant situation, commonly discovering that what she perceived as awful or scary turns out to be not so bad after all. With each experience, the feared situation becomes more familiar and avoidance weakens. Often, a child finds a sense of triumph; what was once a feared situation now becomes pleasant, even enjoyable. Overcoming unpleasant circumstances, perhaps just surviving them at times, are the essential ingredients for the development of self-esteem in children as well as adults.

Just like SPRd, extinction of an avoidance behavior must be carried out in a quiet, confident, and insistent manner. There are other similarities. Your child will likely attempt to get you to interact with him, just as in the PAUSE phase of SPRd. He may complain that you are unfair or unreasonable and may attempt to hit, holler, or escape. The more you interact with your child, the less effective the approach will be. The more you reassure, the more you display your discomfort with what the child has to face, the more resistant your child will become to doing what's necessary. Proceed quietly, confidently, and persistently.

A guideline for parents to remember when going through the elimation process or when dealing with a stressed child is *Comfort, but Don't Fix.* Parents play their most useful role when they provide succor and comfort when a child experiences an unpleasant emotion. If you fix the situation to suit the child, you've taken over responsibility for the situation and abandoned your comforting role, and the child has learned nothing useful from the experience. Comforting is quite different from fixing a child's feelings. A parent comforting a child communicates that they know the child sees something as hard. Comforting acknowledges and accepts their distress, but does not attempt to cure it. We can comfort by simply saying, "I'm sorry, honey. I know it's hard, but you can do it." Or you can comfort by putting your arms around your child, holding him, telling him that you can understand his distress. Comfort may include some adult wisdom, or a story from your own past, or aphorisms and family sayings that help share the child's grief without taking responsibility for it.

For example, Jon has a speech to give to his social studies class about Anne Frank. Jon goes to his Dad, complaining that he is nervous and has a stomach full of butterflies. He says, "I don't know if I can do it. I'm just too nervous. Dad, would you call Mrs. Ricker and see if I can give it to her in private?" Dad's reaction is to put his arm around Jon and say, "Jon, I know it's a pain, but you can do it and you have to. No, I won't call Mrs. Ricker. This will be good practice for you." He does nothing to try to remove Jon from his difficult plight, or to change or modify his feelings. Jon is left to find his own solution to his anxiety. But he is also left with the comforting warmth of his father's love, belief, and concern.

Allowing your child to come up with his own way of handling emotions sends the child one step down the path to independence. Jon, though stressed by the experience, has become a little stronger. He now has learned something about what he is capable of doing, and the experience has taught him he can deal with his anxiety.

Any new situation or challenge scared Brian. From swimming lessons to ski lessons, he would beg to get out of the situation, feign illness, or throw a fit. His parents never gave in, but acknowledged his distress. As he got older, his protests became weaker and his parents could say to him, "Brian, haven't we been here before? Haven't things always worked out okay when you were scared of something new?" In the end, Brian could say this to himself when he faced an anxiety-provoking situation, and he began to take on new activities easily, confident of his ability to survive.

The Role of Positive Reinforcement

When parents pay attention to the things they want their children to do, they are using one of the most powerful tools they have in raising well-adapted children. Unfortunately, many parents find themselves paying endless attention to their children, but for all the wrong reasons and not often enough for the right reasons. What's wrong here?

Sylvia Rimm, author of several books on children, likes to talk about the overwelcome child. The overwelcome child is the child parents have waited so long for, who gets undivided parental attention from the moment of birth. Dr. Rimm speaks of these children as "attention addicted." Her phrase is excellent; these children cannot do anything unless they receive continuous, uninterrupted attention from someone. They often underachieve or achieve only because of the endless attention they get in the process. They do what gets attention, not what they have chosen to do themselves, following their own interests. With the societal emphasis on positive reinforcement and positive parenting, combined with small family size, many children become attention-addicted, unable to pursue their own course except to attract the attention of others. When young, these children feel they are at the center of the universe, but they become a sad and despondent lot as they grow up, always dependent on others for their kudos and raves, never self-satisfied by their own pursuit of their own goals. Kids need our love and attention, but we shouldn't heap these things on them for every little thing they do. They need the time, the solitude, to find their own reinforcers, to pursue their own interests, to thrill in their own independent discoveries. And, if they are going to find their own happiness in life, they need to find out early that they are not the center of the known universe but just another important and valuable human being.

Positive reinforcement can be useful in dealing with misbehavior, but almost never without setting limits as well. Positive reinforcement will not decrease an avoidance response, nor will it make any permanent change in attention-getting misbehavior. Attention paid to acceptable behavior while limiting (SPRd or extinction) undesired behavior will speed up the process immeasurably. But if children are noncompliant, reinforcing them each time they are compliant won't be enough. Most noncompliant children who demonstrate repetitive misbehavior do what they do, in part, because they get attention for their misbehavior. These children may provide us with few opportunities to reinforce desirable behavior positively until we have made progress in stopping misbehavior. It is essential that we pay attention to our children when they're behaving appropriately, but exclusive reliance on positive reinforcement just doesn't work. Remember your long-term goal: a child or teen who really doesn't need a huge amount of attention from others to pursue his own life goals.

To be effective, positive reinforcement must be immediate: The child exhibits the desired behavior, and the parent instantaneously provides positive reinforcement. The most powerful positive reinforcer we have as parents is our attention. As with SPRd, positive reinforcement should be done quietly and matter-of-factly. A wink, a pat on the back, a brief comment describing what you are observing in your child—these are generally reinforcing for most children. Delayed praising statements may communicate a value, but they are unlikely to effect much change in behavior. For example, Kay has just completed her homework and brings it downstairs for her parents' review. They look over the homework and tell her she has done an excellent job. That comment is much too delayed to increase significantly the likelihood of more effort in the future (if, for example, Kay doesn't like to do homework). The behaviors that went into producing an excellent job occurred much earlier. Praising your child for an "A" on a spelling test will communicate a value, but it is not likely to alter dramatically the probability of a similar future performance. Studying for the spelling test occurred throughout the week and the night before the test. For maximum effect, when you see your child studying for a spelling test, you might say, "It looks like you are getting ready for the test tomorrow." Or you might wink at him or give him a thumbs-up as you walk by the child's bedroom as he is preparing for the test.

We strongly recommend that parents stay away from what we call exaggerated praise: "You've done a terrific, wonderful job! You're the greatest!" "That was absolutely the very best!" "That was just fantastic, unbelievable!" Parents who give their child a steady diet of exaggerated praise will likely produce one of two scenarios. In the first scenario, children recognize that what they are doing is not terrific or fantastic. They recognize that they have only done what they are supposed to do. These children will then often develop the feeling that what their parent is doing is trying to "nice" them into behaving; they know they are being patronized, lessening the effectiveness of parental attention. Children may become suspicious of what's coming next: "So, Mom, what is it you want me to do now?"

Some children may believe the exaggerated statements. From their limited perspective, however, they have no way of knowing for sure what it is they have done to win such high praise, and they don't have a clue as to how to reproduce that which the parents have found to be so fantastic. These children may become perfectionistic, immobilized, unable to perform. Worse, they may grow up believing they're the best, the greatest, only to find the world doesn't agree. Be realistic in your praise and, as often as possible, ask your child what she thinks of her performance.

Reinforce children for what they do and not for what they say they are going to do. Reinforcing a verbal statement only results in hearing more statements about the child's planned behavior, but carries no impact on the child's actual behavior. For example, Amy proudly announces to her parents that, unlike in the past, she is going to get all "A's" on her weekly math tests. Feeling excited and hopeful about Amy's intentions, her parents say, "We are so pleased." Will Amy really try harder next semester? Possibly so, and if she did, it was probably not caused her parent's reinforcement. What can be predicted from her parent's reaction is that Amy will make more proclamations about what she will do in the future. Unfortunately, reinforcing a declaration about intended striving will not predictably alter Amy's effort.

The behavior that benefits most from parental positive reinforcement usually is relatively new and just emerging. Continued use of positive reinforcement once the child has learned the behavior only serves to teach dependency. When the child is just learning the new behavior, positive reinforcement should be as frequent as possible. As the behavior becomes more consistent and refined, parents should shift their attention to other new and emerging behavior.

Positive Practice

Positive Practice, a method developed by Nathan Azrin, is very helpful in teaching new behavior. Unlike SPRd, which is used to shut down manipulative behavior directly, Positive Practice teaches an alternative way of behaving. When we suggest the use of Positive Practice, we almost always recommend the use of one of the limit-setting tools as well, like SPRd.

Positive Practice is best used to teach behavior that relies on a cue for its occurrence. The cue can be internal, external, or a behavior in a series that leads to successive behavior. For example, when a child is toilet trained, a combination of all three cue types comes into play: an internal cue (a full bladder) sets in motion a sequence of behaviors (stop playing and hike to the bathroom); when in the bathroom (external cue), undo clothing, void, redo clothing; when done with that sequence of behavior, flush the toilet, wash and dry hands, and return to the interrupted activity. A single external cue can start a complicated sequence of behavior: "Eric, it's time to get ready for school" should result in Eric going through all the steps needed to get ready for his day. In this example, the parental directive started the sequence, but the completion of each behavioral step cues the next.

Behaviors best taught with Positive Practice are those that are routine and automatic—for instance, getting dressed or undressed, getting ready for bed, toilet training, washing hands, putting on a seat belt, crossing the street, having manners at mealtimes, knowing how to behave when being teased, and bringing work home from school. Unfortunately, parents commonly attempt to teach these behaviors by nagging, ever more loudly, with threats of punishment and angry demonstrations as frustration with the child's lack of compliance increases. As a matter of fact, nagging, anger, and threats guarantee increasing unacceptable behavior. How many of us can recall reminding our children over and over again to get dressed, wash their face, or put on their seat belt only to find that we have to do it all over again the next time?

Here's how Positive Practice is done: Simply walk the child repeatedly through the desired behavior (rehearsal). For example, if she is prone to doing anything and everything but what is expected when asked to get ready for bed, you intervene by supervising several rehearsals of the entire bedtime routine each time she doesn't comply. First, when appropriate, seek her input on the sequence of behaviors necessary. Once you both agree on the sequence, you quickly model each step while describing the actions she needs to take. In the bedtime example, pretend to remove your clothes, put on pyjamas, and go into the bathroom, brush your teeth, take care of bodily functions, have a drink, and then return to the bedroom, throw back the blankets, shut off the light, and crawl into bed. Next, have her duplicate your exact sequence of behavior ten or fifteen times. Maintain a humorous and light-hearted manner throughout. A punitive or angry approach won't work. Let her know that learning the sequence will eliminate anger and nagging. With longer and complicated behavioral sequences, it may be necessary to give her verbal prompts: "Good, now what comes next?" or "What did we decide to do here?" or "How should you do this?" Physical prompts may be helpful—looking and nodding or pointing in the direction of the next step. If she performs the behavior properly, acknowledge her success by using a good reinforcement technique (see previous section). Reinforce both her behavioral successes and her correct responses to verbal prompts, fading out both reinforcement and verbal cues as she becomes more successful. If she resists practicing, firmly communicate to her the importance of practice. "Honey, I know this boring, but we need to do it. I think it will make the morning a happier time for both of us," or "We just have a few more to do and then we will be done." If she resists further, do not hesitate to use an SPRd.

Tasks that require a lengthy period of time to accomplish can be taught by simply going through the motions or miming for many of the trials, saving one or two trials at the end to be done completely. For example, when getting ready for school, a procedure that may take fifteen minutes or more, it is not practical to have the child do ten Positive Practice trials. Instead, practice initially by mime, then actually perform the entire sequence.

Each day the child succeeds with the practiced behavior, she does not have to rehearse the behavior anymore that day. If she is unsuccessful, have her do several Positive Practices. If a misbehavior, such as dawdling, occurs, immediately use an SPRd. Unlike SPRd and reinforcement, Positive Practice does not need to be done immediately when there is a problem. You can do Positive Practice at a time convenient for you and the child. You must, however, observe one constraint with Positive Practice: You must practice the behavior sequences exactly the same way each time. Even after a child has achieved reliable performance, continue to use the SPRd and the Positive Practice whenever she misfires. If you don't, the child will start to redevelop the old unwanted habits. The sooner you start the retraining, the more desirable the long-term outcome.

Application of These Techniques

The Oppositional Child

The oppositional child refuses to do what she is asked to do. She will argue about requests and commands, frequently becoming vehement and angry or complaining bitterly. "No" to her is a word from an exotic foreign language, incomprehensible to her. When you do get her started on a task, she may do only part of the work requested. When challenged, she may be deceitful and hide undone parts of the job. Passive/aggressive behavior is common: When sent to her room to clean it, she does only a little bit and ends up playing with the toys she was supposed to pick up, then becomes angry and abusive when confronted. Nothing is ever the fault of the oppositional child, as she is quick to point out. Behaviors that need to be targeted to curtail this child's manipulations are improved compliance with requests, persistence, quality of work, honesty, following of the rules, acceptance of "no," and inhibiting of a behavior when asked to do so.

Jake is an oppositional child. He was eleven years old when we met him. When Jake was asked to do a job around the house, his first response was always to argue. When that didn't work, he would uncork a world-class temper-tantrum, stomping around the house, screaming and hollering, and on occasion, running to his bedroom and trashing it. Jake's behavior at school was better, but he was performing at a level considerably beneath his abilities. Homework was mysteriously "lost," not completed, or not handed in; what was done was rushed, sloppy, and incorrect.

The first behavior we wanted to manage was noncompliance. With the Jakes of this world, there is always a heavy emphasis on SPRd. Here's how it works: A quiet, calm request is made for the child to do something;

compliance is followed with a thank you, noncompliance with an SPRd. The child's behavior is defined as noncompliant if the child has not started to do the assigned task within a few seconds of the request. Parents repeat the SPRds as often as necessary until the child starts to do what is requested. One of Jake's jobs was to take out the trash, and his parents felt that would be as good a place as any to begin. Here's how it went: "Jake, please take out the garbage." "No, can'tcha see I'm watching my show?" "Jake, please sit on the chair over there." It took Jake a good fifteen minutes to settle down and be quiet. "Okay Jake, please take out the garbage." Jake again responded, "No." "Please go back and have a seat on the chair." This time, Jake quieted down more quickly, but twelve SPRds were still required until finally Jake complied with the request.

Each time Jake refused to take out the trash, he was instructed to have a seat on a hard chair away from the TV. During the first go-round of SPRd, Jake screamed at the top of his lungs that his parents hated him, that he hated his parents, and that he couldn't wait until he was old enough to move out. He was also heard to shout, "I will never take out that [expletive deleted] garbage. You can put me in this chair for one thousand years and I will never take it out. I will never do it, no matter what you do to me." Each time Jake was asked to park it, he would become angry all over again. Gradually, however, the length of his temper outburst decreased, as did the intensity of his hollering and screaming. On some occasions, he would try to nice his way out of the situation: "Oh, I'm sorry, I didn't hear you." He also tried a trick that most kids try (sorry, Jake, it's not an original with you): When told to have a seat, he quickly scurried off to do the job. His parents were wise to this one—they had seen it before—so they caught him and parked him again. Jake blew his cork this time. His sister was unfortunate enough to walk by to get the telephone, so Jake poured forth his vitriol on her, calling her a nerd and a scumbag. Fortunately, she knew not to respond, got the phone, and peeled out of the kitchen.

When you implement SPRd with an oppositional child, you can expect to set off behavior similar to Jake's at first. (As a matter of fact, if you don't, worry and reexamine how you're doing the procedure.) The oppositional child has to pull out everything he has to control the situation, and then abjectly fail to control, if change is going to happen. Once the firestorm is over, expect behavior to change. Through his parents' persistent application of SPRds, Jake learned to be much more compliant. With noncompliant children, try to catch every noncompliant behavior that happens and implement SPRd immediately.

Jake's dad, Bill, had an especially hard time doing the SPRds. His natural response was to yell and threaten if Jake didn't comply. Bill's response was automatic and practiced over many years. Jake's mother found the whole process much easier to learn. But Bill's habit had to be interrupted. They decided that when Bill yelled, Jake's mom would do something to cue Bill into doing an SPRd. Sometimes she would cough, catch Bill's eye, touch him on the back, or just say "Bill" to interrupt his behavior. Bill would then drop his thunderous roar by fifty decibels and would calmly ask Jake to have a seat. On those rare occasions when Bill carried on an SPRd calmly and without anger, Jake's mom would give him a thumbs-up or wink at him. We also asked Bill to identify those situations that gave him the most trouble. What we found was that Bill was prone to remind Jake repeatedly that he had a job to do. After the second or third reminder, he would become angry and start yelling. That realization helped Bill to start using the SPRds after the first request rather than waiting until he had become exasperated. We encouraged Bill to rehearse mentally what he was going to do. Bill would sit down in a quite place and imagine Jake noncomplying—something that didn't take much effort. He would form a mental image of Jakes's behavior and his response to it—a calm quiet administration of an SPRd right after Jake misbehaved. He rehearsed that scenario until he didn't have to think about what he was to do. He paid close attention to what Jake did after a request was made. Between cues from Jake's mom, cognitive rehearsal, and sheer determination, Bill learned to do SPRds calmly and effectively.

Within a day or two, Bill asked his wife to stop cueing him. He said, "I didn't want to rely on her. I became concerned that I would become dependent on her. I need to be able to do this myself, because Jake has two parents, not one. We both need to do right by our son." Bill, of course, was absolutely right. Continued reliance on his wife to remind him to do an SPRd could be dependency-producing if it continued beyond a few days.

Jake also lacked persistence, another avoidance behavior. If one is successful at delaying the job, reducing it, or eliminating it, negative reinforcement occurs. The general approach to dealing with lack of persistence is for the parents to administer an SPRd whenever they find that the child is not doing what they directed the child to do, and monitoring the performance frequently at first, to catch the child off task. If the child is caught on task, the parent makes an affirming comment, touches the child, or gives a positive sign. This approach is quite different from what most parents of impersistent children do. The more typical response to impersistence is nagging, cajoling, begging, threatening, and hollering—parental behaviors sure to reinforce impersistance! So the child gets both negative reinforcement by avoiding the job, and positive reinforcement, and the parents' undivided attention for being off task—a double whammy. No wonder impersistence is so difficult to treat.

Jake, when asked to get dressed, do his homework, or clean his room, would give up easily, if he started at all. He could be found watching cartoons when he was supposed to be getting dressed or playing a game when he was supposed to be doing homework. Cleaning his room would often take up to three hours, much of the time devoted to playing with his toys or organizing his X-men cards. Anything was fair game if it meant he could get out of work. Jake's father constantly found himself nagging Jake to get going. The reminders would start out in a quiet and gentle way. After about the fifth reminder, they ceased to be gentle—angry, loud threats took their place. Jake's parents couldn't focus on their own part of the housework; instead, they wandered up and down the halls trying to keep Jake on task.

Initially Jake's parents spent about as much time with the new technique as the old, because it was easy to catch Jake off task. Sent to clean his room, he would be found playing with his Nintendo, playing basketball by throwing his dirty clothes into the trash, or just sitting on the floor and staring at the walls. Each time they caught Jake, his parents quietly implemented SPRd. "Jake, please go sit on your bed." Jake's response was to complain that his parents' actions were not justified: "I was just taking a break." Sometimes he would complain that he was not his parents' slave, that their behavior was excessive and abusive and, after all, this was his room, not theirs. After Jake had settled down, his parents would quietly redirect him: "Jake, go clean your room."

After fifty or so SPRds, Jake became much more efficient at cleaning his room. Usually he did it in less than an hour. As Jake's behavior improved, his parents reduced the number of supervisory visits they made to his room, though they continued on an unpredictable schedule.

In addition to the SPRd, Jake's parents used some positive reinforcement at first. When they found him doing what he was supposed to be doing, they would wink at him or say, "You're moving along today," or "I see you are putting your dirty clothes in the hamper." Jake's parents would make these comments only when he was on task or within one or two seconds after he completed a task—and they didn't overdo it.

Jake was prone to do jobs he didn't want to do in a sloppy fashion. He would claim he was done, but upon inspection, his parents would find his dirty clothes stuffed under his bed, his Legos shoved into the closet, and his clean clothes hanging out of drawers. Jake's parents used SPRd when they caught him doing his work in a haphazard fashion. If they caught him kicking his Legos under his bed, stuffing his clean clothes in the dirty clothes hamper, or walking away from his chest of drawers with the clean clothes dangling out, they gave him an SPRd. But that was not always possible. Again, supervision became the key. They always inspected Jake's work, and they made him redo any job that was poorly done, until they were satisfied with it. This meant that they inspected Jake's drawers and closet and under his bed before declaring that the job was done.

Many parents have their children do their homework at the kitchen table, where Mom and/or Dad can supervise while cleaning up the kitchen or preparing a meal. But this also means that Mom or Dad are available to nag the child into doing the homework or to be drawn inadvertently into doing the homework for the child. Homework is better done in the child's room or some other area equipped for study, where the child can be alone. We have found that the use of SPRd and the extinction procedure, coupled with unpredictable periodic checkups to see whether the work is being done, will improve persistence markedly. Start out with the goal that the child will work on the homework as long as it is necessary for a quality result, even if bedtime comes and goes.

Jake had always done his homework at the kitchen table because his bedroom was loaded with toys, lacked a desk, and was at the other end of the house. A convenient, yet out-of-the-way alternative was their dining room, which was out of the mainstream of household traffic, away from the TV, and easily accessible for supervision. Before implementing Jake's study routine, they sat down with him and worked out a schedule. Monday, Tuesday, and Thursday night, Jake was to start his homework at 5:30 P.M. because he had hockey practice at 7:30 P.M. Jake's mother was to supervise. On Sunday and Wednesday night, Jake was to start his homework at 6:30 P.M. with Dad as the supervisor. On evenings when he had hockey, Jake was to get his school work done, and get it done well, before leaving for hockey practice. Priorities were set: homework before hockey. If he finished his homework at 8:00 P.M. and there was enough time to get him to practice, his parents would take him. On some nights, he had no homework, so his parents would assign him review material or give him a reading assignment that required a written summary to be considered complete. Jake's parents felt, as we do, that doing homework on a consistent and routine basis is necessary. School-work that Jake did not do because he did not bring assignments or materials home, Jake's mother collected on Friday, when she routinely picked Jake up at school. On Friday night, his parents asked him to sit down and make up any incomplete work. His parents checked on him frequently, did an SPRd if necessary, commented on his work if he was on task, and made him stay up until he had done all his work well. The first night, Jake was up until one A.M. After just a few nights of this, Jake was getting all his homework done in thirty to sixty minutes.

Throughout these trying weeks with Jake, his parents reassured him of their love for him, and they let him know they understood how difficult this was for him. They were able to comfort and console Jake without ever backing off from the program.

Jake's parents set up some guidelines that they would use to determine whether help for Jake was indicated. Their goal was to provide him with as little assistance as possible and to foster independence when it came to doing school work. When Jake complained that he didn't understand how to do the work, his parents calmly responded with, "Jake, I know it's hard, but you can do it, and you must do it." If, after a good effort, he still could not understand the concepts, they reinstructed him. At no time during their instructions did they use his assigned work as an example, making up their own examples instead. They were careful to avoid teaching material that he was fully capable of understanding himself. In other words, they would not allow themselves to be blindsided by Jake. For Jake, a good effort was defined as a combination of time spent on the assignment and rereading sections of his assignments. When he had done that, help was permitted. It was considered a good effort even if his work contained errors, so long as the mistakes were consistent, suggesting a conceptual misunderstanding of the material.

With continued persistence, Jake's school work gradually started to improve. Finally, he was turning in his assignments on time, and he was doing them well. A nice side affect was observed: Jake's grades started to improve. The battles about doing his homework started to subside. Though he won't quite admit it, Jake has finally gotten to the point where he finds some of the work satisfying; we can now hear him talking about some of the concepts he is learning and asking more in-depth questions.

Jake and his parents' experiences serve as an excellent example of how Extinction of Negative Reinforcement, the Comfort, but Don't Fix rule, Positive Reinforcement, and SPRd can work together. Jake had grown quite dependent on his parents' help when doing homework. Insisting that Jake do his own work without help is extinction; Jake was blocked from avoiding the work. Comfort, but Don't Fix occurred when Jake became emotional over their insistence he do his work. Lack of compliance and persistence yielded to SPRd. Initially, it took a lot of work and dedication on Jake's parents' part, but they would do it all again in a second if they needed to.

The Dishonest Child

Dishonesty is almost universal in manipulative children. It is difficult to deal with, particularly in an oppositional child. Asked, "Who left the pop cans in the living room?" invites a response of denial. Asked whether a school assignment has been completed or has been done with quality, the dishonest child will always reply in the affirmative, despite the truth.

Lying is the quintessential avoidance behavior, so the techniques we've been talking about have a clear role in dealing with it. To deal with dishonesty, parents must get comfortable with being a bit arbitrary, relying on their gut instincts, doubts, and suspicions about the child's veracity. Err on the side of the liberal use of SPRd when you doubt what the child is saying. Sometimes you may mistakenly implement SPRd when the child is telling the truth, but this won't significantly reduce the likelihood of truthfulness in the future. If you make a mistake, admit it and apologize to the child—you're just modeling appropriate behavior. To err occassionally, for the sake of improving your parenting and raising your child more effectively, is well worth it. But remember, if lying goes unchallenged, dishonest behavior will increase dramatically.

Asking children who have problems with honesty why they lied has the predictable result: It breeds more dishonesty. You're asking them to justify or excuse their behavior. This approach serves only to cloud the issue. Children quickly learn to tell you only what you want to hear or what will allow them to avoid trouble.

The general rules for dealing with dishonesty are these: Don't ask "why" (instead, use an SPRd when you suspect lying); confront lies discovered after the fact, and restate the requirement for honesty; when appropriate, ask the child to do what is ethically correct (such as apologize).

At her sixth grade conference, Carrie's parents learned that on several occasions she had claimed she had been sick so as to be excused from some late assignments. Her parents knew she hadn't been sick at all. After her conference, Carrie's parents held a one-sided conversation during which they confronted her with her lack of truthfulness. They reiterated the family value of honesty; they instructed Carrie to write a letter of apology to her teacher and to make up the late work—despite the fact that she would not get credit for it. Carrie's parents immediately interrupted her attempts to justify her actions, telling her they didn't really want to hear it, and they again clarified the family rules. They contacted her teacher to verify the apology and then followed up to ensure that Carrie did nothing else until she turned in the late work.

Jake was quite dishonest. Nothing was ever his fault. The fault was always his teacher's, his sister's, the bus driver's, his friend's, or his parents'. Asked who ate the last piece of chocolate cake, he replied that it was his sister. Asked why chocolate cake crumbs were in his bedroom, he would claim that his sister had eaten the cake in his room to get him into trouble. Even when caught red-handed, he would deny his involvement.

We asked Jake's parents to eliminate Jake's opportunity to lie through the "why" question. We told them to pay attention to how they felt when they listened to his story. If they were confident that he was telling the truth, they dropped the issue. If they were mildly suspicious, they confronted him. They could use humor, saying, "Jake! Give me a break! Do I look that dumb? I'm not buying that for one moment," Or they could use a more serious approach such as, "I have some real doubts about what you are saying." If their doubts about the honesty of Jake's statement were clearer, they were to do an SPRd. If they caught Jake in the midst of the lie, they interrupted him. After redirecting him, they said "Jake, in our family, you must be honest." If there was some corrective action they could ask Jake to take, they asked him to do it. So, if pop cans were left in the family room, they sent him to pick them up and put them into the recycling bin. If an apology was needed, they asked him to apologize.

Jake typically responded to the SPRd by complaining that he wasn't trusted and that he was treated unfairly—and then he attempted to justify his lie. His parents withheld any response to this. After many SPRds, Jake's lying disappeared and Jake could be heard complaining when someone else wasn't telling the truth. Messes left in the family room were admitted; blaming others was no longer automatic. Jake was now at a point where they could start to trust what he was saying.

Household Rule Breakers

The child who won't accept no for an answer, the child who breaks household rules, or the child who won't stop doing something when asked—all respond well to SPRd. Its use is straightforward; immediately stop the offending behavior with no preamble, and complete the sequence. Mark, a determined seven-year-old, always responded to "no" by doing everything in his power to force a change to "yes." He had experienced frequent success at this, so he had become incredibly persistent in his efforts. Mark's parents had always tried to reason with him so that he would understand why they were saying "no." Unfortunately, their strategy backfired—Mark became a master negotiator; he was usually one step ahead of them in their reasoning with him. Mark's parents first had to become comfortable with their parental responsibility to make decisions and carry them out without justification to Mark. They needed to deal with the fact that Mark would not like having any influence over their decisions. They found it helpful to identify clearly, in their own minds, negotiable versus non-negotiable issues and decisions. Once they had done this, they could tell Mark at the outset that their decision was not negotiable or they could lay a decision on the table for discussion. We asked Mark's parents to respond to attempts at bargaining or arguing the non-negotiable by saying, "Sorry, but the answer is 'no' and we won't discuss it further." Other similar statements of non-negotiability can be used as well. If Mark tried to badger his parents further, they quickly parked him. At first, when they parked him on the couch, he cried and claimed that no one would listen to him and his parents were not fair, they hated him, and he hated them—for thirty minutes. Many SPRds (and many vitriolic protests) later, Mark learned quietly to accept "no" for an answer.

Following household rules was always hard for Mark. Asked to stop roughhousing in the living room, he would momentarily pause, then resume his play just as vigorously. Mark's parents found themselves reminding him over and over to settle down and knock it off. Mark's household behavior just got worse as he got older—it was as if he owned the house, made the rules, and his parents were just there to make the meals and pick up after him.

We suggested the following approach: First, request that Mark settle down; if additional roughhousing occurred, immediately do an SPRd. After the first few times they did this, they were to omit the cue to settle down and just do an SPRd. During the REDIRECT, they were to tell him to go play, but not roughly. Predictably, Mark loudly protested his parents unfairness and promised he wouldn't roughhouse any more, but his parents waited until he was quiet before redirecting him. Mark began to discover that his parents were actually going to stick by the rules they had established and, with that realization, things improved.

Mark had one other problem that needed to be addressed. He never put on his seat belt until his parents asked him to. Only when requested to do so did he cheerfully buckle up. His parents combined SPRd, Positive Practice, and reinforcement to modify this unsafe and dependency-producing behavior. Mark's dad modeled for him what was expected when Mark entered the family car. The procedure was this: open the door, push the seat forward, get in the car, close the door, sit down, pull the front seat back into position, and buckle his seat belt. Mark practiced the buckling-up procedure ten times the first day, with only one minimal coaching from his dad. From that point on, as soon as the car was set in motion (the car was still in the driveway), his dad said something like, "You did it today," "Way to go, you remembered!" or, "I'm having a hard time catching you without it." If Mark was not buckled up, his father did an SPRd immediately in the stopped car, by having Mark put his head down briefly. After the SPRd, his father redirected Mark to fasten his seat belt and reminded him that when they arrived at day care, Mark would need to practice. Once at their destination, Mark's dad got out of the car and had Mark practice ten to fifteen trials, depending on the days' time constraints.

Within a few days, Mark was reliably fastening his seat belt without reminders. In all, there were only sixty Positive Practice trials and about five SPRds.

The Victimized Child

We all know of children who allow themselves to be victimized by a sibling, a neighbor kid, or a bully on the bus or at school. The tools we've discussed can all help in changing victim behavior.

Brianna is an eight-year-old girl at a local elementary school. She is bright, charming, clever, verbal, and highly reactive. The slightest teasing resulted in an emotional outburst, ranging from an angry verbal retort to a quiet, tearful withdrawal. Every day when her mother picked her up from school, she complained about how other children mistreated her. As the year progressed, Brianna's complaints grew from a few sorrowful comments into a two-hour-long pity party. Mother's phone calls to the school and complaints to the principal did little to change Brianna's plight. All the motherly advice to Brianna to ignore the offending children's teasing or to tell the teacher about it, only seemed to make matters worse.

To assist Brianna, we consulted with her parents, John and Judy. Judy, at first, was especially taken aback by what we had to say and was a reluctant participant. She clearly saw Brianna as a victim and in need of protection rather than strong and able to handle the most adverse circumstances. After considerable discussion, Judy began to realize that Brianna had untapped strengths. We advised Brianna's parents to put an end to the after-school "they are so mean to me" complaint sessions. We asked Judy to use Comfort, but Don't Fix and Positive Practice. Judy and John were also to meet with the school principal, Brianna's teacher, and the playground supervisors to discuss managing her victim behavior. When Brianna was in a loud conflict with a peer, they promptly parked both offending parties—Brianna for overreacting and the peer for teasing. At the termination of the SPRd, both were redirected to get along with one another. Any attempts at justifying the children's behavior was interrupted quickly, and they were sent on their way. The increased vigilance at school soon uncovered the fact that Brianna was not the innocent victim, rather, she was doing her fair share of tormenting.

The Comfort, Don't Fix tool was used to put an end to Brianna's constant complaining about her peers. When Judy picked up Brianna, Judy asked, "How was your day?" The instant Brianna began to complain about a peer, Judy said quietly, "I know honey, it's hard; but you are the only one who can handle the problem. It's up to you to learn how to get along with other kids." Since by nature Brianna was so reactive, we believed that she would benefit from Positive Practice. Teasing, a cue for an emotional outpouring, had to be changed to a stimulus that elicited an alternative behavior.

Both of Brianna's parents sat down with her and discussed the impact her reactivity was having on the other children. Her parents explained that an emotional outburst was an invitation to tease again. She was told that, contrary to her parents' previous suggestions, ignoring didn't work very well because it was so hard to ignore a child who was determined to get a reaction from her. John and Judy let Brianna know she was going to have to behave differently: At first she would feel uncomfortable and, like anything else, she would have to practice to get it right, and she would learn by doing a little playacting. When she was teased, she was going to smile, agree, and if she could think of a clever way to do it, exaggerate the put-down. When it was all over, she was to remind herself that the nasty remark was not true and go on with life. Brianna and her parents put together a list of the most common and hurtful behaviors, giving her an opportunity to think of some clever exaggerations.

John was selected to practice with Brianna, since he was the most skilled at teasing. From Brianna's list, he selected just a few comments to get started. He called Brianna a nerd and, at first, Brianna wanted to call names back or denied she was a nerd. John coached her through the first response: smiling and agreeing with the insult. After about eight to ten trials, Brianna started to catch on and smiled at the insult, was more relaxed, and responded with some clever exaggerations. At the end of the first practice session, John and Brianna were laughing and giggling. As Brianna went to bed that night, she was warned that both Mom and Dad would be making a concerted effort to provide her with lots of unannounced opportunities to practice her new skills.

Each time Brianna complained about being teased, or responded with emotional upset when taunted by her parents, they gave her a practice session later that evening. They told her, "They are still getting to you. You need more practice. You can do it." They held practice sessions daily for the first week. And over the next two weeks, she reported problem interactions on only two occasions, and when taunted at home, she responded with a smile and witty exaggerations. Within a month, Brianna was a different girl. She was still innately reactive, but was now able to use her reactive temperament to her advantage. Now, when she was picked up from school, there were no more pity parties. Rather, she talked of what she and friends were doing or shared how she managed a difficult encounter. She looked calm and less depressed, and had gained a sense of control and mastery over her environment. Her peers no longer determined her emotions. She was now in charge of her emotions and had gained a significant measure of independence.

Changing a child's manipulative life-style is not easy. Shutting down each behavior takes a great deal of effort and time. Both parents and child will experience a fair bit of stress throughout the process. The rewards, however, are great. Behavior improves, grades improve, interest in a wider range of activities suddenly appears, and attitudes change from "do it for me" to "I can do it."

The Anxious and Fearful Child

Many of the children we see can be characterized as anxious or fearful. Children may learn to manage their anxiety by controlling everything and everyone around them—situations, friends, parents, relatives, and teachers are all subject to their attempts to control. New situations are often horribly anxiety provoking because these children feel threatened by lack of control. Anxious children worry about school work, what the plans are for the evening or weekend, or who will be at a friend's birthday party. Anything can be grist for the worrier's mill. Frequently perfectionistic, their school work must be exactly correct; they are devastated when their grade is less than perfect. The prospect of giving a presentation in front of the class terrifies them. Any unforeseen change in family routine upsets them terribly. Parents of these children often resort to massive doses of reassurance, avoid changing plans—fearing a major upset—and commonly take great pains to prepare a child well in advance of any new activity. These strategies are counterproductive; real life is, by its very nature, uncontrollable and unpredictable. Anxious children must learn to cope effectively with this reality.

For the anxious and fearful child, SPRd, Extinction of Negative Reinforcement, and Comfort, but Don't Fix are all useful. Our efforts are directed at making it impossible to avoid or escape anxiety-provoking situations while supporting the child through the process. Through repeated exposure to the feared, anxiety-provoking situation, the child learns to quell the anxious response and discovers new coping skills that have wide application.

Andy was an anxious and fearful six-year-old. He wouldn't go to bed at night. He complained that he was afraid of the dark, that he saw shadows that scared him. Andy would do anything he could think of to get somebody to be with him in bed or to get him out of his bedroom. Making multiple trips to the bathroom or kitchen to get a drink, thinking of something important to tell Mom or Dad just before lights out, cajoling his brother to sleep with him, or stealthily crawling into bed with his parents after they had fallen into an exhausted sleep were all part of his repertoire.

Andy's parents had already tried many ways to solve his nighttime problems. Rewards and bribes, repeated reassurance, reasoning, cajoling, threats, anger, and yelling: Nothing worked. Most of the time, one of his parents would have to lie next to him until he fell asleep, but often they awoke to find him in bed with them.

We recommended an Extinction of Negative Reinforcement procedure. Andy's parents were instructed to inform Andy, in the light of day, that he was going to sleep in his room, that he was not going to be permitted to leave his room. Before he went to bed, he was to get a drink and go to the bathroom. No longer could he crawl into his parents' bed in the middle of the night—they locked their bedroom door for a few nights. That evening, after a story, kisses and hugs, a drink, and a visit to the bathroom, Andy was escorted to bed and tucked in; then his parents turned off the light and closed the door. He immediately came out of his room. His mother, who was sitting in the hall with a magazine, immediately escorted him back without saying anything or making eye contact. Her manner, well coached, was quiet, firm, and determined. During the evening, his parents took turns escorting Andy back to bed many times until he finally stayed put. The first few nights were tough for both Andy and his parents. The process lasted three or four hours on the first night, but things rapidly improved. Andy needed to be escorted back to bed later that night when he threw a temper-tantrum at his parents' locked bedroom door.

Over the next ten days, Andy's bedtime behavior improved until he finally went off to bed happily without even a protest. Over the course of the next two months, Andy would occasionally climb into his parents' bed, but they promptly returned him to his bed with minimal fanfare. His grand-parents noticed a nice side effect: They said that he was in a better mood, was easier to be around, and seemed to have a better outlook on life. Amazing what a good night's rest will do!

As luck would have it, several months later, Andy went off to bed, as usual, by himself. A few minutes later, Andy's Mom heard him frantically yelling, "Mom, there is something in my room." She thought to herself, "What do you know, he's trying his old tricks." Andy cried out again, only more loudly and frantically, "Mom, there really is something in my room." She didn't respond. Now, with a tinge of panic in his voice, he cried, "Mom there is something in my room." Suddenly, all was quiet for a moment; then he said, "Mom, I can't believe it. There's a cat in my room." She went to his room and found the neighbor's cat crawling out from under Andy's bed. She removed the cat and put it outside, and Andy settled into his bed for the rest of the night. No relapse occurred over the following nights. Even though Andy had been legitimately frightened, he had developed enough confidence in himself to overcome the fear. Andy was clearly on the road to independence.

Sarah was a kindergartner when we first met her. Her teacher had noted right away that she found it extremely difficult to separate from her mother, who brought her to school. Once she was left in the classroom, she routinely isolated herself from the other pupils. Sarah spoke softly. Although healthy, she somehow presented herself to adults in a way that aroused one's protective instincts. Sarah just seemed delicate. She was a constant worrier, prone to anxiety when routines changed. She enjoyed empathetic adult attention, wanting repeated reassurance. When this wasn't enough, she would try to have the rules changed to alleviate her anxiety.

To ward off Sarah's worrying and fearfulness, her parents always warned her of impending changes in family routines. They reasoned and reassured to help her cope with any change. Sarah said, "I can't" before she even tried to do anything she saw as new or challenging. She had not developed some of the normal skills expected of kindergartners: She didn't dress or undress herself without help, claiming, "I can't do it" or "I don't know how." She asked for help brushing her teeth and combing her hair. When asked to go to an area of the house where she would be alone, she tried charming or coaxing her brother to come along with her, complaining that she was afraid to go into the bathroom, bedroom, living room, or family room alone. Sarah was afraid to go outside alone. An encounter with an ant, June bug, or mosquito sent her scurrying indoors for cover. On school nights, she repeatedly asked whether she had to go to school. When told she had to go, she dissolved into a puddle of tears, whereupon her parents reassured her. Breakfast was an exercise in procrastination to avoid getting dressed for school. Sarah's parents observed that the more they reassured, the worse things seemed to get.

We worked with Sarah's parents to help them learn SPRd effectively, then apply it first to her problems with school. On school nights, her complaints were met with, "I'm sorry, Sarah. I know you are afraid of school, but you're going to go. You'll survive." We told her parents to stop, altogether, reassuring and rationalizing with her. Instead, they could acknowledge her fears and express their confidence that she could handle them, letting her know that they would not change things to make her less worried. If she continued to try to get more reassurance or change her parents' decisions, they used SPRd immediately.

Her dawdling with dressing and brushing her hair and teeth also needed quick attention. At first, they got her up an hour earlier than usual so that they would not have a time bind. And they interrupted each of her stall tactics with an SPRd.

Sarah's parents also used SPRd when Sarah wouldn't go to some part of the house alone. Charming her little brother into accompanying her wasn't allowed. So, if Sarah didn't go, as requested, to the family room to get the dog's leash, for instance, they used an SPRd and then asked her to go again.

We asked her parents to find more jobs for Sarah to do around the house. They instructed her to clear the table, take the paper goods into the bathroom, take her clean clothes to the bedroom, and take the cat litter to the garage (all these are age-appropriate tasks for a five- to six-year-old). Any attempt to avoid doing these chores was interrupted by an SPRd. Finally, if Sarah complained she was afraid, they did not offer reassurance but rather, "I'm sorry, I know you are afraid. But you'll have to deal with it—I know you can." Further complaints were to be followed with an SPRd. We wanted to increase Sarah's responsibilities for two reasons: Each time she went about the house by herself, she learned to deal with her fears a little more. But Sarah also needed to learn to do as she was asked—her fears had become an excuse to get out of work she didn't want to do.

Within a couple of weeks, Sarah was getting dressed independently and without reminders. She was voluntarily and freely going about the house—doing so when she was requested as well as when she wanted something from another room. She now went to the bathroom independently. She soon learned to go outside and play in her backyard, even alone. Her parents had treated going outside just like her other difficulties and were amazed to find that, after a couple of days, Sarah started asking to go outside—she had found the outdoors quite enjoyable. She had found her own reinforcement and was no longer as dependent on her parents for their attention.

Luckily, Sarah's teacher was amenable to a plan developed for her problems in school. Sarah's mother dropped her off at school in the morning, gave her a quick kiss, peeled Sarah off, and handed her over to the teacher, who then took her into the classroom. She was allowed to sit by herself and cry until she settled herself down. Her teacher was instructed to ignore her fastidiously until she made an advance toward the other children. The result of this was predictable: Within a few weeks, Sarah was able to separate from her mother with ease, engage herself with the other children, and cooperate with the classroom routine.

Sibling rivalry was a problem for Sarah, and as her other behavior improved, this became a focus for treatment. Her little brother simply had her number. He could get Sarah to react to the slightest provocation. Alex and Sarah exhibited typical sibling interaction difficulty: One would tease; the other would react with bloodcurdling screams. Alex tended to be the usual protagonist in this game. In the usual sibling situation, there are teasers and victims: The teaser does something to get the victim to react, and the teaser is reinforced by the victim's reaction to the teasing, but the reaction also brings parents into play, with the victim sitting back watching the fireworks that follow. Sarah and Alex's parents sat down with both children and told them that they were free to have conflicts but they would have to work them out by themselves. How they worked them out, though, had rules they must follow—conflicts must be solved quietly and without aggressive behavior. If the children did not follow these rules, the mother or father would intervene. The secret to their success with this plan was in how they intervened. Instead of trying to figure out who did what to whom, refereeing the battle or assigning blame, they merely broke up the conflict with an SPRd for both kids. Once both children were settled, they were directed to go solve the problem in the bathroom or outside. Tattling was initially a problem, but quickly disappeared when the tattler routinely got parked. Quiet conflict was ignored—as long as it stayed quiet. Sarah and Alex learned to get along with one another better. Teasing and overreaction melted away, and they began to negotiate solutions to their difficulties.

We asked Sarah's parents to have her do age-appropriate tasks that required social involvement, such as returning videos to the video store, paying for items at the store, or asking the store clerk for the location of an item in the store. She did all this under the watchful eye of her parents standing some distance away. With this practice, her confidence in strange situations increased dramatically.

At school, she was asked to do things to stimulate anxiety. She was sent to the school secretary with the daily report of absences or to the custodial area to get the classroom erasers cleaned. Since she didn't raise her hand in class, her teacher called on her at least two or three times a day. Periodically, she was asked to do show and tell. Other children were not permitted to enable her shyness: They could not speak for her or make it easier for Sarah in other ways. Sarah began to learn to be assertive. Since their neighborhood was devoid of other children, playmates for Sarah had to be imported. Sarah was coached in how to invite other children to her home and then asked to do it. Sarah began to learn the give-and-take of social relationships.

Though still tentative at first, Sarah's social interactions improved substantially. She now has friends she calls and invites over to her house without parental prompting. And she has learned to assert herself on the playground. At first, if other children rejected her overtures to play, Sarah gave up and went to her retreat on the monkey bars. This was not permitted and was interrupted with an SPRd; then she was sent on her merry way to find someone else with whom to play. Gradually, she was successful, and more importantly, Sarah learned to deal with failure.

Today, Sarah is a much different girl than when we first met her. She has a few close friends and several acquaintances. She is still quick to become anxious, but has learned to cope effectively. Certainly, some of Sarah's anxieties were learned during a long history of avoidance behavior, but we also believe that Sarah's propensity for anxiety was part of the original equipment installed at the factory. By having many experiences with overcoming her anxiety, she has adopted an "I can do it" approach to life. On several occasions, Sarah's mother reported hearing Sarah say "I'm scared, but I can do it" when faced with a fearful situation.

Methods that Don't Work

Probably you have noticed that nowhere was the use of rewards, threats, bribes, or punishment described in managing behavior. These are manipulative techniques to be avoided. While they may change behavior in the short run, their beneficial effects do not endure, but they do teach a child to operate in a manipulative environment—just exactly what we don't want to do.

Rewards and incentives can change behavior over the short haul, but their effects generally last only as long as the reward or incentive is available and continues to be desirable to the child. Sometimes behavior change brought about by rewards will generalize, be satisfying to the child, and thus persist, but that is not usual. Rewards and incentives will not overcome avoidance behavior under any condition.

Bribes are even less effective in changing behavior. Bribes are a little like rewards, but there is a major difference. With bribes, a reward is offered in return for a behavior, and once an agreement is made that the behavior will occur, the reward is provided. With bribes, the inducement is provided even before a behavior occurs. For example, "John if you do your homework on a regular basis, I will buy you a Super Nintendo." John agrees to do his homework, and he is then given a Super Nintendo. John is given the reward just by agreeing to do his homework. All John has to do to get the reward is to agree, yet he doesn't have to actually *produce* the behavior. This mode of operation virtually guarantees that future bargains will be struck with little or no intent of follow-through.

The effects of threats are a little like rewards. When a child is threatened, she is told that if she behaves in a certain unacceptable manner, something awful and unpleasant will happen—for example "April, if you don't get your bedroom clean, you will not be able to have Becky stay overnight." The effect on behavior change is similar to that of rewards. That is, the threat must be present before the behavior occurs. With threats, frequently the behavior will change for as long as the threat remains in place or as long as the child perceives that there is a threat present. Once the threat is removed, behavior returns to the way it was before. April might clean her room tonight, but future performance is in doubt. Both threats and rewards foster dependence. To get the child to behave appropiately, someone else has to offer the threat or reward. This behavior is not initiated by the child.

Punishments, such as removal of a privilege, so-called "logical consequences," physical consequences, or verbal reprimands, don't work. Punishment does not usually alter behavior in any predictable way, particularly if the "consequences" provided are harsh and delayed—for example, "Albert, you got another D on your report card. You might as well kiss the TV good-bye for the remainder of the school year." Parents hope that by making a consequence severe enough, the child's behavior will change. Behavior may change, but not in the ways parents hope for.

In our population of children, parents and teachers alike often make a diligent search to find just the right punishment that will alter a child's behavior. They may often feel that if they are just creative enough, the punishment will work: longer in-school suspensions or time-outs; longer groundings; more work—even harsher physical punishment. And when increasing the *intensity* of the punishment doesn't work, then some people try other punishments, moving from one to another. In our view, all of this is abusive, not to mention ineffectual. Imagine your employer treating you this way. What does he get for his efforts? An enthusiastic, devoted employee or a devious, guarded employee who watches the want ads a lot? Physical punishment appears to have worked well years ago because it produced avoidance behavior and empowered parents to be heard and taken seriously by their children. It worked well because it was used within the framework of strict conditions: Rules were simple, clear, and consistently enforced. It was not used by parents as a frustrated, angry last resort, but as the procedure of first choice. But like all forms of punishment, it was often used inappropriately and to excess. We, however, do not advocate the use of physical—or any form—of punishment as a method of managing behavior simply because it doesn't work in the long run. We've found that parents can get results with equally good success, without having to resort to punishment.

CHAPTER 8

Raising Children
Who Believe in Themselves

The techniques used to shut down manipulative behavior that were discussed in chapter 7—SPRd; Comfort, but Don't Fix; and Extinction of Negative Reinforcement—if practiced effectively, can have a powerful role in teaching children to adapt. But their use is only part of the story. In this last chapter, we want to integrate everything we've said up to now into a useful whole. First, we'll consider what parents can do to ensure the development of self-esteem in their children.

Self-Esteem

Self-esteem is a realistic and enduring set of beliefs about oneself that, on the whole, offers a positive view of one's worth and competence in the world. In other words, over a prolonged period of time, even though a person realistically recognizes his frailties and shortcomings, he nonetheless views himself as having worth and competence. Some elements of this definition deserve our attention:

A realistic view of oneself is essential. Persons with self-esteem do not have an overinflated view of themselves. They are not cocky or arrogant. Nor do these people have a deflated view of themselves, with the self-deprecatory view of someone who can never get the world to be the way it should be. Instead, they realistically understand that there are areas of skill that are beyond their competence, training, capabilities, interest, or desire. They also recognize their own competence in the areas to which they have committed themselves: They can judge their own competence fairly. They view failure in an area of competence as a challenge, not a devastation, and they re-double their efforts to achieve excellence. Failure does produce uncomfort-able feelings, but these are normal, healthy human emotions. People with healthy self-esteem are resilient.

This positive view of self is enduring. It does not depend on a steady stream of attention and adulation from others, but instead thrives without outside comments and compliments. Compliments are appreciated, and good feelings may result from them, but they are not essential because the person with self-esteem already knows he's done his best, he's lived up to his stan-dards. Terry Waite, the envoy from the Anglican Church held hostage in Lebanon, went voluntarily back to meet with his former captors after his initial release. He knew that it was likely he would be taken hostage again, but he knew that some of his fellow hostages were sick and perhaps dying. Mr. Waite felt he was needed, that perhaps he could help in some way, so meeting with the hostage takers was the right, and therefore the only, thing he could do. He was again taken hostage. After a year of torture at the hands of his captors, he was told he was to be executed and had six hours to live. He was told he could write one last letter, which he addressed to his employer, the Archbishop of Canterbury. In it he wrote, "Do not feel badly for me, I am at peace. I have done my best." Now that's real self-esteem.

People with self-esteem are independent. They pursue their own goals, sometimes against odds that are formidable. They believe that the product of their efforts is worthwhile. They are honest and own their successes and failures. No one else has done their jobs for them. They give themselves credit for their successes, and when they fail, they don't blame others for their mistakes. They accept the failure as their own. People with good self-esteem do not lay claim to successes that are not truly their own. They give credit to others who may have assisted them with a success. People with self-esteem are honest with themselves and others. They do not sacrifice their personal integrity to remove conflict or anxiety. They are principle-directed. Like Terry Waite, they do what they believe is right, recognizing that there may be a personal cost.

Self-esteem is not a birthright, present from the beginning. Rather, it is acquired through experience and honest evaluation of experience. Develop-ment of self-esteem does not occur overnight, nor is it derived from a few significant experiences; it is the cumulative result of a lifetime of experiences.

Self-esteem is a state of being that is worked for and maintained. It is not static, but dynamic. It waxes and wanes over time as conditions change, as effort and energy are put into its maintenance. It cannot be addressed directly, as in telling yourself that you really are a wonderful person. Instead, it is a result of addressing other issues of life such as values and one's integrity with them. Like Terry Waite, persons with self-esteem know what they believe is right and follow their beliefs.

The key life experiences that foster the development of self-esteem are those that present challenge, (that is, experiences in which there is a clear risk of failure and a chance for success). Often, these are situations we would just as soon avoid. For example, if a child finds her math assignment tedious and difficult, but nevertheless does it to the best of her ability, she makes a small contribution to her self-esteem. Or consider the child who's working on a troublesome reading assignment and asks his parents to help with the difficult words. His parents quietly demur, saying that they're quite sure he can sound them out on his own. The child complains, but plugs away and gets the job done. This experience builds self-esteem.

Self-esteem is often fostered in challenging situations, regardless of success or failure. The outcome may be insignificant compared to the sense of mastery that comes from the effort expended on what a person believes is right, particularly when one is tempted to give up. From this, we can learn something about our capacities. An honest acknowledgment of failure and an assessment of the cause of the failure enables a person to make corrections so that success has a chance to occur. And when it finally does, self-esteem receives a big boost. No one feels good about failure, but without it there can be no real successes. People with self-esteem know they put forth their best effort, they met the challenge, they did the right thing, despite failure; and this keeps them going until they succeed. And they learn something else of immense, enduring personal value: They learn that they can survive failure.

Manipulative behavior systematically destroys self-esteem. Both the dishonesty inherent in manipulative behavior and the dependence given rise to are incompatible with self-esteem. A steady diet of easy successes will destroy self-esteem, yet parents and teachers often engineer easy successes for a child, believing this will enhance the child's self-esteem. When they do this, they have confused the child's momentary happiness—or relief—with self-esteem, a fatal error if they want children to develop enduring and realistic self-worth. Children often know what it will take to meet a challenge. If we allow them to avoid a troublesome problem, to take an easy way out (like getting help when they could have done it themselves), we have made the child happy at the expense of his self-esteem. Worse, we've made it more likely that the child will find his way around similar challenges in the future; we've taught him to manipulate us to avoid frustrating and frightening challenges. Patronizing of children breeds dependence and a weak sense of self.

Michael is a fourth grader. Monday, in school, his teacher assigned fifty math homework problems to do that evening. Math is Mike's best subject. After dinner, he sat down to do the work and recognized that he understood in general what the assignment was about. He saw that the whole experience would be boring and tedious. Besides, his dad was watching Monday Night Football. If he had had no homework, he and his dad would be enjoying watching the game together. So he started to rush through the work to get it out of the way. He was done in ten minutes flat, but his work was sloppy and loaded with errors. Mike knew his family's expectation: Whatever you do, try your hardest. If you tried your hardest and did poorly, that was okay. If you tried your hardest and did very well, that was wonderful. After completing the assignment, Mike went downstairs feeling a little guilty about his sloppy job, rationalizing that, after all, the assignment was boring, silly and, besides, it was unreasonable for his teacher to expect him to do such mundane work. The next day, Mike got a C- on his paper, and he justified his grade to himself by saying, "The assignment was really stupid and besides, math is easy for me." But Mike soon found other excuses for doing hurried, sloppy work on several succeeding math assignments. Mike has an excellent teacher, and she noticed the problem. After the fourth sloppy assignment, she called him to her desk and said she was disappointed in his recent work and expected him to do it all over. She gave him a deadline and suggested he might want to stay in from recess to get it done. She didn't ask why he wasn't doing his homework as well as he should be—she didn't consider that any of her business—and she didn't threaten punitive action. She didn't even call Mike's parents—this was between Mike and herself, teacher and pupil. Mike got his work done properly and promptly, and returned to his usual solid performance.

Mike had started to learn to take the easy way out of an onerous chore. When it worked, providing the TV time he wanted, he became more prone to do it again. He knew he had violated a family value, and didn't feel good about it, but he continued his sloppy work anyway. If his teacher had asked why he did it, he would have spouted justifications for his behavior, but she didn't give him the chance. She just stated her expectations and moved on—thank goodness!

This episode was a rare example of avoidance behavior for Mike, so he was able to recover and move on. For another child who practiced avoidance regularly, correction of this behavior would have required a huge struggle. Each time avoidance behavior happens, every time a child is able to manipulate, the strength of these behaviors is enhanced. As avoidance and manipulation become entrenched, as children break the values held by their family, dishonesty with self and others becomes more common and self-esteem deteriorates.

Implicit and explicit messages given children by well-meaning adults can be quite destructive to a child's self-concept, especially when they are backed by authority or commonly repeated. Parents, for instance, who talk long and hard (read: lecture) to their child about his unacceptable behavior may be sending the message, "You're a bad person." With repeated, prolonged attention paid to unacceptable behavior in this way, the message gets through. It is much better to stop unacceptable behavior immediately, wait for the child to compose himself, quickly redirect, and go on with life as if nothing happened. Children are children; they need training, not retribution, reasoning, or rationalization. The less time spent on misbehavior, the better.

Explicit messages are, nonetheless, easier for children to handle than implicit messages. At least all the cards are on the table, without hidden assumptions or conclusions that are so effective in subtly undermining a person's self-concept.

Sometimes, serendipitously, explicit messages have the opposite effect of what was intended. Peter was a high school freshman, a laconic youngster with a deadpan expression who hails from a working-class family. We began treatment for ADHD when he was in the sixth grade, and his progress in school improved a fair bit. In eighth grade he decided he wanted to take advanced math (algebra). His math progress so far had been pretty good, and he felt he was ready for a challenge. When he asked to take this course, the teachers involved told him he wasn't ready, reciting his academic record. They told him he should take regular pre-algebra. This angered Peter, and he quietly simmered through the entire semester of pre-algebra. We saw him in May and learned of this whole business. Not very professionally, we expressed our dismay and anger about the school's decision. We couldn't believe it!

During the summer, Peter obtained a copy of the algebra text and studied two hours every day on his own. When school reconvened in the fall, he asked to take the algebra final, which he was allowed to do, and passed it with an excellent grade, then demanded admission into Algebra II. We heard about all this when he came in for a visit in the late fall. He quietly smiled and told us he was getting an A in the course. We laughed with him and cheered him on.

Brian was nine when he first asked his father to play racquetball with him. He has always been excited by a challenge. His father told him he was too little to play, but he said Brian could bring along a friend to swim in the pool with him while he played racquetball. Brian brought his friend, and they had a good time swimming. Over several years, this scene played out many times. Finally, when Brian was thirteen, his father gave him a racquet of his own and said that he was old enough to try playing. Brian's father did not let Brian win; he played hard and competitively. At age sixteen, Brian finally beat his father in a game, and a prouder and more triumphant boy there never was. Brian's father hadn't pandered or patronized his son, hadn't tried to make him feel good; he had just been honest with Brian. Brian worked hard for years to meet this challenge, and he finally succeeded after years of failure. Brian's father had set up an irresistable challenge for Brian. He met the challenge head on and took one more step on the road to self-esteem.

While we wouldn't tout explicit negative messages as a reliable method to motivate children, they are at least tangible, available for processing in some way. Some children find it irresistibly challenging when an adult tells them that something is too hard for them or that they can't do something because they're too little. They want to prove the adult wrong.

Implicit messages may be far more destructive. Because of their insidious nature, it is virtually impossible for a child to deal with them. They are often sugar-coated, intended to protect a child's feelings, so no one realizes what's being said. The typical implicit message comes from someone's unstated conclusion that a child does not have the capability to master a task or situation.

Jonathan, a fifth grader of average intelligence, had studied little for his spelling tests for the first six weeks of school. He managed to get more wrong than right on the tests. Jonathan's teacher, feeling bad about his performance, was concerned that continued failure would damage Jonathan's self-esteem. She felt Jonathan needed some successes and decided to engineer them by reducing his word list from twenty to ten words. Her intentions were good, but clearly misguided. By reducing Jonathan's workload, she told him implicitly that she believed he was not capable of doing the work or that he couldn't put in more effort. That is, Jonathan was unable to correct the problem. Unfortunately, Jonathan bought the plan—after all, it reduced the amount of work required of him. He got eight out of ten words correct for awhile, but his performance declined later, even with such reduced expectations, and his self-confidence took a real nosedive. Unfortunately, the problem wasn't his capability to do the work, but his unwillingness to do the work required. But that wasn't the message Jonathan got in the end.

Self-esteem is commonly confused with feeling good. While people with healthy self-esteem may feel happy and content some of the time, they are more likely to take on difficult tasks and, like anyone else who is struggling, not feel particularly happy during a stressful period. This is just as true of children as adults. It behooves us to realize that it is not our job to eliminate a child's struggle to cure the "bad" feelings; if we do this, we are patronizing the child and sending the implicit message that we don't have faith in them. It is our job to support children when they are struggling with a difficult task, be understanding of their emotional flip-flops along the way, refuse to bail them out and, finally, celebrate their eventual successes with them: "All right! I knew you could do it!"

The Role of Parents

Boundaries

Defining and placing boundaries on your role as a parent is vitally important. What you conclude your role to be flows out of your assumptions about your children. If you are secure in the knowledge that children are survivors, can adapt to practically anything, including finding their own happiness and developing a sense of well-being, you will feel responsible to provide those things children cannot provide for themselves, but little more. Parents must be responsible for food, shelter, clothing, medical care, good schools, protection from real threats and dangers, and, most importantly, the elements of family structure.

Parents can also give children gifts, arrange parties and entertainment for them, and take vacations with them, but parents should see these things as extras, not fundamental responsibilities of parenthood.

A Vision for Your Child

Family structure is the values, ethical principles, and goals that guide you in all the things you do with your children, in all the rules and decisions you make, in all the things you try to teach them. Children learn to live by and accommodate to the structure you create, so your values and goals become a vision for your child. Who do you want your child to become? What is your vision for your children? Do you want them to be responsible? Honest? Reliable? To do their best, even in the face of failure? Do you want them to know how to have fun, friends, and a career that is satisfying? Do you want them, as adults, to be independent, resourceful, and strong? We are not suggesting that parents should ever try to make decisions that are rightfully the child's, like choosing a future occupation or a spouse. But a child raised in a consistent family structure will be equipped to make these decisions well, to adapt, survive, and thrive in whatever world she finds.

Your thoughtful long-term vision for your children provides the day-to-day guidance you need to raise them. Your vision makes it possible to define right and wrong. For example, if you envision your children becoming adults with unimpeachable integrity, then you must insist upon their honesty, while demonstrating it yourself, now and throughout their years with you. You cannot be dishonest with your children nor tolerate dishonesty from them, regardless of circumstance or rationale. If you value resourcefulness, don't remove opportunities for your child to find a solution to a thorny problem. Instead, have faith in them, put the problem squarely in their lap, support them through the process, be patient, and celebrate with them the solution they discover. This means refusing to solve problems that would be simple and easy for you. If you value responsibility for self, instead of asking "Why?," ask "How are you going to handle it next time?" or, "What was your part in this; what do you need to change?" In this vision, blaming others for mistakes and failures is never acceptable. If you want to teach this to your children, you should not only deal with their behavior, but you must also demonstrate this trait yourself.

You need to maintain your vision for your children even when times are tough. For example, if you value honesty, you cannot discard truth when it would be easy to fudge a little. If you provide steady and consistent feedback like this over many years, your child will learn to behave in a manner consistent with your vision. If you provide feedback that is inconsistent, a values vacuum will be created that will surely be filled from random outside sources like peer groups, TV, and societal pressures; the outcome will be haphazard and unpredictable.

Last night, we were working with the parents of a client at a pediatric clinic. We were talking about honesty in families, and they related this story: As they were walking into the clinic building with their four-year-old daughter, they noticed some vomit on the front steps. Our client's mother commented, to no one in particular "Looks like someone must have been pretty sick and vomited." Another woman, who was just then leaving the office with her three-year-old child in tow, whispered, "We aren't calling it vomit, we're saying someone spilled their Pepsi" while nodding toward her daughter.

This lady was being dishonest with her child because she assumed she was incapable of handling the truth. She disguised reality to protect her child from the uncomfortable feelings she might have felt upon learning someone had vomited on the steps. If we can't be honest about something as ordinary as throwing up, where and when do we start being honest? How do we choose what to be honest about? How will this child learn about honesty when the simplest truths are disguised?

Providing Opportunities

Opportunities to acquire life skills are available in both organized programs for children and day-to-day family living. Parents can provide these opportunities both by arranging for their children's participation in organized activities like art classes, music lessons, sports, and boys' and girls' clubs, or through family activities and hobbies. There are innumerable opportunities in day-to-day family living to enhance a child's skills in life, but parents may overlook them just because the opportunities seem so mundane. For instance, when parents ask children to take on jobs and chores around the house, they learn something about being responsible for themselves and others, particularly if the family ethic stresses shared responsibility for household work. Some parents avoid asking children to participate in the daily work of a household because the parents can do what's necessary quicker and they receive too much flak when they ask the children to participate. They are missing a golden opportunity to teach their children some essential skills. Besides, household chores are rarely very interesting, and learning to accept the monotony and boredom of mundane tasks is good preparation for some of what life will bring. Children should be involved in the work of running a house early and continuously.

When seeking opportunities for a child, parents should look not just for those that appeal because of the child's familiarity or strength, but those that will be challenging, particularly in an area of weakness. The child who is not physically gifted needs practice in sports, and the future Olympian might benefit from music lessons. A shy and fearful child will benefit immeasurably from experiences he cannot avoid. Asking your shy child to bargain over the price of something, especially if it involves her own money, or allowing a child to return a defective toy for exchange, are examples of simple daily activities that teach assertiveness and self-reliance. Since self-esteem is built on a foundation of mastered challenges, children who do only the things they feel sure about, and avoid the unfamiliar and the threatening, miss many opportunities to broaden the base of their feeling of competence.

Scott was six when his family went skiing in Jackson Hole. On previous ski trips, he had spent time in the day care at the base of the mountain, sliding on the bunny hill, taking walks, and playing inside. This year, his parents decided that he was going to take ski lessons for the first time. Scott was the oldest child, so he didn't have the opportunity to watch and follow siblings learning to ski. When his parents told him of their decision, he argued, cried, and flat refused to participate in ski lessons. He said he loved day care, he already knew how to ski, he'd take lessons next year—Scott tried everything he could think of to avoid ski lessons. The next morning, his parents got him dressed, hauled him to the ski hill, put on his skis, and deposited him at the ski school, all against his will, loudly proclaimed from the first sock Scott put on until the final dreadful moment when his parents beat a fast exit to the nearest chair lift.

On their second ride up the chair lift, his parents saw Scott and the other students skiing down the bunny hill. Scott was laughing and having great fun, and the rest is history. Scott, now a sophomore in college, is a great skier today. But more importantly, several other similar episodes with new activities taught Scott that he could overcome things he was afraid of, and as he grew older, his parents merely needed to remind him of previous examples of situations that caused him initial panic. Scott learned to do this for himself as he got older. Today he is a self-confident young man who can face any challenge put before him.

Many parents try to ensure their childrens' success by presenting children with opportunities requiring minimal effort. They hold the belief that self-esteem will be enhanced if the child has a string of successes, despite the fact that these successes required only minimal effort and little perseverance on the child's part. Unfortunately, minimal effort resulting in a success is likely to produce only minimal effort in the future, with a distorted valuation of one's capacities. Worse, children may be devastated by failure when their previous experiences consist mainly of easy successes. A lot of effort resulting in success teaches persistence. Substantial effort resulting in failure tells us something about our capacities, and that there is life after failure. Minimal effort resulting in failure helps us understand what it takes to achieve.

The skill-building opportunities we have been discussing must be consistent with the family value system. Allowing your child to pursue an activity that runs counter to the family value system because he wants to is not helpful. It's more than okay to say "no" to a child who wants to hang around the shopping mall or go to an unsupervised party, even though your child might not like your decision. It may be years before your child appreciates some of the positions you take on the basis of your family code.

Parents must set priorities based on their belief system. For example, suppose that your son plays soccer very well and is essential to his team. There's a game tonight, but his homework isn't done, and you know he'll be too tired to do it after the game. He could have done it after school, but he talked on the phone all afternoon, shot a few baskets, and watched TV for a while. Do you let him go or make him stay home to do his homework? What are your priorities? Your decision will send a powerful message about your family's values and the priorities that follow from them. Parents not only need to be clear about the values they hold, but the precedence of the values.

Several years ago, Sean, age ten, was invited to spend Saturday with a boy he knew but wasn't good friends with. He accepted, but later in the week a good friend invited him to come over on the same day, so he decided to tell the first boy he couldn't come. He had an excuse all planned, and mentioned this to his father. His father knew he really preferred to go to his friend's house and knew Sean would be upset if he was not allowed to pull off this deceitful switch. Sean's father thought about it for a moment and said, "Sean, you've made a commitment to Joey. In our family, we live by our commitments, so I expect you to stick with yours. In addition, your method of getting out of your commitment isn't honest." Sean argued vigorously, and finally agreed to live up to his commitment. Several years later, Sean's father was amused to hear Sean complaining angrily about soccer teammates who didn't show up for practice reliably, "They don't understand that they've made a commitment to the team. Even if it's not so convenient, they should live up to it."

The Importance of Failing

Failure is essential to the development of self-esteem and independence. Failure tells us what we need to work on, helps us correct what we do, and tells us that we're up against difficulties worthy of our continued effort. Self-esteem cannot really endure without considerable experience in surviving failure, especially if several failures lead to appropriate practice, changes, and eventual success. Effective parents will allow their children to fail, supporting them through recovery and opposing those who see failure as dangerous and the concomitant emotions as toxic. Standing by your children when they are struggling isn't easy. The temptation to jump in and solve the problem for your child is sometimes almost unbearable. Adults, who've had much more experience in life, may find the answers to a child's problems obvious, but the solution may not be so obvious to the child. If we can let them figure it out on their own, they will learn much more from their experiences.

A word of caution: A common way to deal with failure is to shift blame elsewhere. Both children and parents are liable to do this. "Wilbur, you are really pretty smart and I think that the reason you failed your math test was because your teacher simply made the test too hard." Or "Sarah, I think you're having a hard time in getting along with Amelia because she's threatened by you." Ask instead what Wilbur thinks he ought to do next time so that he's better prepared for his math test, or what Sarah thinks she could do to get along better with Amelia. The message contained in the latter is "You have some control over your life and circumstances; you can have some influence over the outcome if you want; you're not a victim. But making change in your life requires you to change, not others."

We commonly see children who are failing in school who do some of their work but don't manage to get it turned in. Often they feel that it is okay to fail as long as they did so without effort; there's no need to be responsible for a failure if they didn't care and try in the first place. The child who avoids challenges this way may respond to your insistence that he do his work, with careful follow-up to be certain the work is actually done and handed in.

When a child experiences a failure, it is not uncommon for someone to attempt a rescue. While this serves to relieve the misery of the moment, it removes the opportunity to build self-esteem. Rescue can come from a parent, a sibling, school personnel, grandparents, neighbors, and even strangers. Rescue attempts need to be stopped calmly and tactfully with the message that you have every reason to believe your child will survive.

Putting It All to Work

Putting all this to work requires three steps to be successful. Most of what we are going to suggest sounds simple, but in practice all of it takes considerable effort and staying power. Raising children to be good, responsible, independent, and self-controlled human beings—people with character—is often hard work, and the payoff doesn't come for years. Along the way, you'll have many enjoyable times, but you'll also feel anguish and doubt. If you keep your eye on the long-term goals you've set, your course will have fewer detours.

Step One: Positive Assumptions

First, work to put positive assumptions about your children into place. Review the end of chapter 6, where we list empowering assumptions. Positive assumptions about children are quite different from positive parenting. If you hold positive assumptions about your children, then you believe in your children and in their ability to survive, thrive, and take care of themselves. Positive parenting, on the other hand, suggests just the opposite—that children can only survive if we create just the right atmosphere for them. If you don't really believe that your children are survivors, that they can adapt and thrive, nothing else we say here will help.

To put positive assumptions into place, examine your own thinking about, and behavior toward, your children. Without considerable introspection and self-observation, you'll find it easy to slip into a pessimistic pattern; you'll find yourself caretaking rather than caring. Pessimistic assumptions and the behavior they engender are not undone overnight. Contract with your spouse to help, examine one another's behavior, and learn together. Put up a sign, THEY AREN'T GOING TO BREAK, as a reminder. Say to yourself daily, "The worst damage I can do is to send my child unprepared into young adulthood because I've protected them from the realities of life." Children must develop independently and be encouraged to be their own person, live their own life; you can't possibly do it for them.

Step Two: Value Guidance

What, or who, guides and directs your family? Do you spend your time negotiating and debating in a pitched battle over who's in control? Are decisions made by attrition, by who wears out first? Do you find yourself flip-flopping between passively giving in to your children's demands and autocratically demanding your children's compliance with your wishes? Do you make an unpopular decision and then spend days attempting to justify your position through reason? How often do you find yourself trying to avoid upsetting someone—keeping the peace—using discussion, explanation, and placation, all the while not confronting something that is not right? Do you dream of a family in which everything is worked out rationally, in which consensus results from a "reasonable approach"? Do you believe that the rules of the world can be understood and taught through reason?

These questions are about how families operate. They get at the heart of problems that face—and paralyze—many American families. Everyone who has a public voice—from experts to politicians—has a pet culprit for our difficulties. Most agree that the family is somehow involved. How and what can we do about it in our own families is the big question.

Family Dysfunction

Most people, even experts, would have a difficult time composing a clear, concise, and understandable definition of the characteristics of family dysfunction. This word, "dysfunction," is associated with the problems of alcohol, drugs, and child abuse. Yet many families untroubled by alcoholism and abuse are unhappy, their children trying, unproductive, and irresponsible. We believe there is a need to look at the problems these families face from a different perspective. We think there is a more optimistic perspective that can tell us, in terms we can understand and use, what we need to do to change our families for the better.

Lately, family values have become emphasized in political rhetoric. While all this talk has brought the topic into the public arena, what we would like to say here is different than what most politicians are saying. They're talking about some mythical set of beliefs that supposedly made this country great. They're trying to tell you that a certain set of beliefs are correct and if we all would just believe as they do, everything would be just dandy. Not so!

We're going to focus on what values do for us, how they influence families and the lives of family members. We don't want to discuss your values or ours. Your values are your private domain and should remain so.

We started by asking you a series of questions about control in your family. Families are guided in two different ways: Some families are mostly influenced by the conditions that exist at the moment; others receive their guidance primarily from a standard of beliefs and values. Functionally, the difference is striking.

In the study mentioned in chapter 4, researchers were able to demonstrate clearly that families that used a set of values to guide their decisions and actions produced children who did considerably better in the long run. Value-guided families, without regard to the specifics of their values, worked better than expediency-guided families. As far as we are concerned, one could substitute functional and dysfunctional for value-guided and expediency-guided, though considerable clarity would be lost in the translation.

Value-Guided Versus Expediency-Guided Families

Let's compare and contrast these two kinds of families.

Value-guided families embody the following characteristics:

- Everyone's behavior is compared to the standards of the family beliefs and value system. No one is exempt. If Dad is impolite or disrespectful and the family code does not accept that sort of behavior, others point out his transgression. Children are expected to follow the code and are allowed to speak up when the code is broken.

- No one's personal convenience is more important than the code of ethics that exists within the family. Confrontations about behavior are never avoided just because someone might become upset. Another's feelings are seen as personal business, not the primary concern of the confronter. The family may stress diplomacy when approaching someone about something they've done, but the message in the confrontation is not obfuscated by tact.

- Members talk in terms of their beliefs. Conversations contain frequent references to the family standards. This creates a sense of family identity—a feeling that your family stands for something. These families often treasure their stories and history, and in their telling and retelling, the message comes across: "We have a past to live up to; we have an exciting future to look forward to; you can be proud to be part of this family."

- Children are sent out into the world as representatives of their family. Their behavior is expected to be consistent with family values outside the home, and transgressions are given timely, brief, and undivided attention. Once dealt with, the issue is dropped, and the person is welcomed back to the fold. The sense of pride in the family acts to deter many impulsive acts that would reflect poorly upon the family.

- Parents have a vision for their children; they are goal-oriented. The vision may be as simple as "Do your best in whatever you do" or much more complex, but this vision is apparent to the children, and they are motivated to live up to it.

- Children are raised consistently over time. Rules, decisions, and consequences all derive from the family ethic, and this provides continuity as children grow up. A family ethic anchors the parents, gives them a reference point that changes little as they navigate their way through raising their children. That's why it works.

In *expendiency-guided families*, on the other hand, these characteristics prevail:

- Decisions and rules are based on the convenience of the moment. Who's grumpy, who's tired, who's irritable and unapproachable, who's had too much to drink, who'll get angry and abusive, are all primary considerations for decision-making, rather than right and wrong as defined by the family code. In many expediency-guided families, most everything is negotiable if just the right tactics are used. Negotiable and nonnegotiable issues are not clearly defined. Children in these families may learn to be quite persistent in trying to get someone else to do it their way. Personal feelings are commonly public property, and a goodly amount of effort may be put into avoiding conflict and confrontation that might upset someone. Caretaking is common in these families; they are often dominated by someone who causes everyone discomfort when he or she is upset.

- There is a limited vision of the family. Family stories may not be common, and those related often do not illustrate family beliefs. The family value system is not an inherent part of many conversations. Family identity, consequently, does not develop well; pride in who the family is is stunted.

- Social position, inconvenience, embarrassment, avoidance of distress, and other measures of momentary importance are used as the yardstick of behavior. When children misbehave, explanations follow, excuses prevail, and the never-ending question "Why?" is again asked and (temporarily) answered. The child is not held up to the family values, confronted, and accepted back into the fold. Parents in these families do not see parenting as training, but seek permanent, quick solutions to problems. When that approach fails, these parents become enraged and resort to major punitive consequences.

Perhaps the most distressing feature of expediency-guided families is the outcome for their children. Since values have not been preeminent in guiding the parents, decisions and rules have not been consistent over time. Instead, children learn to be opportunistic, to take advantage of others, to manipulate as a way of life. They carry these lessons into the world with devastating consequences. It is not possible to be consistent over the eighteen or so years it takes to raise a child without continual reference to a value system, and children don't do well without long-term consistency.

It is quite possible to be guided firmly by values and be loving and forgiving at the same time. Being value-guided does not mean being authoritarian or dictatorial—just the opposite. Parents who fear being authoritarian have often set themselves up to become authoritarian when their lives and their childrens' lives are so out of control that some action must be taken.

What Do We Do?

The steps involved in becoming a value-guided family are easy to describe, but require a bit of work to accomplish. Each step must be done well. If you decide to follow these steps, make a long-term commitment to this process—the final product is well worth the effort invested. Parents who've followed these steps often find it very satisfying. This is not a set-it-and-forget-it program, but one that requires continuous reinvestment and revision over the years.

The first step requires creation of statements of personal values. Each partner in a couple must write down what they believe; creating this personal code should be done without consultation. Try to be clear, specific, and concise. Consider the following possible areas and add others if necessary: honesty; personal responsibility (toward others and toward self); respect for others; the value and importance of work; quality of work; the relationship of work and play; personal boundaries and privacy; property (ownership and respect for); values that extend outside the family (that is, environment, sportsmanship, the relationship of the family and the individual to community, and so on); equality and what it means; spiritual beliefs and teachings; money and material possessions; relationships between people; authority and law. This is not an exhaustive list; you may want to include other areas.

Very often people have not seriously thought about what they believe and the conflicts inherent in their belief system. For instance, it is easy to say you believe in honesty and you also believe in not hurting the feelings of others. How do you resolve the problem of being honest about something that will upset another person? Which is more important? How do you resolve this inherent conflict? One way this might be handled would be to identify the beliefs that are absolute, of highest priority. State them as such, and state lesser-priority beliefs as subject to the dictates of the more absolute ethics. The proposed dilemma might be resolved this way: One must always be honest. Other people's feelings should be considered in whatever we do, as long as honesty is not compromised. Thus, tactful behavior toward others is desired, but never at the expense of honesty.

Second, reconcile the differences in value statements of both members of a couple. Single parents will find that others can help here. When others look at our value systems, they will often see conflict that we didn't notice. Since our value statements are going to be real-world guidelines, we need to put a lot of thought into understanding how they will work in real-world situations. Reconciling a couple's values may be simple, requiring only prioritization and restatement. At the worst, this effort may end in stalemate over major issues. Generally, discussion of how the values actually operate in the world will help. It may be necessary for a couple to agree to disagree, but be honest about this.

Third, prepare a family statement of values. This statement should be as concise and clear as possible, with primary and secondary values identified. From this statement, a set of house rules can be derived, if you want. This is valuable for families with children old enough to learn the rules verbally.

Fourth, present the values to the family. Illustrative stories from the family's past is one of the best ways to communicate the meaning of each statement. Your values identify the family as a distinct entity: "These are our values; these are what we stand for. Everyone in this family is expected to follow and adhere to these values both at home and away. Take pride in being part of a family with such wonderful standards."

Fifth, put the values into effect. Really use them as your guide, even when doing so is not comfortable. When an infraction occurs, immediately stop the person, pause until calmed down, and discuss the infraction in terms of the family's code of beliefs. Children will not learn, for instance, what respect means unless we stop disrespectful behavior on the spot, identify it by name, and then describe the expected behavior. One event like this virtually never teaches the whole lesson; only consistent repetition over time can do this. Children are developing; they must revisit principles many times over in the light of new experience, to learn how these principles actually work. Your child may not understand what you're talking about when you use words like honesty, respect, or even work. The real meaning of these words is for you to teach; as children learn more about their world, you will find it necessary to help them integrate the old lessons into their new understanding. There is no point to this whole exercise if we preach a set of values to our children without also taking the time and effort to deal immediately with behavior that is inconsistent with these values.

It is vitally important to realize that these values apply to children and adults alike. If you are unwilling to be challenged about behavior that is inconsistent with the family values you want to put into place, you may as well not bother with this whole exercise. "Do as I say, not as I do" just won't work. Your willingness to be open to respectful observations on your behavior, to assertive comments from your children or spouse, is absolutely necessary for this system to work.

Sixth, revise your statement periodically as necessary, and go through the fourth step. As much as possible, use stories to illustrate. Over the years, modifications and clarifications will be necessary, and house rules will have to be revised as children get older and situations change.

Finally, use every opportunity to teach the family values. Don't assume that just stating the values will make children understand them or how they work. Children won't learn the things we'd like to teach them unless we're willing to put forth the effort, consistently, over time.

Step Three: Methods and Technique

Most of the parents we deal with are very good at paying attention to their children. Most, in fact, pay too much attention to their children, their children becoming used to being at center stage all the time. In Sylvia Rimm's words, author of several books on child rearing, these children are attention-addicted. What a burden these children carry, expecting to be in the limelight as they venture out into the world, not understanding why the spotlight isn't on them anymore unless they're getting in trouble. Children need time by themselves, need time to find and pursue their own interests and endeavors, even if they don't like it at the time. If your child must constantly be at your side, you've got a problem, and so does she. So go ahead and put your toddler in a playpen or insist your preschooler go play alone for a while everyday.

Most of the people we see need to learn to pay attention to the things their children do that are desirable, that are developmentally and morally appropriate. Most also find that they are paying lots of attention to misbehavior and don't know how to stop. What we all need is an effective means of setting limits for our children—they cannot learn to adapt well without it.

Setting Limits—the Missing Piece of the Puzzle

We described a method of limit setting in chapter 7 that works well if you dedicate yourself to it; becomes gentle, quiet, and brief with practice; and doesn't wear out with time. This method is not the only way to do the job, but it is the way that successful parents and teachers commonly go about teaching children to obey values and rules—even though they don't call what they are doing Stop, Pause, and Redirect. Without an effective method of teaching children to observe limits, we cannot hope to teach them to become strong, independent, adaptable adults. Anarchy works no better in families than it does in society. Intentions may be good, and values may be clear, but many families struggle with finding a method to accomplish their goals.

Stop, Pause, and Redirect is no quick fix, but a lifelong style to be adopted and used routinely. It is not manipulative, nor based on punishment or incentives, but on guidance with limits. It assumes the child needs training that inculcates the consistent message of the values and rules of a family. It supports the development of independence, self-motivation, and self-direction. While this method is very firm and clear, it is in no way abusive. It is very simple to conceptualize, but very difficult to learn to do because it requires us to change radically the way we operate. And, like any other parenting approach, it will produce good results only if mated to and guided by an overriding set of family principles. Well used, it is virtually all you'll ever need as a disciplinary technique. We have reproduced in Appendix C a quick reference guide about the technique that many of our families find useful.

Perseverance

Perseverance in achieving the goals for your children is the key to success. The road to success is by no means smooth, but don't look for easy detours. Your child must learn to navigate for himself. During periods of distress, don't give up. Keep going. Even with the approaches that we encourage parents to use, consistency and frequent use is required. Rearing a child is a little like carving a statue out of wood. To do a good job, you carefully remove the wood in thin layers. You continue to do so until the carving looks like your desired goal. If you get impatient and try to take off too much wood at one time, the statue takes on a different character than you had planned. Fortunately, raising children is more forgiving; you must make the same error over and over to do irreparable damage.

Guidance with Limit Setting

If you can set limits persistently and consistently, and if the limits you set are value-guided, you give your child the opportunity to learn self-fulfillment. If your attention is focused on adaptive, appropriate, and wanted behavior and you merely interrupt undesirable, maladaptive behavior, you are teaching your child the necessities for a successful life. When you support, through your directed and immediate attention, your child's own interests and pursuits, you are helping him to persist at his own endeavors. When you teach your child that there are rules he must follow, values he must heed, you are giving him irreplaceable lessons in life that will allow him to participate independently in the many new situations to come in his future. This approach to childrearing we call Guidance with Limit Setting.

Conclusion

Stephen Covey, in his wonderful book, *The 7 Habits of Highly Effective People,* offers an exhaustive review of American "success" literature (pop psychology, self-improvement, and self-help literature) from the 1800s to the present. He reports a striking change in this literature that began after the conclusion of World War I. Prior to that time, authors of this genre focused their efforts on development of character, on integrating ethics into daily life. After World War I, writers in the field dropped this emphasis, favoring the development of personality traits over individual character. Such things as appearance, positive thinking, power strategies, communication skills, social image, and behavior became the predominant topics. Quick fixes without lasting merit became the fare of the day; fundamental problems of integrity and purpose were addressed perfunctorily or not at all. He goes on to tell how personality ethic thinking affected his wife and his approach to one of their children, getting in the way of parenting this child with unconditional love and acceptance. He and his wife had seen one of their children as not measuring up socially. They compared him to the standards of the personality ethic, and their approach to this child became conditional on this child's social behavior—his outward appearance to the world. The child's self-worth plummeted, and his problems grew worse. After considerable thought, they recognized the mistake they were making; they had ignored their basic values in favor of superficial personality standards. This caused them to get back in touch with their deeply held beliefs, and their behavior toward their son changed fundamentally. They forgot about social comparisons and lived within their family value system. Their son soon began to thrive.

There are lessons here for us to heed: Our values are important; they will determine our effectiveness as parents. Unconditional love is fundamental for our children. Boundaries between parents and children are essential; trying to make children into what we want them to be without regard to their interests and proclivities is invasive. Insisting they try things that frighten them and deal with situations they abhor is essential to their well-being. Finding the middle ground between the two is one of the most difficult balancing acts we perform as parents. We can teach them the values that guide our lives, allowing them to explore and develop their future with our support. We can teach them to see reality and deal with it; we can teach them to participate by teaching them the skills of compliance. We can teach them to overcome fear and anxiety, to accept daunting challenges. We can build their character so that they can pursue their own life course. Self-esteem is hard-won. We can't give it to our children, but we can help them develop the skills they need to find it.

Define your job as a parent this way: Love your children without condition; provide them with the things they can't really provide for themselves; don't let them avoid worthwhile experiences out of fear or because work is involved; set limits on their behavior clearly and persistently; and teach them the values that guide your family's life. With all this, they will find their way and their character will be secured.

Epilogue: Schools and Other Places

The lessons provided in this book work well as long as parents have good control of a child's environment. Unfortunately, transferring them to the child's larger world sometimes presents almost insurmountable difficulty. Teachers, day-care personnel, coaches, and scout and youth leaders may not be willing to address issues in the same way that parents address them at home, and may easily fall prey to a child's manipulations. Here are some suggestions that may help:

Never try to train your child to behave properly in a public place until you have successfully trained him to behave that way at home. For instance, it is much better to teach a child to get his angry outburst under control at home before trying the same thing at the local supermarket. And, until you have practiced SPRd at home, don't try it at the ball field.

Don't suggest that someone else park your child until your child is doing it willingly at home. If you are going to ask a teacher or coach to use this technique, always tell them that the technique that works well for you at home might be useful in the teacher's or coach's venue. Describe SPRd simply and exactly, and give the teacher or coach the option, supported by you, to use it. Few people are going to stop your child's manipulative, rule-breaking behavior unless they can depend on your backing. No one will do SPRd well unless they chose to of their own accord. We have had varying degrees of success in trying to get teachers to cooperate in managing children's behavior. When we—and the child—are lucky, we get wholehearted and enthusiastic participation, even to the extent of the teacher using the technique on the entire class. Other times, when the teacher or coach doesn't agree, it is probably better to leave well enough alone. If things are not going well and the person is not going to change his or her approach, it may be best to arrange a change of teacher or coach, if possible.

Explain that you are working on shutting down manipulative behavior and identifying the sort of behavior your child typically uses, and that you would welcome the teacher's participation. Let the teacher know about your child's temperament, explaining the connection between temperament and the child's manipulative behavior. Ask about the manipulative behavior that the teacher sees in the classroom. Again, discuss the approach you find helpful.

Choose nursery schools and day care with an eye to how they manage behavior. Do they just stop misbehavior or make a production of it? Are the personnel comfortable with the idea that they are training children to get along in groups, to cooperate in group activities, as well as to accomplish individual tasks? Does an academic agenda outweigh a behavioral agenda? Go observe and see how they handle the children. Are the rules clear? In a good nursery school or day-care environment, you'll see little management of misbehavior taking place because the teachers have already established their leadership and taught the rules of conduct. If you see lots of behavior management taking place, question whether the teacher is really in control of the group. Day-care and nursery schools should be happy places just because the staff is clearly in charge and children are involved in fun, often productive, activity.

Teachers and parents who act in concert will make considerably more headway than if they are at cross-purposes. But you must remember a few things about teachers. They commonly feel very vulnerable. Our society has made it very difficult for them to assume a dominant role in the classroom. They fear parental complaints, lawsuits, and harassment from unsupportive administrators. School administrations are essentially political, and teachers often suspect they will be unsupported by the administration when a parent conflict arises. Teachers are often warned of the dangers of touching children, and many are unwilling to intervene physically even when safety is an issue, let alone simply insist that children do as they are told—such as being parked on the playground. Teachers must know you support them if progress is to be made.

Teacher training in behavior management is sometimes very limited. We have seen many programs to manage classroom behavior, but few work well and none work as well as the teacher who is unwilling to relinquish his dominant role in the classroom: This teacher is determined to achieve his teaching goals and will not get bogged down discussing the why of a child's misbehavior. Unfortunately, highly successful teachers have not been studied extensively so that their technical expertise can be modeled by younger teachers. Instead, teachers have often been instructed to use manipulative tactics in the classroom—reward and punishment systems—that any competent manipulative child can completely destroy without even breathing hard. It may be up to you to ask the teacher not to use such a system with your child because it is manipulative. Unfortunately, the teacher in question may not have an alternative plan that will work.

In the ideal world, teaching and learning would occur between teacher and student without third-party involvement. Parents would play a supportive role, doing all the things necessary for a child to go to school and be prepared to learn, but leaving the teaching and the managing of the child's classroom behavior up to the teacher. Such a teacher would be held in high regard by both parent and child. Parents would be available to act as surrogate teachers with homework, but would spend little time ensuring that children do their homework—that would be between teacher and pupil. When school is very successful, this scenario exists. But when things are not going well at school, parents quickly take on the role of intermediary between teacher and child, and the manipulative child quickly learns to use this situation to her benefit. Parents suddenly become responsible for overseeing that she does her homework—work they didn't assign in the first place. As this fails, elaborate communication methods are set up between parent and teacher to try to ensure that the child does her work. This effort fails because it requires too much of everyone involved—except the child. Confidence is lost in the teacher and school, the teacher-parent teamwork suffers, the teacher is not held in high regard, parent support dwindles, and the essential teacher-pupil relationship is lost.

The conundrum this presents is difficult to solve. Many teachers seem to expect parents to ensure that homework will be done, and they are relieved of the responsibility of expecting student performance. Perhaps the best solution is prevention. We suggest the following:

Establish a routine for doing homework early in a child's school career. Many different routines will work, depending on the family situation. If a parent is home when the child comes home from school, it may be best for the child to do homework before doing anything else. If the child goes to an after-school activity or is on his own until a parent comes home from work, he is less likely to do his homework during this time, so after dinner will be better. Whatever, chose the time and stick to it.

Chose the place carefully. Studying at the kitchen table promotes dependence on the parent to supervise, to keep the child on task, and to become overinvolved in the actual work. We suggest someplace quiet with a desk and light and limited distractions. Ideally, this is in the child's room.

Observe the rule "Homework first, then other activities." Turn off the TV, and intercept the phone during homework time. Pay your bills or read a book—provide a good model. If there's a favorite TV show, record it for later. Remember the motto "Do what you gotta do before you do what you wanna do."

Let your child's teacher know that homework is first and foremost a teacher-pupil arrangement. If your child is not doing his homework, tell the teacher that you will be glad to support her in whatever she needs to do to get the child to do the homework—including allowing the teacher to limit recess, keep the child after school, or assign extra work. But let the teacher know that you won't become an intermediary between her and your child.

Review your child's completed homework to praise the work or catch sloppy and inaccurate work. Let your child know by both of these interventions that you expect her to do the best she can.

All this works very well for the child who is doing well in school and feels accomplished at school work. But for the child who is having a terrible time in school, another bad grade just doesn't matter. For a short time you may need to become more actively involved until she is getting the work done. Let your child know you are confident that if she does the work, her grades will improve. Pull out of this role as quickly as possible.

Let your child know your priorities. A child active in sports or other avocations must know that schoolwork comes first. If her schoolwork falters, she must cease her other activities until she is doing her schoolwork satisfactorily—not as punishment but as a matter of priority. (For more guidance, read Sylvia Rimm's excellent book, *The Underachievement Syndrome*.)

Parents often get the distinct impression that school personnel expect them to punish a child at home for misbehavior at school. We suggest that you make sure your child understands what he has done and accepts personal responsibility for his actions. Clearly explain to the child your expectations for behavior at school, but don't punish a child for misdeeds at school. To do so will only promote more rebellion and manipulation. Moral consequences, such as letters of apology, may be very helpful. Meanwhile, let the teachers know you support them in doing whatever they need to do to deal with your child's misdeeds at school. However, since you are not at school when the misdeeds occur, you can do little about them other than the above. Schools won't necessarily like that, but hold firm. Delayed punishment promotes deviousness but rarely improves behavior. Above all, don't ask your child to explain his behavior and don't accept any explanations offered. Children who explain the reasons for their behavior are generally not accepting responsibility for their behavior.

Unfortunately, many behavior management programs used in schools are fundamentally manipulative. Rewards and incentives, threats and punishments are commonly used in classrooms and fail to improve significantly the behavior of children having difficulties. But, worse, they may teach children to manipulate back, to work the system. If you can, discourage the use of such systems with your child. You may find, however, that you are swimming upstream with many teachers on this issue.

Some time ago, one of the authors gave a talk to the PTO (Parent Teacher Organization) at a local school. In it, he stressed the importance of value guidance in parenting and in teaching. After the talk, the principal came up and said, "I agree with your points, but you used the 'V' word." For many schools, values are a hot potato. They have found themselves embroiled in controversy over values, particularly as regards sex education in the schools. Schools are left in limbo with no overall ethic to follow except, perhaps, the best interest of the child. Meanwhile government at all levels has imposed rules and expectations on schools that are often substituted for values. Goals to achieve and values to guide their achievement are essential if enterprises are to work well; we're not surprised that schools are having such difficulty. Because schools are essentially political, we don't expect to see change in the nature of schools, except where strong leadership prevails, in the near future. Understanding this point may help you see the plight of the teacher who is just there trying to do a good job within a system that doesn't always provide the necessary support. Active participation in parent-teacher organizations can impact this for your local school and benefit your child.

If your child is having a great deal of behavioral difficulty at school, you'll probably be asked to meet with some sort of team of school personnel. When you arrive, you'll be feeling guilty, as if your child's difficulties are all the fault of your misguided parenting. When you find yourself sitting in a meeting room with eight or ten people representing various different disciplines from the school, perhaps you'll feel more intimidated than you ever have in your life. We are often asked to attend these awful gatherings, more to lend support to overwhelmed parents than to provide anything substantive. Unfortunately, meetings like this may not result in much real change for the child, but they sure scare the pants off the parents.

We suggest that you ask for an agenda of the meeting beforehand—at least a statement of what is to be accomplished. Ask for the principal to attend, and sit next to him or her if you can. Do your best to keep the meeting focused on what is going on in school and what the school is going to do about it. Try to come away with a specific management plan that you can support wholeheartedly. Remember that all these people are hired to service the needs of your child; that's their job, and you must ask them to do it. If you feel you are being blamed for your child's difficulties and you're told you must do something about them, don't let that be the conclusion of the meeting. Ask repeatedly what the school is going to do in its own environment. Ask whether they really intend to say that what is going on at school is really your fault, your problem. Point out that you expect to come away with a plan, that you're willing to do your part, but that you can't quite accept an unclear management plan for school. Demand specifics. If the school proposes some sort of assessment, agree, but ask for a specific interim plan. Part of the school agenda may be to recommend that you seek outside help—which you may accept or reject. Don't let that be the only plan—ask for a clear understanding of how the school is going to handle day-to-day problems. If you get nowhere, try the advocacy organizations for parents that exist in many communities; they can help you get the school's attention. Unfortunately, in some schools, the way to make progress is through blind, assertive, if irritating, persistence.

Sometimes the only way to manage a child who is having behavioral difficulty in school is to put the child in a different school, especially a private or parochial school. Private schools have more leeway to handle a child's behavior, are often much more clearly value-guided than public schools, and may work more closely with you to do the right thing for your child. In our experience, this has been a good move for many frustrated parents, though it is not always successful. If you contemplate a move like this, interview several schools and meet the principal or headmaster. You want a principal or headmaster who is strong, supports the staff to do the work that needs to be done, and shares your view of what your child needs. Difficult children need committed, strong, goal-directed, value-guided management by teachers who know they'll be backed up by administration and parents—that everybody is on the same team, pulling in the same direction. One parent who shifted his child to a parochial school in sixth grade (from a public seventh grade) said, grinning, "The first three months were sort of like boot camp, and he just hated it. But then he began to come around, and now he likes school and likes his teacher, and his grades are much better.

Thank goodness the principal was there when he was needed by all of us. We can really work with him." This child has done very well in the succeeding years and smiles when asked about how school is going. An excellent outcome resulted from a very hard parental decision and tireless teamwork between school and parents.

Good Luck!

Milestones of Adaptive Development

Age	Task	Successful Outcome	Symptoms of Failure
0–6	Communication	Develops good verbal interactive skills.	Absent or aberrant—develops skills to control others: crying, whining, etc.
	Physical Laws	Increasing skills of movement, balance.	Withdraws from practice. Poor physical skill development; allows others to do everything.
	Imposed limits on behavior	Adapts to new sets of limits quickly; tests limits and incorporates easily.	Controls others, gets rules changed rather than adapting.
	Rudimentary peer relations	Learns to participate and initiate play/ interaction. Compromise learned.	Controls; bossy, bullying, physically aggressive. Withdraws to protector.
	Reality vs. fantasy	Learns to perceive difference.	Contructs own view of reality; selective modification.
	Reason	Uses to attack a problem requiring understanding.	Argues, negotiates to get own way.
School-age	School environment School work	Adapts to school rules. Learns to overcome fear, frustration— produces work.	Behavior problems; asks for help, doubts ability, develops fear, gives up.

MILESTONES OF ADAPTIVE DEVELOPMENT (continued)

Age	Task	Successful Outcome	Symptoms of Failure
	Peers	Learns to participate, cooperate, engage in peer activities, lead; develops lots of friends.	Tries to control; has fewer friends. Finally isolated from peer group, imposes own rules, can't participate, withdraws.
	Sports	Plays, learns to fail, lose, and succeed; sportsmanlike behavior.	Imposes own rules, can't participate, withdraws; unsportsmanlike.
	Clubs	Participates and can lead activity.	Tries to control rules of games—frustrated—gives up and shifts blame, expresses dislike for game.
	Home	Learns to accept responsibility at home: chores, personal effects, etc.	Controls to get things done for him—learns to shift responsibility for work or mistakes.
	Values	Learns family values govern rules and decisions. Accepts consequences of actions; owns up to deeds and misdeeds.	Denies values or argues with them. Shifts or denies blame and responsibility for misdeeds.
Adolescent	School	Performs at ability level. Pushes self to perform, is proud of performance.	School: "boring," "irrelevant"; "I hate it." Underperforms or performs only when likes teacher or subject.
	Homework	First priority.	Not done or not turned in.
	Sports	Enjoys participation. Dislikes but accepts losing. Does not cheat. Persists at sports activities.	Drops out of activity. Hates or fears athletic competition.
	Peer/social	Widens group/enjoys friends. Participates in peer activities enthusiastically.	Withdraws; isolated, few friends. Joins adolescent subculture group. Others good/bad—no gray area.
	Student government activities	May participate; involved.	Student government is "dumb"—withdraws.
	Job	Successful, if decides to work.	Job failures, excuses; "bad boss," "dumb job."

MILESTONES OF ADAPTIVE DEVELOPMENT (continued)

Age	Task	Successful Outcome	Symptoms of Failure
	Adults	Finds mentors/ adult models.	Disdains adult relationships.
	Intimacy	Close relationship with friends and members of opposite sex. Full appreciation of others. Not judgmental in black/ white way.	Sexual activity (irresponsible and usurious); seeks sex thrills, but no real intimacy. Dependent relationships, few lasting relationships.
	College	Plans made for life work (may change); uses mentors to develop.	Few decisions about future, few goals to develop.
	Avocation	Intense interest in world/hobbies/ activities.	Disinterested in world activities or may be intensely interested in only one activity (i.e., computers, hunting, surfing, etc.).
	Values	Reexamination of family/parental values. Begins development of own values system— explores values of others, especially mentors. Generally practices own values, which tend to be mono-chromatic.	Discounts/rebels against parental values, adopts peer subculture or flexible situational values when convenient.
	Self-esteem	Confident, knows a lot about self-competence; not preoccupied with self but with world at large. Feels good when successful at participation.	Preoccupied with self; function, figure, face; self-conscious/ blatant dress affectations. Self-esteem low; feels good only when controlling.
	Emotions	Experiences wide and varied range and sees them as his own.	Narrow range of emotions: anger, happiness, melancholy, hate, fear; displaces them upon others/not own responsibility.
	Problems	Conflict with parents over values.	As above: eating disorders, drugs, underachievement, depression, suicide, etc.

MILESTONES OF ADAPTIVE DEVELOPMENT (continued)

Age	Task	Successful Outcome	Symptoms of Failure
Young adult	Outcome	Self-confident, functional, ethical, goal-directed, independent, interested in world; definition of self advances greatly; job/college success. Intimacy without sacrifice of personal goals. Responsible to and for self; self-motivated.	Bitter; drugs or other involvements; aimless, angry; looking for easy way out; adopts easy self-definition: pregnancy/marriage/job/figure, etc. Opportunistic rather than ethical; dependent; shifts responsibility for self to others.

Parenting Styles

Incentive-Punishment	Guidance with Limits
Based on rewards, incentives for good behavior; threats, and retributive punishment for undesirable behavior. Rules often unclear, poorly defined. Emotions very important; how child feels about punishment or reward determines effectiveness.	Based on clearly defining rules and expectations (that is, the outside limits on behavior). Child explores inside these limits. How the child feels about limits, rules, and family values is of secondary importance.
Less freedom of choice for child, with poor definition of child's choices	Child is given great freedom to choose within limits of family goals and values.
Parent vacillates between niceness and harshness.	Uniformly quiet and gentle niceness when well practiced.
Manipulative	Inherently nonmanipulative
Often dishonest	Stringently honest
Punishments often poorly timed for any desirable effect; often escalates out of control	Timing is all-important; parents rarely give up opportunity to redefine limits.
Intensity of reward or punishment varies.	Frequency, not intensity, varies as needed.
Response to threat or punishment varies over time: decreases or produces retaliatory reactions, angry or manipulative behavior	Response to limits, stopping behavior predictable; does not fade with time and use, but improves with practice and consistency
Will not overcome avoidance behavior	Stops avoidance behavior
When works will not produce persistent effect	Guidance and limits lead to goal, produce lasting effect

PARENTING STYLES (continued)

Incentive-Punishment	Guidance with Limits
Requires extensive and systematic planning, high degree of adult involvement	Vision, goals, values, rules clear: child finds way within them.
Not adult-adult consistent	Technique simple: consistent
Punishment, or threat of punishment does not confer power to the parent, often becomes reinforcing to child.	Parents gain respect because they are consistent over time and are seen as determined and nonmanipulable.
Disrespectful, judgmental	Respectful, accepting
Results in lots of verbal interaction over behavior: arguments, negotiation, justification, blaming; as process escalates, any guidance from values tends to disappear.	Little verbal interaction about behavior, few arguments and less negotiation; not blaming, but identifies where responsibility rests; values→rules→limits
Product: dependent, manipulative person focused on control of others to gain short-term advantage	*Product: independent, self-controlled, ethical person focused on achievement of own goals*

Quick Review: Rules for STOP, PAUSE, and REDIRECT

STOP

1. Before you react to a misbehavior in any way, you must first stop the misbehavior. Ignoring this rule renders **your effort** useless.

2. Misbehavior is anything the child is doing that you have decided you don't want him to do. This may be behavior you've dealt with before, behavior that is entirely new, or any behavior other than what you've asked the child to do.

3. Never use SPRd after the fact—it is not a punishment. Remember this.

PAUSE

1. During the pause phase, the child must settle himself before any further interaction takes place. Do not respond to anything the child does except to bring him back physically to where he was originally placed. Interaction before the child has settled himself down merely pushes the reset button and wastes your effort.

2. The pause is not a punishment! It lasts only as long as it takes for the child to settle himself. Longer is not better, but if it takes forty-five minutes for him to compose himself, that's how long it lasts.

3. With practice, your child will learn to settle down quickly and quietly, and the whole procedure will be very brief and quiet, even surreptitious. This is the goal you should strive for; the more times you do it, the earlier you'll reach this goal. Practice makes perfect.

REDIRECT

1. Make your redirect short and direct. Do not harangue the child; merely state, if you want, what he did wrong, and send him off to do whatever it is that you want him to be doing: "Go play," "Go pick up your toys," "Go apologize to your brother," and so forth. Long-winded redirects don't make the procedure more effective. Explanations of the reasons behind your actions don't help and should be avoided.

2. Remember, this is training about behavioral limits. It is not supposed to elicit unpleasant emotions, though sometimes when you are just beginning to use it, it will. Success is obtained through frequent use, not more elaborate methods.

3. If you want to talk to your child about his behavior, to discuss rules, values, reasons, and so on, do it at a different time—never in the heat of battle.

EXAMPLE

George, a second grader, is running around wildly at a church gathering. His mother, Amy, talking to a friend, notices that his behavior is out of control. She interrupts her conversation momentarily, calls to George to come over, and resumes her conversation. George arrives, and she continues her conversation until he is calmed down for twenty or thirty seconds. She then bends over and whispers in his ear, "You're getting too wild. Go ahead and play, but no running or screaming." This is SPRd done to perfection.

A Final Word

SPRd works well, doesn't wear out, establishes that you are in charge, and is gentle and quiet. But be wary of this: If it is not done exactly as we've described, it will not work. If you go back to your old ways as soon as you've had a little success with this procedure, you'll quickly be back where you started. Good Luck!

Suggested Readings

Azrin, Nathan H., and Besalel, Victoria A. *A Parent's Guide to Bedwetting Control: A Step by Step Method*. New York: Simon and Schuster, 1979.

Bennett, William J. *The Book of Virtues*. New York: Simon and Schuster, 1993.

————.*The Book of Virtues for Young People: A Treasury of Great Moral Stories*. Parsippany, N.J.: Silver Burdett Press, 1996.

————.*The Children's Book of Virtues*. New York: Simon and Schuster, 1995.

Collins, Marva, and Tamarkin, Civia. *Marva Collins' Way*. New York: Jeremy P. Tarcher (distributed by St. Martin's Press), 1982.

Covey, Stephen R. *The 7 Habits of Highly Effective People*. New York: Fireside Press, 1989.

Erikson, Erik H. *Childhood and Society* (2nd edition). New York: Norton, 1964.

Rimm, Sylvia B. *The Underachievement Syndrome: Causes and Cures*. Watertown, Wis.: Apple Publishing Co., 1989.

Rosemond, John K. *Six Point Plan to Raising Happy Healthy Children*. Kansas City, Mo.: Andrews and McMeel, 1989.

————.*Parent Power!: A Common Sense Approach to Parenting in the 90's*. Kansas City, Mo: Andrews and McMeel, 1990.

Sykes, Charles J. *A Nation of Victims,* New York: St. Martin's Press, 1992.

Szasz, Thomas. *The Myth of Psychotherapy.* Syracuse, N.Y.: Syracuse University Press, 1988.

Thomas, Elizabeth M. *The Hidden Life of Dogs.* New York: Pocket Star Books, 1993.

Index